PURPOSE

PURPOSE

AN
IMMIGRANT'S
STORY

WYCLEF JEAN

WITH ANTHONY BOZZA

itbooks

AN IMPRINT OF HARPERCOLLINS PUBLISHERS

HarperCollins books may be purchased for educational, business, or sales promotional use. For information please write: Special Markets Department, HarperCollins Publishers, 10 East 53rd Street, New York, NY 10022.

FIRST EDITION

Designed by Renato Stanisic

Library of Congress Cataloging-in-Publication Data is available upon request.

ISBN 978-0-06-196686-6

12 13 14 15 16   OV/RRD   10 9 8 7 6 5 4 3 2 1

This book is dedicated to the Creator,
for without my creation,
none of this would have ever been.
I dedicate my book to my mother,
Yolanda Jean, and my father,
the late and greatly missed Gesner Jean.
Most of all, I'd like to thank
the woman that has stood beside me
since I was nineteen years old:
Claudinette Jean, I would not be here without
you or our beautiful daughter, Angelina.

There is no problem without a solution; therefore there is no solution without a problem. As the earth turns, I maintain my balance, so if the earth was to stop, I would lose my balance. Why try to control the uncontrollable? What you seek is right in front of you, so open your hands and read your palms. If we ever converse, tell me not the words of others, just words that are your own.

JEANNEL WYCLEF JEAN

CONTENTS

PURPOSE

INTRODUCTION

THE INVISIBLE MAN

My first thought was extraordinary: "Look, there's my uncle Ray. He's on TV." I stood at the control board in Studio A at Platinum Sounds, the recording studio I've owned and made records in since 2000. Platinum is an institution founded on my success with the Fugees. It's a fitting legacy for a group that has sold over 15 million copies but released just one major-label album. *The Score* was recorded in a damp, smoke-filled basement on a tough stretch of Clinton Street in East Orange, New Jersey, on the only equipment we could afford, but nothing limited our soul and imagination. Platinum is a palace compared to that basement. I brought none of that old gear along, but the same spark of invention is there. Many hip-hop hits have been recorded there—by everyone from T.I. to DMX. Classic tracks by a true cross-section of artists have been laid down in those rooms, too: U2 did most of their last album there. Tom Jones has recorded there, and so has Patti LaBelle.

That evening, I was working on a song called "Two Strangers in the Night." I don't come into the studio with anything more than a few lyrical ideas on paper usually, or melodies I've recorded in voice mails that I leave for myself. I always have the song concept in mind, and then I let the raw spirit of the music and the moment guide me until it becomes what it is meant to be. I play piano, guitar, and can figure out any instrument with strings, so I always have too many options.

"Two Strangers in the Night" was bound for a mix tape called *Toussaint St. Jean: From the Hut to the Projects to the Mansion*. It never made it on there because the events of that evening changed everything, but it will see the light of day in some form or another soon. I like rapping as Toussaint St. Jean. He is an alias I created when I needed to get back to my street roots. Back when the Fugees released *Blunted on Reality*, raw street style was the only way I did it. I evolved from there on *The Score, The Carnival*, and my work since then. But the time I'd been spending in Haiti with kids whose streets were tougher than any of those I'd known brought me back in time and somewhere further. I needed the proper voice to tell those tales, and I didn't know how. So I created Toussaint. He's a gritty gangster; he tells it like it is. He's a revolutionary and a mercenary. I had some things to say about hip-hop and the world, and Toussaint was the man for the job.

I'd had enough of the clownishness that had taken over the game. Hip-hop was an art form born of protest in the late seventies; it was the voice of the outsiders and the underprivileged in the South Bronx. They were hungry and they were struggling, but their spirit would not be held down. Hip-hop culture brought together break-dancing, rapping, DJs, Caribbean rhythms, and American rebellion. It grew. It became a commodity and an industry of its own years ago, but even at its worst, I'd always found new voices worth listening to. There have always been legends in the game and young guns coming up with something to say.

In 2009, though, I was no longer impressed. All I heard from the youth on the streets were soundtracks fit for strip clubs. Instead of raw humanity there were only synthesized voices, instead of real-life street tales, only insincere bragging. Toussaint needed to make a state-of-the-union address.

I couldn't hear Uncle Ray because the television was on mute. "Uncle Ray looks good, man," I said aloud, more to myself than anyone else in the room. I do this a lot.

It wasn't unusual to see him on television being interviewed live in Washington, DC, because he lives there. My uncle, Raymond Joseph, is Haiti's ambassador to the United States. He is my mother's brother and though I didn't know him much growing up, my perception of him was always that he was a serious man. My mother always reminded us that he had translated the Bible from English into Creole for publication. That is a serious undertaking. I got to know my uncle Raymond when I was in my late teens, when my dad and I were butting heads because of the music I was doing. My father called hip-hop of any kind "bum music." He associated it with the drug dealers and criminals in our neighborhood who listened to it and never understood the possibility that the music could do more than just celebrate the lowlife. My uncle Raymond was brought in to talk to me, since my dad and I had stopped communicating altogether. I wasn't expecting him to see my side at all, but after Uncle Raymond talked to me and listened to my music, he went back to my dad and told him, "This is America, Gesner. Your son isn't doing anything wrong. He's just making music, which is keeping him off the streets. His music is not a bad thing." It didn't do much to change my dad's mind but I never forgot my uncle Raymond for that. I thought it was really cool that he stood up for me the best he could.

I reached for the remote to turn the volume up, but my buzzing phone intercepted my attention.

The incoming text said, "We've been hit."

I looked back to the TV and saw the graphic in blazing red: 7.1 MAGNITUDE EARTHQUAKE IN HAITI. I turned up the volume.

"It's getting dark there now," Uncle Ray was saying. "Our phone contact has been severed. I was on the line with the president just a few minutes ago and I heard cries and people shouting. It was chaotic. Our concern is that night is falling and we don't know what will happen once it is dark." Now I noticed the deep lines of worry on his face.

I picked up the phone and called one of the most reliable members of my Yéle team in Port-au-Prince. Miraculously he answered my call. There was noise on the line but I heard the fear in his voice loud and clear.

"What's goin' on, man?" I asked.

"We've been hit! I gotta find my kids. My kids are in school! My kids! My—" Then the phone went dead.

I am the kind of man who never sits still and I have always been this way. I had spent the last year musically working with the likes of T.I. and Estelle; I'd done soundtrack work and was renegotiating my publishing contract with Sony in anticipation of the release of my next album. I'd gotten my face on a Western Union card—the first-ever celebrity to be offered that—and had seen my line of Yéle Timberlands come out. I'd spent most of my year politicking to make Yéle a truly global relief effort. None of that mattered anymore: I knew what I had to do. I had to be in Haiti before the sun came up. I had to help any way I could, not as Wyclef Jean, but as a Haitian. I had to stand side-by-side with my countrymen and help save lives.

My cell phone vibrated again. I looked at my Twitter feed: "Jimmy O, R.I.P."

Time stopped for me. I stared at the screen, ignoring the calls and texts that began to come in one after the other. This couldn't be true—not Jimmy O. He was one of my best Yéle soldiers in Haiti and the toughest dude I've ever known.

I met Jimmy O after President Jean-Bertrand Aristide was ousted in a coup d'état in 2004. I went down in 2005, and that is when I met him.

If you see the documentary *Ghosts of Cité Soleil*, you will understand who he was. The film is about an extremely impoverished community in Port-au-Prince that has no running water, electricity, health care, or stores of any kind. It is commonly regarded as one of the most dangerous and poorest areas in the Western Hemisphere and it is the biggest slum in the entire Northern Hemisphere. A human life there is less valuable than a meal. People do whatever they must do to survive and everything is controlled by ruthless gangs, most of them just kids. Jimmy O was one of them once upon a time.

That year, I started a project called We're All in the Same Gang. We took kids who were involved with hard-core gangs all over Haiti and brought them into a recording studio to record a song called "Peace for the Streets." Jimmy O was one of those kids. He and I connected immediately, and I started speaking to him a lot beyond the program. His biggest wish was to get a visa so that he could travel to America and do some recording. He would drop verses for anybody, so long as he made some money he could bring home to feed his family. Jimmy was in his late twenties and he had three children.

At the time, Creole rap was really taking off and Haiti was doing well, but that wasn't enough to earn Jimmy a visa, so I suggested that he work for a social foundation, like mine. I needed someone like Jimmy O to increase awareness of Yéle in the streets. We launched a hip-hop program called Clean Streets and I put Jimmy O at the center of it.

The plan was to go into the roughest communities in Haiti to select the best rappers we could find. We'd ask them to write a rap about cleaning up the streets. Their rhymes had to be environmentally themed, about clearing the garbage, the proper disposal of waste, and how garbage can be turned to energy if handled and disposed of the right way. We wanted them to look at their surroundings and learn how they could turn the worst aspects of their surroundings to their advantage—if they put in the work. Their rap had to carry a message of empowerment.

Jimmy O put the entire project together; he oversaw everything and became the face of the movement. He worked with different radio stations across the country and went to every single one of the roughest areas to speak to the local rappers and gang members face-to-face.

I've lived in the notorious Marlboro Projects of Brooklyn, New York, and in East Orange, New Jersey, which was a jungle of its own. I've known killers, gangsters, thugs, and sociopaths, and I still believe that the kids who entered our program were by far the toughest I've met in my lifetime. And we got them to rap about cleaning up the environment and changing the world.

The program was such a success that we launched another program with Jimmy O that was an AIDS initiative. He'd become known all over the country, so he was the perfect spokesman, which is what makes the message in Haiti. It was called the Hip Hop Truck and it drove throughout the country handing out free condoms, giving HIV tests, and educating people about the disease. Jimmy transformed his life and began doing so much work for Yéle that eventually I was able to get him a visa to come to the States without a problem.

It was an incredible day for us both when I brought him to New York to record at Platinum. His eyes lit up when he saw the place. I got him on a track with me and the Game and the kid was beside himself with happiness. *Rolling Stone* did a little article about us recording that song, so Jimmy O was officially the first Creole rapper to be mentioned in a magazine that means something in America.

I took Jimmy to California with me, too, when I went to work with Anthony Mandler, the music-video director who did the clip for "Let Me Touch Your Button," a song I did in 2008 with Will.i.am, which featured Jimmy O. Anthony couldn't believe that Jimmy was from Haiti.

"Yo, Clef, this guy looks like a Crip from LA. Who is this guy?"

"He's from Haiti, man. He's straight Creole."

"Has this kid thought about doing movies?"

"I'm telling you, this kid can do anything."

Jimmy O was loved wherever I brought him, so we started working on a system where he would go back to Haiti for a while to work and then come back and record with artists here. We had to because of the visa system, but we had a plan. He was really starting to get a career going in America: he had a crew in Philadelphia that he recorded with, and he was starting to put together a solo album that was shaping up to be something. Every time he called me he'd say, "Father, what's next?" He didn't call me brother, he didn't call me homie, he called me *father*: to him this was the deepest respect he could show me.

About six months before the earthquake, Jimmy felt that he'd been in America too long and was losing steam back in Haiti. He wanted to return home for a while to do a Creole mix tape and keep up his presence there. He saw it as a responsibility to the community, not just to himself. He was devoted to his roots. After he fulfilled that, he would return to America and finish recording his debut album, which he had decided to call *Destiny*.

I saw Jimmy O for the last time in December 2009, when I went down to Haiti to pass out gifts dressed as Santa Claus. I stayed at the Hotel Montana during that trip, as I always did. Two weeks later the hotel would be a pile of dust on the ground. Every single day I realize that if I'd stayed two weeks longer, my wife, my daughter, and I would probably be dead.

The three of us spent our time that trip giving out gifts to as many kids as possible. Claudinette and I were happy to have our little girl, Angelina, along because we felt that she was old enough to start learning about her heritage and about giving back first-hand. I saw Jimmy O on that trip and I told him to call me after the holidays so we could start planning his record release. Now here I was, two weeks later, reading texts that he had died, crushed in his car by a building.

Haiti is the land of rumors and I refused to believe this one. I believed what I read on the TV screen: an earthquake larger than any in the history of Haiti had leveled Port-au-Prince. But I refused to believe that it had taken Jimmy O. If there ever was a guy who could defy Mother Nature, it was Jimmy.

I am a man with many interests, but when I set myself on a goal, I have no other focus. I become a man on a mission; I go into high gear, as I did that night. It didn't matter what had happened. I would be in Port-au-Prince by morning and I would find Jimmy O wherever he was. I began making the necessary calls, first to my business partner, Brad Horowitz, with whom I'm a partner in a mobile phone company called Voilà. Brad is a renegade. He was in the Dominican Republic, and he told me that he had a private plane to fly us into Haiti if we could get to him. That was all I needed to hear. My next call was to my wife, then to my cousin Jerry Duples-sis and to two other Haitians I knew would want to go down with us to help out on the ground: Encinto, who plays in a group called Fantom, and Isola, who is rapper with a group called B.C. Isola had just come in that day, but he'd heard that his family's house had collapsed and that they were trapped in the rubble, so he turned right back around and flew down with us.

I stopped by the CNN studios in Manhattan on my way to the airport to do an interview with Anderson Cooper, who was heading out to Haiti as well. I told him all about Jimmy O because that was all I could think about. Now, with time on my side, I understand why. I could not wrap my mind around what had happened. Haiti was barely holding on no matter how much aid Yéle and the world provided. This earthquake was a hardship from which the country might never recover. I could not face that possibility, so Jimmy O's well-being became symbolic to me: he had to be alive, because he represented the soul of my homeland. He was the future; he was their hope. Haiti deserved a chance, and if one young gangster could change his ways, all hope was not lost. With enough heart, we could cure our own ills. He had to be alive.

MY PARTY LEFT ON a commercial flight out of JFK to the Dominican Republic and then hopped the plane Brad had arranged to get us into Port-au-Prince. Our pilot flew as low as possible, because without air traffic control, there was a chance that we might hit a larger plane above us. It was a risk, but the journey would have taken us two days or more by car and I wasn't willing to wait.

As we approached the airport, the morning sun cut through the dust clouds that hung unnaturally above the city. We saw one or two other small planes landing, all of the traffic being directed by a few men standing alone on the tarmac. They had become air traffic control in the crippled airport. Below us the runways were cracked and the terminal lay in a heap; the control tower was a pile of rocks. Planes were parked wherever there was enough runway left to hold them.

When I got out of the plane, the smell hit me. I was used to the heat—that was familiar—but this did not smell like Haiti. It did not smell like anything. The smell of the sea and vegetation was gone. All I could smell was a thick odor somewhat like smoke and rotting meat.

I immediately noticed officials from Venezuela on the tarmac, including President Chávez. Then I saw the prime minister of Haiti, Jean-Max Bellerive. He looked like he'd seen a ghost. As he and his wife greeted us, she began speaking in gibberish.

"You don't understand," she said. She kept stammering, "You

must see the street. You must see the street. Everything is . . . You must see."

Those members of the Haitian parliament who had escaped before the building collapsed stood around on the runway. They had been evacuated to the airport because it was the only open space safe from falling buildings. The tarmac had become Haiti's capitol.

We arrived down there homeless, with nothing. We could have waited for some sort of vehicle to arrive, but I didn't want to delay. I wanted to help—however I could, immediately. So we started to walk into the city. We knew that the hotel La Villa Créole was still standing and that we would be able to stay there. We figured that it would be the headquarters from which we would organize our Yéle teams and begin to feed the hungry. Our small group set out, leaving the officials, the airplanes, and the last we'd see of anything resembling civilization behind.

A thick fog of dust hung over the city, clinging to the humid, tropical air. It dried our eyes and scratched our throats as we walked onto the streets of Port-au-Prince. Nothing looked familiar, as reality hit my consciousness. I understood that all I'd known of Haiti was history in just one moment. Nothing drove this home more personally than my own sudden invisibility.

For the past fifteen years, Haiti was the one place in the world where I could never ever walk anonymously. That day Haiti was gone and Wyclef Jean was a ghost. I was a man, any man, on a ruined street, staring into an abyss. I knew why the prime minister's wife was unable to make any sense. There were not words to explain what I saw. Shadows lay on all sides; civilization was reduced to piles of darkness. Through the dust, the shapes of men and women emerged. They wandered past us as if we did not exist, and neither did they.

I saw a man with a broken arm dangling from the socket. I saw a woman hobbling along, the cartilage of both kneecaps exposed. A mother with a baby in her arms ran past us screaming, the dead infant's broken neck bobbing up and down along her forearm. The darkness and dust mutated the sounds around us. We heard disembodied voices crying out but couldn't see where they came from. We walked on, losing all sense of direction.

I heard the sound of an engine ahead of us. There are colorful buses in Haiti called tap-taps that we use as public transportation, and one of them emerged slowly from the smoke. It was a converted pickup truck with benches in the back and a few injured sitting there. I thought it was a mirage. As we drove through the city, I began to see, as if the way you do when your eyes grow accustomed to the darkness. We were surrounded by dead bodies in the streets.

"Why are these bodies everywhere? We got to start getting these bodies to the graveyard," I said. "Where is the hospital?"

"It's gone," the driver said, as if in a trance. "There's one clinic. I can take you there."

We picked up more injured along the way until the tap-tap was full. But we had to make room for another. As we drove, I saw a girl trapped in the rubble, calling out to us.

"Stop the bus!"

"I can't find my mom," she sobbed as my wife and I freed her from the concrete on top of her. "I can't find my dad. My sister . . . They're dead. They were inside."

She couldn't move her legs. I thought she was paralyzed but I didn't want to tell her so.

"Hold on, sister, it's going to be okay," I said. "We're going to the hospital. They will take care of you."

As we drove past the remains of one hospital, then another, I felt my self-control slipping away. I felt angry, I felt helpless, and I wanted to scream. Who would help these people? They could not be left to die like this.

The nearest clinic that hadn't been destroyed was located on the outskirts of town. It was built to handle about fifty people a day; outside the building was a crowd of two thousand or more. The living and the dead lay beside each other. A man stood there patiently, holding the remains of his left hand in his right hand. There were no doctors or nurses in sight. There were only the hurt, side by side, in a mass surrounding the small building.

I cannot explain what came over me, but I had reached my breaking point. I lost all sense of logic and became consumed with purpose. Like Jimmy O, the girl we had found must live if Haiti were to survive. I was convinced of this. If she were saved, everything would be okay. We had found her because she was destined to live. She had unfulfilled purpose here.

I took the girl in my arms and carefully worked my way through the crowd, all the way into the clinic. I was the invisible man in a land where I'd once been known to all. I was ordinary now; she was special.

The interior of the small clinic looked like photos I'd seen of field hospitals in Vietnam. Bodies covered in dirt and blood were everywhere, some partially bandaged, others being stitched where they stood, a few deceased but not yet removed. I found my way to a doctor.

"You've got to see this girl," I said to him.

"We will get to her," he replied. He was weary.

"No, you don't understand me, man!" I yelled. "You've got to see this fucking girl now!"

The doctor stopped tending to his patient and looked into my wild eyes.

"You've got to calm down," he said. "Give her to me. I will look at her."

"It's going to be okay," I said to the girl, whose name I never knew. I handed her over as carefully as if she were my own daughter.

I left one of my Yéle faithful with her in the hospital, because now that she was safe, I had to move on. I had to find Jimmy O.

When the tap-tap pulled up to La Villa Créole in Petionville we found that the most beautiful hotel in the country had, by the force of need, become a field clinic. The hotel is at the top of a hill along a winding road, with a beautiful view of Port-au-Prince. From the hotel driveway, I'd always thought the maze of buildings below to be as much a marvel as the Grand Canyon and layered with an equally rich history. But on this day the familiar view was shrouded, and what I could see looked like crumpled cardboard boxes. Behind me, bodies were everywhere, resting on whatever they could find to insulate them from the rocky earth. They had torn their clothes into bandages to stop the bleeding as they sat in silence, patiently waiting for medical aid. Doctors, nurses, and volunteers, most of them trained on the spot, made their way through the masses, doing what they could to clean wounds and ease pain.

The lobby was now the emergency room; the larger suites in which I'd stayed in the past were now the operating rooms. My wife, my cousin, and I stood inside the entrance among the injured, as one of our group sought out whomever was in charge. We wanted them to know we were here and that Yéle was ready to rally our surviving staff and to pool our resources. We wanted to use the hotel as our headquarters until we could organize one of our own. We had put word out to our people to gather at the hotel, but we wanted them to know that even if all of our staff had died, we were alive, and we would work as long as we could be useful.

As all of these thoughts spun through my head, I felt a tug at the hem of my shirt.

"Clef . . . is that you?"

I looked down at the young man on the stretcher next to me, one of the lucky few with something to rest on. The thin sheet over him trembled as his body shivered violently. A dead man lay beside him, his jaw open and his eyelids closed.

"Clef . . . you're not going to let me die here," he said. His eyes were blood red. "Don't let me die . . ."

"It's going to be okay," I said to him. "You've got to stay calm. Close your eyes and listen to my voice. I am here with you."

He closed his eyes.

"You must think of peace, my brother. Everything is going to be okay."

"Stay with me, man . . . Please stay with me . . . I can't see anything. My heart . . . it is beating so fast. I'm going to die. I am going to die." His breath came quicker now.

"Stay calm. Be peaceful, my friend. You are not alone," I said. "The doctor is coming. It will be okay."

I knew he would not live much longer so I searched for something more to say. Words did not come, so I remained silent. I put one hand on his heart and I held his other hand in mine. I closed my eyes and tried to send him peace. When I opened them again, he was gone. I pray that I helped him ascend to the other side.

· · · ·

WE SPENT THE NEXT few hours assisting the doctors at La Villa Créole, waiting for our Yéle team to gather there. We weren't sure who was dead and who was alive, so every hour brought us both good and bad news. We had spent the past few years developing our organization, preparing ourselves for tragedy, and stockpiling emergency rations. But we were hit by surprise the same way everyone else was; all of our supplies were buried when our warehouse was destroyed. Every other relief agency was in the same boat. We had nothing to give, but it didn't matter because every which way we looked there was much to do. We were all equal that day. There were people dying all around us and it was our duty to bring them to the nearest hospital, to find them water, to dig them out of the rubble.

But first I needed to know something.

"Yo," I said, interrupting one of my Yéle staff. "Where is Jimmy O?"

Silence.

"Jimmy O is dead, Clef."

"If he is dead, tell me, how did he die?" I asked.

"His car was crushed by a building."

"Did you see this?"

"I did not, but it is true."

"How do you know this?"

"One of our cars was behind him. He was pulled over by the police. When the earthquake hit, the building next to his car fell over. It killed the police and it killed Jimmy O. We drove away . . . "

"Where is his car?"

"You can't get him out, Clef. He is trapped in the car. He is dead. He is buried."

"Where is his car?" I said.

"In the city."

"Take me there."

We wound through the maze of Port-au-Prince, to an intersection where two buildings had fallen across the road. There was only one path through. At one corner the tail end of a car could be seen. One of our Yéle family had spray-painted JIMMY O on it. He was under a thousand pounds of rock. Digging by hand would take days. But I didn't care.

I stood there with my Yéle family around me. "We need a Caterpillar," I said.

"Clef, take a look around," someone said. "This is impossible. There were only one or two in the entire city to begin with. They are probably buried, too."

"Nothing is impossible," I said. "We must bury Jimmy O. He is gone. He was one of us."

One of us had salvaged a few electric drills that we used to build houses. I took one and began to break rocks, one at a time. After many hours, we were able to pull Jimmy's body from the wreckage of his car.

I could no longer retreat into my fantasy: here in front of me was Jimmy O and he was dead. I did not know what any of our actions meant anymore, but I knew we must honor him if we were to move on. In my mind, burying this one soldier would restore order. It would put things right.

We took his body to the closest graveyard, which had become a marketplace: with so many bodies and limited space, the grave-digger was charging families a premium to bury their dead. The city had fallen, but human greed lived on. This man was hustling those who had nothing left but their own loss. The gates to the cemetery had been closed and locked, because if they weren't the people would have flooded the place and created even more chaos.

The only reason I was able to get inside is that I was with a kid named Izolan, who is one of my closest allies in Haiti. In Haiti, Izolan is known by everyone; he is their 50 Cent or Lil Wayne, combined with the mentality of Che Guevara. Through this entire time, he was like an apostle to me, like Peter was to Christ: he was the man taking care of business. Izolan went up to the gate and they opened it for him. Then as we were walking in, we saw FaFa, who was one of my capos in Yéle. I couldn't believe my eyes, because FaFa had just lost his daughter in the earthquake. Yet there he was, devoted to our mission to help, devoted to his fellow man.

I smiled at FaFa and he smiled at me, and we hugged, creating a moment of peace in the storm. "What are you doing here, man?" I asked. "You just lost your little girl."

"She is gone and I can't change this," he said. "But I can change how many more will be gone if I sit around and do nothing."

FaFa had a massive presence, kind of like André the Giant, not that huge physically but in spirit. He was a tall, good-looking kid with a big bushy afro. He had chiseled cheeks, he was beautiful; if he had grown up in New York he would have been a model. It was his eyes that made him ten feet tall: they were more intense than anyone else's I'd ever seen, and when he was angry or upset, one look from him would send a man crawling into a hole. He was the type of kid who would walk up to you in a gunfight, crack your gun in half, and beat you up without blinking. FaFa was my right-hand man in Yéle and in Haiti, and I kept him close by me whenever I traveled through the more dangerous parts of the country because I could rely on him in every way. I was also the only one who could talk to him when he got out of control, which he did a lot. I got plenty of calls in New York when FaFa got out of control.

I met FaFa in one of the worst slums in all of Haiti, back in 2005, around the time I met Jimmy O. FaFa wasn't into music or anything like that; he was a militant type to the bone. He was very hotheaded, but he had a lot of love in his heart. If he had been discovered by any country's army earlier in life he could have been trained to be the perfect soldier. I met him through a Yéle project in his area, after which he approached me to ask how he could help us out. He was willing to do anything—pick up boxes, carry supplies, hand out rice—whatever it took to be part of the team. He wanted to see his slum rise from the depths of poverty and become a real community.

Yéle gave him that opportunity and in return he began to refer to himself as a Wyclef diehard. This had less to do with me than with what I stood for. Fafa was leading by example, showing the kids out there in the slums that they could live another way and follow another road. My name became a symbol, and I was proud of that. He was proof that aid organizations weren't just providing handouts; some of us were offering the path to a new future.

I was FaFa's lifeline and that was deep to me. I made sure he always had a job with us and he never shied away from the hardcore work. He became one of the leaders of our distribution team, the ones who make sure that rice gets delivered intact to the starving. He carried our flag through the toughest territory and always came through. There were times when other nongovernmental aid organizations couldn't get into the most gang-ridden slums to feed the hungry. Whenever they got close, the volunteers would get shot up and their supplies would be stolen by slumlords who kept everything for themselves. FaFa was the type of man who made it his business to make sure that didn't happen to Yéle. He spearheaded talks with the gang leaders to insure that no harm would come to anyone working for Yéle. This kid had nothing then: FaFa's home was a small lean-to shack with a roof made of scrap metal. His bed was a mattress he had fashioned out of tinfoil.

I remember seeing him after I'd been away from Haiti for a while and he came up to me with a big smile on his face.

"Look at my arm," he said.

On one forearm he'd gotten WYCLEF tattooed. On the other, JEAN.

I was touched, really touched. FaFa was a tough guy, though, so I made a joke out of it.

"Hey man," I said. "I'm glad you got a tattoo of me, because I'm not going to get a tattoo of you."

We both had a laugh, but when I looked in his eyes he knew how I really felt. I treat all of my leaders in Yéle like they are my kids. I take them in because they are part of my extended family. Opening your doors fully is the only way to take a bad situation and make it good.

FaFa worked for Yéle tirelessly until the day he died. And the way he died is the kind of injustice that all Haitians have known firsthand at some point in their lives. Haitians know that life is not fair and that death can come to anyone at any time, no matter how good they are.

Like every other kid who wants to improve his community, Fafa wanted to see the rest of the world to learn how he could return and help his country. He and I talked about him getting out to see America.

I made that happen with a visa to be in America for the night I performed at the MTV New Year's Eve party in 2008. FaFa stayed with me for a few days afterward, too, and anyone who saw that performance knows that on air I invited everyone back to my house. I didn't give out the address, but let me tell you, everyone who knows where I live in Saddle River, New Jersey, showed up. We had seven hundred people in my backyard until the sun came up! FaFa was there and he couldn't believe it. I'd never seen him so excited and I wasn't far behind.

"Anything is possible, you know."

"Why is that, FaFa?"

"Because here I am standing in a mansion. In Haiti, they make you think you could never set foot in a mansion; you could never be good enough to do that. Well here I am. I am in a mansion. Look how simple it is for me to stand in the middle of a mansion."

"This is true, my brother. Here you are. And what do you think of it?"

"I think one day I'm gonna have my own mansion. If it's possible that I'm standing here at all, it's possible that I can have one of my own. The only thing people with mansions have over me is the opportunity to travel. If I get that opportunity, I'm going to go to school. I'm going to be a big businessman and I'm going to help my daughter and my mom."

"You can do it all, my brother. I know you can."

Back in that graveyard, FaFa, Izolan, Jerry, and I watched as people tossed bodies into graves. The undertaker recognized us and came over to greet us. We had five or six bodies in a wheelbarrow. We paid the undertaker, who told us they'd each get their own grave, and then we left them there to get more bodies.

At the gate, we were pulled aside by one of the undertaker's workers. "Clef, don't trust him," he said. "By the time you get back, they will all be in one hole."

I turned right back around and walked up to the guy. "I gave you money to put each person in their own hole and you're going to do that."

"Don't worry about that. It will happen."

At that moment, I lost it. I grabbed him by the collar. "One of your own men said you're not burying the people in their own holes. Don't you lie to me! One hole for each body that I gave you, do you understand?"

"I understand!"

I turned to FaFa. "Stay here and make sure each one of them gets their own grave."

"I'll dig them myself if I have to," FaFa said. That is the kind of man he was.

After we returned, FaFa left in his pickup truck to begin taking bodies from the rubble to the graveyard; it was a four-wheeled ferry for the dead. During one of these trips, he was carjacked by some gangbangers. He refused to get out of the truck, so they shot him in the chest twice and drove off. We know this because the guy riding with FaFa slipped out the other door and got away.

When the guy who survived came to us and told us what had happened I went completely insane. I forgot who I was, all that I had done, everything. I didn't care about any of it; I only cared about killing FaFa's killers. I can't lie. I decided that I probably wouldn't make it back to America and in that moment I was okay with that. Nothing else mattered. I was going to kill them or die trying because the injustice of his death was too much for me to bear.

It wasn't a fantasy; I was ready and able to do this. I had all kind of guns and weapons at my disposal and my only mission became putting FaFa's killers underground. As I got ready to leave with my team, my wife started screaming at me.

"You can't do this! You can't do this!"

"Yes I can!"

"Keep in mind why you're here! Keep in mind what you came here for. There is a lot of tension but you have to stay above it! You are going to ruin everything you've done here over this! Stop it right now. You will destroy your life in one second. These people need you. Think of them—not of yourself!"

"Get off of me! I'm going to handle this."

She was right of course. And I heard her, but I wasn't going to stop what I was doing. My wife is such a good woman that in the end she came along with us rather than see me go out there alone. She's my ride or die. She and her friend Cynthia Debeaux came along. And with those two on your side, you don't need anyone else.

We loaded up the car with arms and went out to find the killer. We drove around for hours but we never found a trace. We couldn't find the truck; we didn't find his body. We didn't find anything. The killers were so scared of retribution that they made FaFa just disappear. To this day his body has never been recovered and nothing else has been learned about who did it. They must have known from the start that if we tracked down FaFa's body, we would figure out who killed him and come for them.

Over the next three days my wife and I spent our waking hours loading bodies onto trucks until our hands burned. When someone dies, the body releases all of its toxins. When you pile bodies on top of each other under the blazing sun, those toxins become a corrosive acid, as the chemical reaction that comes with rot sets in. We worked through it, washing our hands as often as we could, because we had no gloves.

We spent our nights strategizing on a large scale, plotting how we could bring international aid into the country as quickly as possible. After a few days on the ground, Yéle was up again and running, providing safe drinking water and food, and clearing the streets of the dead before disease took hold. There would be no end to the work, but I realized that I could do greater good back in America, promoting the relief effort.

I did not know how long I had been gone as I set out for the airport, because it was all still a blur. In front of La Villa Créole, I saw a member of my Yéle family that I'd not seen since my first day on the ground.

"How are you, brother?" I asked him.

"She lived, Clef," he said, smiling at me. I didn't know whom he was talking about at first.

"The girl, in the clinic, she lived."

Her face came to me, and that intense moment which was so intense returned. It had happened just a few days ago, but I felt like I was recalling something from long ago. "I'm so glad to hear that, brother. I'm glad she's alright."

"It's better than that, Clef. She can walk, too."

The girl we had pulled from the rubble—she had survived. Her legs were not paralyzed; they were only traumatized, the nerves damaged by the impact of the debris. The numbness was so severe that her legs were temporarily useless, but after a few days the feeling came back, and after that her motor skills. She had grown strong and left her hospital bed.

She didn't go far though, because she had nowhere to go. She had been saved and she was grateful, so she did the only thing that made sense to her: she helped the doctors to repay her debt to them. She worked to rebuild, in whatever small way she could, the spirit of Haiti. In the days and months that followed, I kept her memory in my heart. Like an eternal flame at the Tomb of the Unknown Soldier, it gave me the strength to go on and to never forget that there was always more work to do. No one could do it alone; we would all need to lean on each other.

I

THE VILLAGE

I was born in Croix-des-Bouquets, a village that lies in the Ouest Department of Haiti, about ten miles from the nation's capital, Port-au-Prince. It once was a coastal village but, like the lost city of Atlantis, the original Croix-des-Bouquets fell into the sea during one of the many earthquakes that have rocked Haiti since the dawn of time. The Port-au-Prince earthquake of June 3, 1770, was so strong that the tsunami waves it caused turned the earth along the coast into mud incapable of supporting buildings, and so the entire town slipped under the water. According to the history books, only three hundred people were killed by the tremor itself because a deep rumbling preceded it. They were warned that time. But in the fires and famine that followed, an estimated thirty thousand escaped slaves perished. What can I say? Mother Nature has never given Haiti a break.

My ancestors relocated Croix-des-Bouquets inland to the Plaine du Cul-de-Sac, a valley that extends all the way across the island, into the Dominican Republic. The soil there is naturally fertile and the valley is known for its agriculture. This changed the focus of the villagers from fishing to farming. Over the next two hundred years, the town evolved into two distinct halves: one was agricultural and the other industrial. They were divided by the center of town, literally and symbolically. In the middle was where all commerce was done, along a crowded section of road crammed with vendors selling their goods. The vendors built shacks there and later low buildings with storefronts.

Over time, the two sides of town also came to divide the "haves" from the "have-nots." Those families who tended farms and passed them down through the generations were wealthy, because their land provided food to the rest of the country. Those who made clothes or other goods by hand weren't as lucky. As the rest of the world industrialized and handmade items became outdated, those families fell further behind.

I was born on October 17, 1972. My family lived in the formerly industrial side of the village, in a place called La Serre, which by that time resembled the Juhu slums of Mumbai that were captured so well in the film *Slumdog Millionaire*. There was no infrastructure to speak of, so neighbors looked out for each other as best they could. We did not have electricity; we did not have centralized health care or local clinics of any kind. My mother will be the first to tell you that my birth was not an easy one.

I was not a small baby, so she was in pain. And I did not come quickly, so her pain was not brief. After hours of contractions, she was near delirious, but I would still not come because my large head (so I am told) had become stuck in her birth canal. The village midwife did what she could: she used forceps to grip the sides of my skull but she could still not guide me clear. It's not like there were superprofessionals doing this stuff in Croix-des-Bouquets.

As the clock ticked and my mother continued to cry out in pain, the midwife lost her patience.

"Woman!" she yelled, right in my mother's face. "Shut your trap now! Do not yell at me! I am not the one who got you pregnant!"

My father waited outside the hut, pacing and listening, unsure

of what to do. Inactivity did not sit well with my father, because he
was a man of action and a man of words, like his father before him.
The two of them represent the pillars of my character. My grandfather had devoted himself to leading his village as their Vodou
priest. My father chose to lead as well, devoting himself instead to
Christianity, against his father's wishes. In this moment of need, he
turned to his faith.

As my mother continued to cry out helplessly, my father sat quietly and prayed until he found the answer. He entered the hut, put
some water on the fire to boil, and sat down beside my mother.
He opened his Bible to Psalm 23 and tore out the page. He cut the
paper into small pieces, dropped them into the water, and stirred
the concoction as the women stared in disbelief.

The midwife said what my mother could not. "Are you crazy?
Why are you cutting your Bible?"

"Silence!" he shouted.

When the psalm had dissolved, he let the water cool.

Then he made my mother drink it.

"This will ease your pain," he said.

Two hours later I was born. My father gave me the gift of words
before I even left my mother's womb.

PSALM 23

The Lord is my shepherd, I shall not be in want.
He makes me lie down in green pastures,
He leads me beside quiet waters.
He restores my soul.
He guides me in paths of righteousness
for His name's sake.
Even though I walk

through the valley of the shadow of death,
I will fear no evil,
for You are with me;
Your rod and Your staff,
they comfort me.
You prepare a table before me
in the presence of my enemies.
You anoint my head with oil;
my cup overflows.
Surely goodness and love will follow me
all the days of my life,
and I will dwell in the house of the Lord forever.

My parents named me Jeannel Wyclef Jean, a name that honors
two rebel leaders in the history of man. The first is John Wycliffe,
who was born in England in the 1320s and became a theologian, a
preacher, and a religious reformer. Wycliffe and his followers were
called the Lollards and they did not agree with the Roman Catholic
Church's idea of the role of the clergy. At the time, the Bible used
by the Catholic Church was Latin, which allowed the church to
control how its meaning was interpreted. The average churchgoer
in England didn't speak Latin, so they believed what they were told.

Wycliffe did not believe that a select group of men should be allowed to withhold the words of the Bible from their fellow men. He
believed that they should be free to learn from the book directly.
He believed, as I do, that all men must be their own teachers and
be free to discover knowledge from the source because this is the
only path to truth.

John Wycliffe has been referred to in religious history as the
Morning Star of the Reformation. He was the earliest to question the rule of the clergy over the lives of man. He was ahead
of his time: his writings planted the seeds of the Protestant

Reformation that took hold in Western Europe two hundred years later. He was a man of both words and action, so in his fifty years on Earth, he put his beliefs into practice by initiating the first translation of the Bible into everyday English. In the scholarly Christian circles of his day, he argued that the scriptures be held in higher authority over both the papacy and the monks in man's quest for God. Wycliffe began a translation of the Bible from the Vulgate, the fifth-century Latin version of the Bible used by the Catholic Church of the day. There is no way for historians to be certain, but they believe that John Wycliffe translated the Gospels of Matthew, Mark, Luke, and John himself and perhaps he completed the entire New Testament. His associates and his assistant, John Purvey, worked on translating the Old Testament and finished the resulting Wycliffe's Bible in 1384.

His Bible, written in everyday English, had great influence due to the clarity, beauty, and strength of its language. Wycliffe taught that the privileged hierarchy of the clergy should be replaced with priests who chose a life of poverty, so his followers took no vows and received no consecration. They walked the countryside barefoot, in pairs, wearing long red robes and carrying staffs, preaching the sovereignty of God.

The other man I am named after is Toussaint L'Ouverture, a slave who became a general of the people and led Haiti to freedom from foreign rule in the late 1700s. He was freed by his French master and became a high-ranking officer in the Freemason organization in Saint-Dominigue, a French colony on the island of Hispaniola, would eventually become Haiti. L'Ouverture organized thousands of slaves in the area into a guerilla army that rebelled against the French colonial rulers. This was the first step toward the emancipation of the nation. It is fitting that the name *Toussaint* means "all souls opening."

My father fused theology and leadership in my name, and it is no accident that he chose a rebel like Toussaint L'Ouverture to represent strength. My father was man of faith like his father, yet he chose to rebel against him. Where my grandfather found his path in life through Vodou, the native religion of the Haitian people, my father found his by embracing Christ—and defying his father's beliefs. In that way, my father, Gesner Jean, was a typical teenager.

One day when he was eighteen, Gesner passed the Nazarene Church while he was walking through the streets of Port-au-Prince. According to him, he experienced a revelation. He saw the house of God with its doors opened before him and suddenly felt a light ignite inside him. Beyond the shadow of a doubt he understood what he must do with his life: he must become Protestant. He must "protest" Vodou and follow a path apart from his family's beliefs.

Gesner walked into the church and joined their congregation that day. He could have done so and still practiced Vodou, because it isn't uncommon for Haitians to do so. Some churches even integrate Vodou ritual into their Sunday services. But my father wanted no part of that; he wanted a clean break from tradition, so he renounced Vodou for life. There is one thing about my father that all who knew him will tell you: he always did what he vowed he would do. His father wasn't happy to hear this news, but he took it respectfully. He told my father that he would always remain his son, though he saw their spiritual paths permanently diverging. There was definitely tension, because until his dying day, my father never spoke in depth of this decision. It was the moment that defined who he was, because he defied everything that his family had been up to that point. He told me about that time at a point in my life when he and I had our own problems. I was embarking on a path that was different from what he intended for me and we'd come to the crossroads where he, too, knew there was nothing he could do to change my mind. It is an interesting place for a father and a son because it's a standoff. And because you're of the same flesh, you know instinctually that your opponent is not going to give. And so you both walk away with respect and no harm done, because if you do anything else, it will be mutually assured destruction. So what I'm saying to you is that I believe that my grandfather respected my father's decision, but he let it be known that he denounced it completely. Like father, like son: Gesner's father was a spiritual leader, so in the end, he wanted that for his son, and he was willing to accept it, even if that meant that his son was going to become a leader in an institution that he rejected. And in a way, that is what passed between my father and me.

My father, Gesner Jean, was a born leader, just like his father. Even in his youth Gesner was the type of man who commanded the attention of his peers, so it didn't take very long for him to become influential in the congregation of the church he'd just joined. He decided to become a licensed minister, because the Nazarene Church's policy of shared power between the people and the clergy, and between the local churches and the greater denomination, echoed his belief in equality and democracy. The church allows men and women to become ministers and their vow is to teach the word, to administer the holy sacraments, and to guide their community.

My father had been in the church for several years before I was born and had gotten far enough along in his education that he was granted a visa to visit a Nazarene Church in America to continue his studies. The church was founded in 1908, in Pilot Point, Texas, with Haiti accounting for the second-highest number of denominations in the world, after the United States. My father had other plans for that visa, though.

He planned to disappear.

After I was born, and my brother, Sam, two years later, my father's main concern was finding us a better life, somewhere safer than Haiti. He did not see good times ahead after the election of Jean-Claude "Baby Doc" Duvalier, who came to power following his father, François's, death in 1971. Nothing was going to change under the absolute power rule of the younger Duvalier. Speaking out against the government in any form was considered treason. Even a preacher could be arrested and executed without a word if one of his sermons was interpreted as being anti-Duvalier.

Gesner Jean did what he had to do: he deceived the church, he received his visa, and he went with his wife, Yolanda, to America, leaving their two kids, Sam and me, in Haiti. They settled as illegal immigrants among the Haitian community in the Marlboro Projects of Coney Island, Brooklyn, and once they settled, they had my brother Sedek. He had US citizenship by birth, and this in turn allowed my parents to become citizens through what has come to be called "maternity citizenship." When illegal immigrants have a child in the United States, that child becomes what is called an "anchor baby," which allows the parents to remain in the country and the entire family to apply for citizenship behind the infant's legal right as a citizen. In 2008, by one estimate, there were something close to four hundred thousand anchor babies born in the States that year, all of whom allowed immigrant families a chance to bring other relatives into the country, leading to an unstable US population. It isn't as easy as it used to be, but my parents did it, and once they got that foothold, they relocated my brother Sam and me, and then added to our family. My sister Melky came after Sedek and then, in their older days, my parents had my little baby sister, Rose.

FOR THE FIRST TEN years of my life, I was raised by my aunt, Mama Filomen, who was my mother's sister, and my uncle. I thought they were my mother and father. My aunt looked Ethiopian, and she could have been Indian as well—fierce eyes and beautiful bone structure. She wore simple cotton dresses and glasses and I was convinced that she was my mother. I would even call her Mama but she'd always correct me. "Your mother lives in America," she'd say. "She sent you this Bible, and she will come back for you and Sam one day." I never believed it.

We lived with my aunt and uncle and about thirty or forty of our relatives under my grandmother's care in a series of huts that always felt like we were all living underneath just one roof, in one hut—my grandmother's.

She was the matriarch to all of us. She was a short woman, barely five feet tall, whose facial features also looked like a mix of African and Indian. She had eyes of fire but her smile was peaceful. Her voice was always calm, but when she screamed it was louder than thunder. What mattered most to her was keeping the family together; she did not want the tribes to separate. There were many kids under her care, and those with their parents with them were always more valid than those like Sam and me, who didn't have parents there. This created friction among the homes, and it definitely weighed on my brother and me because it made us feel invisible. The only one who made us feel important was our grandmother, my mother's mother.

My parents would send us gifts every Christmas from America, but I never believed the presents were truly from them. When my aunt and uncle would say, "These are from your mother and father." I would nod yes, but I would tell my brother Sam what I really thought: our gifts were from Santa Claus.

I told Sam that Santa couldn't bring his sleigh to our house because we didn't have a chimney to slide down so he dropped our gifts behind the hut as he flew over. Each year we tried to stay awake to catch him, but sleep always won. As any child knows, the moment you fall asleep is the moment Santa Claus arrives.

My brother and I were consumed by the myth that our parents were Santa Claus until the moment they came and got us, which was a pretty strange moment I must say.

My father left us with my aunt, uncle, and grandma when I was one year old and my mother was pregnant with Sam. He flew to the States to preach and do further Nazarene training in the ministry. It wasn't easy on my mother at all; you can imagine the struggle of having a child in those circumstances without her husband present. If it weren't for my grandmother and her sister, she couldn't have done it.

In a basic sense, too, everyday life for my brother and me was far from easy. My family were farmers for the most part; they owned a little piece of land that they tended, but they spent most of their time working the land for other people. When the crops came to bear, we would have a nice landfall and things were good. About once a month they'd take enough home that my grandmother could buy a pig or a goat, and when that happened, we kids knew that the feast of the century was coming. My grandmother would cook every single piece of that pig into dishes so delicious that I remember them all to this day. The animal would be roasted right in our backyard, behind our huts, so you could smell it cooking from a long way off. You could smell the rice simmering, and when you knew it was your family making that feast, you walked proudly through the town. There would be green beans, white rice, and meat, and I remember waiting in anticipation all day long. I loved those smells, but I wanted the food now. It was like being a child on Christmas; I could barely wait until mealtime. Those were nothing like the hard times, when I'd dig into the depths of the rice bowl hoping to scrape a few bits of burnt rice from the metal.

On Sundays, my grandmother would give us *goud* for the collection plate at church. Goud is the Haitian Creole word for money, adapted from *gourde*, the French word for Haitian currency. My mother's mother was a good member of the Christian Nazarene Church and she raised us to be the same, so we went to services three times per week, and we attended the Nazarene school.

In spite of this, the goud did not always make it safely to the collection plate. "Don't you buy candy with this," my grandmother would say to us. "If you do, God will tell me, and he won't be happy."

What can I say? My brother and I were businessmen from the start, and as both street hustlers and CEOs know, you don't succeed in business without taking risks. We would take the goud and go to a man who sold candy in the village. We would give him the coin and take the candy. We liked having one candy between the two of us, but we knew we'd be happier with many candies. After a few weeks, we made the man a proposition.

"This goud is enough for one candy. And we will come and give you a goud for a candy the next five weeks. But if you give us five candies today, we will guarantee you four more goud."

We knew grandma was good for the goud. We just had to be sure we didn't sit beside her in church and let her see us without the goud. In the end, out of the goodness of his heart, the man agreed, and I thank him for giving Sam and me a feast the likes of which we'd never known. To children who'd survived on so little, feasting on candy like that was like serving a starving man a steak.

If you have a best friend or a partner in the worst of times, you find a way to carry each other through anything, and that is what Sam and I did for each other. We were always hungry, but we never felt that we lived in poverty because we were always happy. If you have love, you have the will to survive whatever comes. When there was no food, we ate clusters of the red dirt that made up the floor of our hut. This is common in Haiti. The dirt has some degree of mineral content to nurture you and the bulk of it fills you up when there is no meal to eat.

Things never got too bad in our family because we had cousins on my father's side who lived along the ocean in Arcahaie. Their town was in the middle of a rich agricultural region, so they were never without food, because vegetables grew everywhere. They worked farms and owned land the way we did, but they also lived by the ocean and were free to fish as often as they liked. They were good fishermen so they were never without, and whenever they visited us, they brought us some extra food, which was always a great help.

Those visits were also special because when our cousins came to visit we became the kid pack and we always got into mischief. My

aunt and uncle were strict about Sam and me saying our prayers
before bed every night, but when our cousins visited we never got
around to it, because we never wanted to go to bed. We were having
too much fun to sleep.

My aunt and uncle were wise though, and they came up with
a scheme to get us to bed early and to say our prayers. One night
after we were nestled together to sleep, my uncle took a branch that
he had carved to look like the claw of a dinosaur and extended it
slowly through the door. At least this is what I think happened. I
have never gotten the truth out of my uncle.

As I lay there, I heard scratching in the dirt and opened my eyes
to see this wooden claw making its way toward us. My eyes popped
open, and so did my cousin Nason's and we both started screaming.
The others woke up and they started screaming, too, even louder
when they saw the claw I was pointing at. Suddenly my aunt burst
through the door of the hut with a machete and chopped the claw
in two, yelling at the "creature" to be gone. She was our hero.

She may have only been trying to keep the children under her
watch from misbehaving, but she accomplished much more than
that. I have always enjoyed telling stories, and it did not take long
for me to tell every child in our village about the monster that had
tried to eat us in our sleep. My aunt had told us it was called Alugaw,
the werewolf of the night, and I spread this story far and wide. This
experience taught my cousins and my brother and me that there
are greater powers at work in the world, and through this idea, and
the fear that came with it, we were drawn deeper into our religion.
We now had a reason to pray every night: asking God to protect us
from evil and the demons that might try to eat us.

As an older man, I realize the value of illusions. I understand
why a parent uses them to scare their children into the behavior
that is best for them. But sometimes, when I lie in bed and see
that claw again in my mind, I ask myself, *Where did they get that
idea? And how did they know it would work so well?* They helped the

entire village, because soon afterward, we weren't the only children praying for an hour or more before we put out the oil lamp and lay down to rest.

THERE WERE MANY WAYS for young boys to spend their days in my village before they were old enough to go to school. My favorite activity was hunting because if we were successful, it meant more to eat that day. My brother and I had no guns or knives, so we made slingshots out of branches and thick rubber bands. We would shoot rocks at the small birds that lived in the trees in the village, and I was pretty good. They weren't easy to hit, but it wasn't unusual for us to come home with five or ten of them to eat.

One day, as I took aim at a bird on a branch, I saw the largest bird I had ever seen fly overhead.

"Look!" I said to my brother. "It is a giant eagle! If we can shoot that thing from the sky we will eat forever!"

The two of us flung rocks at the giant eagle as it flew on, its shadow passing over us. It was the first time either of us had ever seen an airplane.

My brother and I loved going to church, not only because it meant we'd get goud to trade for candy, but because there was music there. Haitian churches are where the culture really comes alive. Members of the congregation bring instruments, play songs, and sing as an integral part of worshipping God.

Ever since I was a small child, I've always been a bit of a bully. My parents have a picture of me in a little cowboy outfit holding two toy guns, and in that photo, you see everything you need to know about me. I was the kid who held all of the toys, even if they weren't mine. And if they were mine, everyone else had better look out. Let me give you an example.

By the time I was eight years old, I did not believe that Sam and I had parents at all. I had realized that my aunt and uncle were my aunt and uncle, and I accepted it when they told me that my parents used to be here but now lived in a faraway place called America where I would join them someday. I nodded at them when they said that someday my parents would come for us, but in my heart I never believed them. I thought that our parents did not exist and that eventually my aunt and uncle would tell us this truth. By then I figured my aunt and uncle were Santa Claus, too.

That is not what I wanted to be true, but it is what I believed to be true. When a bicycle arrived in the village for Sam and me, supposedly sent by my parents, it became irrelevant whether they existed or not. All I knew was that this bike was ours and that no one else would ever ride it.

To the children in our village, a bicycle was a Bentley; there was nothing better a kid could have. If you had a bike, everyone wanted to ride it, but I didn't let that happen. It was not because I loved riding it so much, but because it was mine and I was a bully. I would have felt the same way if the bike had been given to someone else in the village: it would still have been mine and I would have ridden it whenever I liked, perhaps even more if I could take it without a fight. The truth is that I got more satisfaction out of holding on to the bike than I did riding it. I've just always liked to be in charge. My cousin once made the mistake of trying to ride my bike around the village. I grabbed the closest rock from the ground and threw it at him as hard as I could, knocking him from the bike. He was one of my best friends, but that didn't matter to me. I got in a lot of trouble and took a beating for it, but no one ever tried to borrow my bike again.

Now that I am older, I realize why I behaved this way. I told myself, and my brother, that we had no parents because in case it was the truth I wanted us to be prepared for that reality. I didn't want that to be the truth, but I had to be ready in case it was. I wanted a mom and a dad just like every child, and I envied every kid who had them. I saw it this way: I couldn't have my friends' parents so they couldn't have my bike. That bike symbolized whether my mom and dad existed or not. The bike was all I had of them, whether they were just an idea or real people, so I kept it close to me at all times. It represented independence for me as a kid, but to me guarding it was also a test. After all, if my parents didn't exist, I would need to be a parent to Sam, and I would need to protect what was ours.

Every day, my brother and I walked a few miles to the Nazarene school in our uniforms. On the outskirts of our town, there was, like there are in many rural villages, a huge shit pond. This is how plumbing works in the third world: there is a ditch that runs downhill into a pond where the townspeople's human waste gathers. Some of it dries out in the sun and turns to dust, but it's always about three feet deep. Our path to school wound along the top of the hill that circled the pond.

One day, my brother and I were making each other laugh on our way to school and just then I slipped, slid down the slope, and landed face first in the shit pond. My head went under and I fell far enough in that I had to swim to get back to the shore. It was the most disgusting thing that ever happened to me. How can I explain to you how horrible the sensation of going under in a pool of human waste was? The smell was everywhere and it didn't leave my skin and hair for days. It didn't feel like water. It didn't feel like mud. It felt like what it was. When you end up paddling through a shit pond, there is no fooling yourself, believe me.

That wasn't one of my better days. I had only one school uniform, so I had to go to the river, take it off and scrub it until the stains came out. Then I had to wait around in my drawers until my clothes dried. By the time I got to school I was half a day late, so my teachers beat me. That is how they handled truancy in my school: the ruler was a learning tool.

. . . .

I HAD MY FIRST musical experience in church, which isn't uncommon, but this was a Haitian church. You have to understand: Haitian Christians are Haitians first, so as I've mentioned, they have no problem practicing both Christianity and Vodou. Religion is religion to Haitians; a relationship with God and powers greater than man are one and the same. Church is the house of God where these relationships are celebrated, so practicing both there makes sense to Haitians.

I'm not sure how old I was at the time, but there was a great controversy in our village surrounding a tamboo drum that someone had brought to church. Haitians always bring instruments to church, because the service is full of music and all of the congregation sings and plays together while they worship. The drum was not out of place, but this one was different. As the service went on, the preacher began to pay attention to the man playing it. He kept singing with us and clapping his hands, but I could tell that he was listening to this one drum out of all of the instruments. I knew this because I was standing directly in front of it. Slowly the preacher made his way toward the drum and stood staring at it, and me, for some time. Then he stopped the music.

"Bring that drum to me," he said.

I froze. I figured he knew about Sam and me hustling goud off Grandma.

"That drum has evil in it," he said. "You, child, bring it to me."

I turned around and looked at everyone in the church, then took hold of the drum and brought it to him. It seemed like every other drum to me.

The preacher carried the tamboo to the front of the church and put his hands on it. He began to pray.

"Evil spirit, leave this drum! Leave this village!" He began rocking the drum back and forth. "I send you out in the name of Jesus Christ!"

It looked like something was moving in the hole in the bottom of the drum. The preacher leaned it to one side and a black snake crawled out. The preacher picked up the snake and brought it to the door of the church.

"Spirit be gone from this village!" he said.

The drum was placed at the back of the church where it would stay until the preacher took it away from the village into the woods. It was forbidden to even go near it. But I never thought rules applied to me if I wasn't hurting anybody, so in the middle of the night, I snuck out of my hut, being careful not to wake my brother. I snuck past all of the dark homes and sleeping villagers and went to the church, because I had to play that drum. I made sure no one saw me as I crept inside, into the dark church. For a minute I thought that this wasn't a good idea.

I got hold of that drum and ran my fingers over the top of it, then down the side. I got scared that another snake would come out, but I tipped it on its edge anyway, and ran my hand along the inside of the hole. I flicked my finger against it and heard the hollow sound it made. I began to pat my fingers against the drum, quietly tapping out rhythms. I wanted to play louder but I didn't dare to. I didn't want to be discovered, not because I was scared of being punished, but because I didn't want to stop playing.

It felt like I played for half an hour, but when I looked up, light was leaking into the church. I knew I had to get home quickly or be caught, but still I couldn't stop. I was in a trance, playing rhythms, and loving the music I was making in a way I never had before. I closed my eyes and kept playing.

Then the pastor came in. He pushed me aside, took the drum from my hands, and poured holy water over it. Then he covered it with a white cloth and took it outside. I followed him like a little boy who had lost his puppy.

"This drum is a curse!" he shouted. He put it into a bag, tied the bag to a donkey, and rode it out of town himself.

That was the last time I saw that drum, but I've never forgotten it. That moment was the first time I experienced "trance mode," which is an incredible place for a musician. In trance mode you become one with your instrument and your thoughts and feelings are directly connected to what you are playing. It's like being on autopilot, but without losing the excitement of flying on your own.

People who know me always say that I'm a different person on-stage, and any fan of mine knows that I've been known to play shows for four hours or more. Quincy Jones himself once said that Prince and Michael Jackson (rest in peace) had better watch out. He said no one should fuck with me onstage because they couldn't keep up. It all started with that drum back in the village. Maybe that snake was left over from a Vodou ceremony the owner had done the day before. Whether it was possessed by a demon or not, that drum possessed me, and I have yet to be released from its spell. I hope I never am.

2

GARDEN STATE PROMISED LAND

I wasn't a very good student in school at any point in my life. Aside from music class, and some pieces of world history, I've never been able to retain anything taught to me in a classroom. It's not that I don't like learning, or that I can't read; it's just that most days in my school, there wasn't much going on that was more interesting than the thoughts in my head or the girls sitting next to me. Even when I wanted to pay attention to the teacher, beautiful girls were like interference causing static on the radio in my mind. The teacher began to sound like the weaker station far away in another town, while the girls were right there, coming through loud and clear. There were a few times when my teacher was herself a pretty young lady, which made it easy for me to pay attention to her, but hard for me to understand what she was saying.

In my Haitian school, I was no stranger to the ruler, because a swift hit to the back of the head was how teachers put an end to daydreaming. The only subject I was any good at was Haitian history, because the stories of our liberation from foreign rule made me proud. Other than that, I was completely useless, just staring out the window or trying to get the girls to smile at me and meet me after class.

When I did get involved in the lesson, I was even worse, because I was that kid who liked to ask the teacher questions that had nothing to do with the subject. I wasn't so much a class clown as I was a rebellious instigator. I would try to lead the teacher into a conversation about life that had nothing to do with school. I was a skinny grade-school philosopher. I especially enjoyed doing this when substitutes or new teachers showed up for their first day. As soon as they'd said hello I was the first kid to put his hand up.

"Who are you?" I'd say. "Why are you here? You're not our teacher."

"No, I'm—"

"Where is our teacher, then?" I'd get all of this out before they could even answer my first question.

I had my reasons for this: by the time I was nine, teachers disappeared regularly from our school. It became accepted for history teachers in particular to disappear and never be heard from again. Most often the new teacher would silence me with a stern look and a slap.

Or they would say something like, "The other teacher is no longer at school because she was a Communist. Do not speak of her again."

All of the kids knew what that meant: the army had taken our teacher away to be executed.

My father's predictions about the young Duvalier had been right. Once he took power, he targeted intellectuals at all levels of society and they began to vanish—schoolteachers, lawyers doctors, writers—anyone smart and well-spoken who might oppose the regime. The side effects of this paranoia destroyed Haiti because it forced the educated class to flee for their lives. If you drive away the best minds of a generation, how can a country hope to move into the future? Our country was already in trouble, so Duvalier's shortsighted cultural holocaust crippled us for life. My father was wise to see this coming, and like many others who would have otherwise stayed and helped Haitian society, he found a way to get out.

Duvalier drove the future away and kept the present in chains through fear, propaganda, and calculated gestures that convinced the poor that he was their benefactor. I remember one of these acts very well because it is among my fondest memories of childhood. It was what American kids experience when they go to an amusement park: a moment when magic seems real to you. A few days after Duvalier took power, he celebrated by sending helicopters over the most impoverished villages in Haiti to drop money from the sky as loudspeakers proclaimed the great wealth in store for us under his rule. That was like God speaking from heaven to a kid like me. My brother Sam and I jumped in the air to catch the bills before they landed and spent the rest of the afternoon searching the ground, picking up as many as we could find.

Of course, Duvalier Jr.'s rule was not the start of a rich and comfortable future for all Haitians. Those with no way to leave the country had to abide by his law or be murdered. The only way to insure your survival and that of your loved ones under Duvalier was to pledge your allegiance to him, and the easiest way to do that was to align yourself with his vast network of volunteer police. They were called Macoutes and they were the neighborhood thugs, with Duvalier at the top like a gang leader. The Macoutes were not formally trained or organized in any way and they operated under one order: to squash all antiregime activity that they observed. The Macoutes made their own rules locally as they saw fit and were feared by their peers in their villages. At any time a Macoute could create a reason to take a citizen and throw him in jail or kill him. Just as the sky was blue, if a Macoute didn't like you, your days were numbered.

Becoming a Macoute or a friend to them was the only way to survive, and if I had grown up in Haiti past my tenth year, and things had stayed as they were politically, I probably would have become one. If there were fifty men in a village, you could bet that forty of them were Macoutes. Half of my mother's brothers were Macoutes, not because they believed in Duvalier; they believed in staying alive. Paying lip service to a dictator and doing whatever deeds they were told to do was the only way to keep their families safe. My mother's family knew that this was the only insurance a Haitian had against violence because one of her older brothers had risen so high in the older Duvalier's regime that he became one of Papa Doc's elite personal bodyguards. He made sure that his family members fell in line and that the men became Macoutes to ensure their survival. He was a fierce, brutal man, feared by all who knew him. His presence alone was enough to keep our family members safe.

I can't share his name, but I can tell you that he was famous across the land because when he was still just a local Macoute, he built a jail cell within his own house where he took any citizen he suspected of crimes against the government. This guy took great pride in his job. He demanded that people in the village pay tribute to him by doing work for him or bringing him things, and if they didn't, he would ask them to report to him at a certain time. Usually they didn't do that, so he would find them and drag them by their arms through the village and lock them up in his jail cell until he decided to let them out. There was no law but his own, and he liked to make a point of it by enforcing it himself, without the help of his soldiers. A man like that has only to do something like this once or twice before the entire village gets the message. Under Duvalier, my mother's brother became a local warlord, then a bodyguard to the man himself, but when Papa Doc's regime fell in 1986, he fled Haiti in fear for his life and never returned.

My father only wanted a safe and peaceful life for his family, so he became a minister not only because it was in his blood, but because it was a way out. As a minister of the Nazarene Church, my father, Gesner, was able to put down roots in America. He joined some of his family who had settled there along with many other Haitians in the Marlboro Houses in Brooklyn, one of the roughest projects in New York City. Marlboro was a horror show back then and it hasn't improved tremendously, but anyplace was safer than Haiti.

My mother and father were able to illegally emigrate to New York because my father's sister already lived there. She hid my mother and father after Gesner's visa ran out and until my mother gave birth to my brother Sedek, qualifying them for citizenship. This was a common hustle among Haitians. Once they'd set down roots legally, they arranged for us to join them.

We heard of this the night before we left for America. My aunt sat us down and said, "Your dad and mom are coming to get you tomorrow."

That was the first time I really believed we had parents. We were going to America.

That morning Sam and I put on our best church clothes, which were the best we had, and we went to the airport to meet them. We were going to stay for a couple of days and then return to our new home. I'll never forget standing at the window in the airport, staring at the big white jet.

"They flew here from America on that plane," my aunt said. "They will be coming down the stairs, so you look for them."

The staircase was rolled out, the door was opened, and people began to file down onto the runway. I didn't even know what kind of person to be looking for.

My aunt started pointing. "There they are! There are your mother and father!"

My father was dressed in a very Western-style suit with a vest and a big belt buckle. He was all in black and he looked like Johnny Cash, with a wild beard. My mother was very neat and well kept; she was wearing a beautiful yellow dress and incredible sunglasses.

I remember her looking like Jackie O. That is all I remember, because they were strangers to me. But I recall saying to myself that my parents were rich. "This is it, Sammy," I said to my brother. "We're going to America!" America was the land of plenty.

I ran up and hugged my mama and dad, and my mom began to cry. Then my dad picked us up and hugged us both a little. He didn't cry; he just asked us if we were okay and how we'd been treated while they'd been gone. It was like stepping outside of anything I had ever known. To Sam and me, an airplane was as strange as a UFO, and until that day we'd never had parents.

My father didn't want to stay in Haiti long, because he had hustled the system down there, too. And he'd left in a hurry, so he didn't want to risk getting caught. On the plane, my father sat next to the two sons he hadn't seen in almost a decade and he talked to us about life the entire way. I've never forgotten what he said, and what I remember of it has become more important to me over time. He spoke to us as if we were young men, not the little boys we were. He gave us something to eat and then he asked us straight up what we wanted out of life. I don't remember what I told him. What does a nine-year-old want out of life? To be a cowboy?

He also asked us to describe how we had lived since the day we were born and Sam and I told him everything we liked to do. We told him about hunting birds and all the dogs in the village, and singing songs in church and stories about every kid we ever knew. And how much we liked the bicycle.

The pilot of the plane was white and so were a few of the stewardesses. We didn't speak a word of English, so when they told us to fasten our seat belts, we heard alien language. Sam and I believed that they could make this bird fly using their powers. We thought they worked together to make it go up in the air. We believed that behind the door in the front of the plane was a secret closet with more white people in uniform who all worked to get this iron bird up in the air.

"That is why they are sitting in the front and the rest of the people are in the back, Sam. They all fly together and they pull this bird. That's why we are sitting and they are still walking around. They are using their language to make it go up into the sky."

It got even stranger for me when the white stewardess served me juice. That was something that had never happened to me: a white person serving me. Coming from my village, I was felt like I was on another planet and these people were the aliens. And these aliens were serving me juice. When I think back, the only white person I remember spending any time with in the village was a missionary. He had a beard and taught us about the Bible, so to me, he wasn't a white man or a Christian: he was Jesus.

Over the course of our flight, I watched out the window as the sky went from light to dark. We had only experienced the passing of a day on the ground, never right before our eyes, up above the clouds. Suddenly, maybe an hour after we were in the air, it was almost night. I thought it was magic.

The first thing Sam and I saw of America were the Twin Towers and the tall red needles on top of them blinking. The lights of the city below, all spread out in lines, didn't look real to us at all. I had no idea what they could be.

"Sam," I said. "Look at this place! We have arrived in the City of Diamonds!"

He smiled and giggled.

"You see those lights below, Sam? They are the diamonds and they are everywhere."

"We are going to be rich," Sam said, nodding his head.

"We will work hard. We will get a bunch of diamonds every day. We will stay here for maybe a year and we must find people to help us get those diamonds on the airplane, but we will do it, and we will bring all the lights and other stuff back to the village."

"That is a good idea," Sam said. He was smiling but suddenly he got serious. "We need lights in the village."

When we landed, Sam and I experienced cold for the first time. It was fall, not even winter yet, but coming from the heat and dust of Haiti, the cold hit me like a wall. The chaos of JFK airport made me dizzy. All around me people were speaking languages I had never heard; there were aliens everywhere. In my mind, I wasn't in an airport, because the only airport I'd seen was the small one in Port-au-Prince, and this place was much too big to be an airport. To me, JFK was America, and all I kept asking my brother and mother was, "Where is everybody going?"

My dad's brother picked us up in his LTD station wagon, which was green, like the Family Truckster from *National Lampoon's Vacation*. We thought that thing was a limo. I could not believe how rich my parents were—first a UFO, then a limo. Life in America was going to be incredible. We loaded into the LTD and drove to our new home in Brooklyn to begin our new lives. We had never seen a maze of buildings like the Marlboro Projects, and I thought that this was how rich people lived. As we walked up to the building, I figured that my father owned the whole thing. I learned the truth when we got into the cramped apartment we now called home. It was packed: me, Sam, my parents, my grandmother, my aunt, and whoever else needed a place to stay, all living in that one-bedroom flat. I remember looking at my dad leaning against the wall, watching all of the activity, deep in thought. I can only imagine what he was thinking, after having jumped fences, dodged immigration, risked his life—all for this moment.

My father had come from Haiti on a missionary visa to do further study in the Nazarene faith. Then, when his visa ran out, he decided that he wasn't going back. He went underground like every immigrant with no papers does after they find their way into America. My father hid out with his brother, down in Brooklyn, and they moved into small apartments all over the place. They lived on Nostrand Avenue, Avenue J, Prospect, and Clarkson. My dad did whatever he could for cash payment: cleaning snow, hauling trash, whatever odd jobs he could lock down. And he steered clear of the police or any other kind of authority, because that could have meant getting sent back. He and his brother moved from apartment to apartment like two outlaws. Especially before it was safe to bring my mom over, they lived like two cowboys on the run. If they got a tip that the INS was going to raid an apartment, they'd leave and find another floor to sleep on that night. His end goal was to make enough money to buy a visa (illegal or otherwise) for my mom so she could join him and they could start a normal life. Back in Haiti, my dad had learned to sew, so he became a tailor and did work among the Haitian community. He also worked in a few sweatshops and got paid under the table. He saved his pennies until he had enough to buy my mom a six-month visa, probably for a few grand, through someone who had connections in the Haitian embassy. When that expired, the two of them hid out. Until she gave birth to my brother Sedek, they hid from everyone.

MY GRANDMOTHER WAS THE matriarch of the first house I came to call home in America in every way, and to prove it she'd make us kids empty the vase she kept by her bed to piss in during the night. This became my job, to keep me humble. It didn't make me humble, but I did empty it. Whatever time it was—morning, late in the evening, afternoon—she'd shout, "Nel! Come take the vase." Nel is an abbreviation of my first name Nelust, and there was never a question what vase she was talking about. The bathroom wasn't very far away, but that wasn't the point. Grandmother was old enough that she had earned the right to have her piss taken care of by her grandchildren. I didn't like doing it, but walking her urine to the toilet was nothing compared to living in the village.

Our new house was a building made of bricks, with an electric refrigerator that kept the milk cold. That refrigerator was magic to my brother and me. For the first three days we were there, we kept opening and closing the door just to watch the light switch on and off. Our second night in America, my brother got out of bed while everyone slept, took the gallon jug of milk from the refrigerator, and drank from it as if he'd been lost in the desert for a week. He'd never tasted anything so delicious as ice-cold milk because we'd never had it before. We had never seen a whole gallon of milk in our entire lives.

"Sam," I said when he got back in bed beside me. "What were you doing with the milk? You shouldn't drink that much."

"I had to," he said, wiping his mouth. It was all over his chin. I had to laugh.

"You drank all of it?"

"No, I only drank half of it," he said. "Listen, we are going to have to stay here longer. We can't go back to Haiti with all the diamonds, yet. This milk is too good. We need to learn how we can take this milk to Haiti."

"So you wanna take all the milk back, too? How that gonna help?"

"I don't care. It's probably not gonna help," he said. "Okay, we can take the diamonds back, but we can't take this milk. Because I'm gonna drink all of it. And you should, too."

"That's greedy, Sam," I said staring up at the ceiling. "The milk is good, and we can't take it with us, but we can take the diamonds and the lights and the other things we need in the village. We need to share and they have so much . . ."

All I heard was heavy breathing. Sam was already asleep, his belly full of milk, a smile on his face.

MY FATHER WAS BORN to be a minister, and leading people was his calling, so it didn't take him long to start a Nazarene ministry church in the projects. There were eight of us living in this apartment once my brother and I joined them, but that didn't matter. My father made space for a congregation to worship in there every Sunday.

My father's services started early in the morning after a few helpers came by to move the furniture and set up a few chairs. From the time I was very young, I always liked to imitate people, and I'm pretty good at it, too. So after about two weeks of services, I started copying my father's every move. While the room was being set up, I would imitate my father's sermon in a corner to entertain myself and my brother.

I held Sam's attention, but my father was incredible to watch. He took his flock on a journey no matter how small or large the church. Gesner Jean had a magical power over his fellow man and from the first time I saw him wield it over the neighborhood faithful, I knew I wanted that same power for myself.

I began to expand my audience beyond Sam in an effort to sharpen my skills. I would get my siblings to sit and listen to me imitate as much of Dad's sermons as I could remember. The one I recited—and bastardized—the most was my father's favorite moral tale, the story of Jonah and the whale.

My father's favorite stories dealt with rebirth, sacrifice, and new beginnings, which were the right stories to tell a collection of immigrants trying to start a new life. They were also very biblical. He would talk about Jonah needing to suffer inside the belly of the whale until he had atoned for the sin of being a false prophet, and how his followers had had to make the sacrifice of casting him into the sea. In my version I got Jonah confused with Elijah the Prophet, whose story comes just before Jonah's in the Bible, so Elijah ended up in the whale for some reason and then ascended to heaven. I acted it out very dramatically so no one minded.

Another of my father's favorite sermons focused on Christ's resurrection, and the theme of rebirth that was at the center of my father's view of the world. He saw a second chance in everyone, so long as they followed the word of Jesus Christ. I can understand his faith better now as a grown man than I could as a teenager. His faith had gotten him through life, and his devotion to the church was the key to our family's survival. All he wanted was to pass this good fortune on in the only way he knew how.

I got really good at imitating my father's theatrics, so good that I'd catch my mom laughing sometimes when she saw me miming his moves. It was like I was doing closed captions for the kids in the room: I knew when my father was going to bang his jacket on the floor, so I'd do it just before he did, and I knew when he was going to hold his hands up to heaven and shake his fists, so I'd do it a little early and I'd keep going after he'd stopped to make fun.

My dad never confronted me about it, but he did come up with a way to focus all of my energy: he bought a bunch of musical instruments and told us to learn to play them. These weren't proper instruments; they were *Muppet Show* instruments, bought at the local Toys "R" Us. Thank you, Jim Henson, for inventing the Muppets and thank you marketing guy who signed off on that licensing deal, because without it, the Jean kids would never have learned to play.

We had a bass, a guitar, some drums, a microphone, and we learned to jam in no time. Eventually, when our parents upgraded us to real instruments, we became a Haitian American Partridge Family. That might sound strange until you realize that the Nazarene Church was Western American, founded in the South, so all of the music in the church came from a country and gospel background.

We had Sedek on drums, my sister Melky singing on the little Muppet microphone, and the rest of us swapping on the rest of the instruments. Even on those toys it didn't take long for us to become the Jean Family Band, entertaining the neighborhood. My siblings and I were blessed with the gift of music; we picked up playing whatever we were given as if it were second nature. To this day, when I play music with my brother or sing with my sister, it's different than when I play with anybody else. My siblings and I share this chemistry that was always there. We don't ever have to talk about it; we already know where the music is taking us. And when we don't, we know that it will.

. . . .

GROWING UP, MY FAMILY lived in some of the toughest, most
dangerous neighborhoods in New York and New Jersey. The Marlboro Houses in Coney Island, where my brother and I began our
adventure here in America back in the eighties, was a war zone
filled with gangs, drugs, and gunfire. The city cleaned them up a
bit in the nineties, but they're not much better today. The murder
rate there is higher than in any other housing project in New York.
There is a reason why every rapper who's lived there mentions it to
prove he's tough.

As soon as they had enough money, our parents moved us out of
there, and for the next few years we house hopped around Flatbush
and other sections of Brooklyn. Both of my parents worked several
jobs until they could afford to buy their first house at 107 South
Clinton Street in East Orange, New Jersey, which was the proud-
est day of my father's life. It didn't matter that the house was in the
middle of the carjacking capital of the world. It was his.

My father was an imposing man. He was of average size, but his
presence was more powerful than any man I've ever met. He commanded respect, even from those who respected nothing. Growing
up I saw my father walk into situations that could easily have ended
his life. He never resorted to violence and he was never scared, because he lived by a rule that he taught me early on: "You must never
fear another man," he said. "No man can take from you what you
don't give him yourself. Only you can give a man the knowledge
that grants him the freedom to take all that is yours."

Over the course of my life, I have seen my father live by this
principle in many situations where it would have been safer to
make an exception to the rule. His devotion to his principles may
have gotten him into danger, but just like his favorite stories in
the Bible, his faith delivered him in the end. That didn't help me,
standing there a few feet away, praying to God that I wasn't about

to see my father shot dead before my eyes. I have never forgotten
that fear, just as I have never forgotten his strength when I have
been tested in life.

The best representation of my father's character was his drive to
start his churches in the toughest neighborhoods he could find. "It
is where God is needed most," he'd say every time I offered to buy
my parents a house in a better neighborhood once I had the money
to do so. "Why would I turn my back on souls that need guidance?"

In areas like that, everyone and everything was a target, so naturally, local thieves tested the waters with Gesner—until they got
to know him, which didn't take long.

This happened every time we moved houses in Brooklyn, because each block was its own village. One of our homes was a very
small three-room house that was also his church, of course. At some
point, a member of the congregation donated a television to the
church. It was kept in the front room, where you could see it from
the street, so at some point soon after that, one of the thugs on the
block stole it. My father had a pretty good idea who it was, so the
next morning he got up, got dressed, walked out of the house with a
real sense of purpose, and went down the street toward the rougher
block where the dudes who ran the area hung out. I ran after him
because I wanted to be there if something happened. There probably wasn't much I would have been able to do, but I wasn't going
to let anyone touch my dad. I prayed that he and I wouldn't end up
dead over some old lady's lame-ass TV.

Gesner walked right up to the guy he was looking for.

"Yo, what's up, Minister? You lost?"

"No, I am not lost," he said looking at the group of them for a
moment. "Do you know where I live?"

The looked at each other sideways, not sure where this was
heading.

"Yeah, you live down there, Minister. Right? You don't know
your own house?"

"I live there, but that is not my house. That is the house of the Lord. It belongs to God and everything in it is his. You do not touch this house. Do you understand? A television was stolen from there last night."

"Oh yeah, Minister? That's fucked up."

"It must be returned. Do you understand what I'm saying to you?"

When a man accuses a known thug of a crime, he'd better be ready to defend himself. No dude like that takes that kind of shit lightly. These guys were feared by everyone on the block and they respected nobody. They stared back at my dad hard, in silence, for a long minute.

"Alright, Minister," one of them said slowly. "We hear that. It won't happen again."

"Thank you," Gesner said. "The church is open to everyone. We have service every Sunday morning. I hope to see you there." Then he turned on his heel like Sidney Poitier meets Dirty Harry and walked back home.

The TV was left on our back porch some time during the night and that next Sunday, I couldn't believe my eyes when I saw one of those cats sneak into the back of church during my father's sermon. He sat as far away from the front as he could, but there was no missing this dude. He stuck out from the rest of the flock like a wolf in a sheep's pen.

I'm not lying to you when I say that my dad had a mystical quality to him, which came from my grandfather. Gesner had turned away from Vodou, but it was in his blood. I believe in greater powers or magic or whatever you want to call it, but even if I didn't, I've seen things happen around my father that had no logical explanation. He was deeply spiritual, and when someone is in touch with God in that way, there is an almost supernatural quality to them.

One time, when we were still living in the Marlboro Houses, a local gang member stopped me while I was walking home from school. I started to weigh my options, deciding which way I would run if I had to.

"Yo, who's that big dude your dad rolls with when he goes out?"

"My dad? My dad don't roll with nobody."

"Yeah, man. Big dude, real tough. He ain't from around here. I see your dad rolling through here all times of day and night and the dude always be walking a few steps behind him, looking out for him."

"My dad don't know no big dude."

"I'm telling you I seen this guy out here walking with your dad."

Whatever you believe it was, Gesner's protector kept him from harm walking in a place where it was easy to die just minding your business.

As a young man watching my father negotiate these situations, I tried to be like him in my own way. I vowed to myself that I would hold my head high when I was tested by kids at school. I wouldn't go looking for trouble, but if it came to me, I would not back down. Being a Haitian with a thick accent, trouble found me.

It started back in Marlboro, where my brother Sam and I got chased home from school every day by a pack of mean, dumb-ass girls. They were older than we were and they were real tough, so they enjoyed beating up the Haitian kids who spoke funny, all the way from the steps of our school to our front door each afternoon.

This went on for a while until I decided we weren't going to take it any more. The two of us had made one friend in the projects who knew his way around, so we asked him what to do. His name was Jeffery; he was a year older than me and he was tough as hell.

"Yo, listen to me. I'm gonna teach you how to slap box," Jeffery said. "Once you learn how, you start slappin' those girls. You do that, they gonna respect you, because they tough like men."

Jeffery gave Sam and me boxing lessons in front of his building in the projects. He made us shadow box. Then we practiced against each other and after a while I got real good. I started to feel like I was ready to retaliate against those girl bullies.

The next day they started in on us the way they always did, the minute we walked out of the building.

"Hey, you ready? We're gonna get you, Haitians. We gonna beat your ass again today, just like we did yesterday."

They liked to let us start running and think we were getting away before they came after us, caught us by the backs of our shirts, and beat us to the ground. I wasn't having that today.

"Y'all ready to run, Haitian?" one of them asked me. "Cuz we gonna get you."

"Nah," I said. "We ain't running."

They all started laughing. "Oh yeah? Okay, Haitian, then you'll get your ass whupped right on the spot."

They came at us and we started using the slap boxing we'd learned. My brother wasn't too good so he got his ass beat, but I was able to keep them off me. I backed their whole crew up with my slap-boxing routine, and they weren't expecting that.

This wasn't some *Karate Kid* moment where I defeated all the bad guys and my brother and I lived happily ever after. They still fucked with us after school, but never as badly as they used to. They'd chase us but not as hard, and when they jumped us, they went easier. If they chose to play that game they'd still win, but they learned that they'd have to take some shots.

In 1985, when my family moved to East Orange, New Jersey, the bullying followed us. I don't know what it was, but the black American kids in my schools growing up loved to hate on Haitians. When I started Nassau Elementary School, I expected it to be the kind of rebirth my dad spoke of in his sermons. The day we moved was a journey worthy of rebirth: it was the first time Sam and I had left Brooklyn since we'd arrived in America. During that car ride we crossed the Brooklyn Bridge, which was the grandest thing

I had ever seen, and then for the first time in our lives, we went through a tunnel. As our LTD station wagon descended into the Holland Tunnel, I thought of Jonah entering the belly of the whale. We were going beneath the sea.

"Are we underwater yet?" I kept asking my dad.

"Not yet."

"Now?"

"No."

"Now?"

"Almost."

"Now?"

"Almost."

"Okay, now we are under the water. We are beneath the Hudson River about to arrive in the Garden State."

Our neighborhood on South Clinton Avenue was a lot like the one portrayed in the movie *Friday*. Within a two-block radius, we had all the same characters: the bully that smacked us in the head every day as we walked to school, the old ladies who knew everybody's business, the dealers, the homeboys—all of it. Two blocks away, on Walnut Street, was a project where the roughest types lived and did their business. All the roughnecks from Jersey came from there: Treach, Vin, and Kay from Naughty by Nature, Apache from Flavor Unit, and lots of other rappers who never made it out.

I started school at Nassau two days after we moved and encountered prejudice for the first time in my life. It began with my family name. The kids in my class refused to pronounce it properly. Instead they pronounced it "jean" as in denim—and they said they were gonna wear me like a dirty pair of Haitian jeans.

I was confused. Coming from Haiti, I saw all black people as brothers and sisters, and I thought of them that way, too. I expected us to share the same ideology and feel the same way about things. I thought those girls back in Marlboro were just mean to us because we were the new kids. Making fun of us being Haitian was like calling us dumb or ugly or skinny. Now I knew there was more to it.

"After school we're gonna beat you down, Haitian," some kid whispered into my ear while I sat in class. "Not just you . . . We gonna beat the whole Jean family down. You boat people gotta know your place."

That's what was waiting for us after school, day one. It made no sense to me that blacks would be prejudiced against other blacks. We weren't a minority in the neighborhood either; there were so many Haitians that they had a bilingual curriculum at school to help us integrate. That set us apart though, so we were easy to pick out. When they saw us in the hallways, those kids taunted us by shouting, "Go back to Jamaica. What's old is what's new!" They called all the immigrant kids "boat people" and told us to go back to our own country. None of them had any idea that Jamaica, Haiti, and the Bahamas were all different. We were all the same to them.

This culminated in what came to be known as Haitian Day, when all the kids in school formed a mob and beat up the Haitian kids, all day long. I held my own on a daily basis, but Haitian Day was too much for my slap-boxing skills. I had to do something to put an end to this bullshit, at least as far as my family being caught up in it. I'd make them leave the Jeans alone.

There was a bully named Walter who was one of those dudes who grew real early. By elementary he was the biggest kid in school and he knew it. Everyone was scared of him and no one tried to fight him. At that age I was still real skinny and not very tall, and Walter was already a few grades ahead of me so this guy looked like André the Giant compared to me. It didn't matter; on Haitian Day I decided that fighting Walter was the only way to end this shit.

School was letting out and I was leaving school to walk home with my sister Melky and my brothers, Sam and Sedek. Walter walked by us with a bunch of his friends and I saw my chance.

"Yo Walter, you guys are punks."

"You talking to me, Haitian?"

"You're punks for jumping all of us in crowds like that. You could never take us one-on-one."

"Oh yeah, you think so?"

"Yeah, that's why I'm gonna whup your ass. If you're a man, you'll fight me one-on-one right now."

"Okay, whatever you want."

Walter tamed his dogs back and I did mine, and we approached each other in the middle of the sidewalk.

I wasn't worried at all because I had a plan. I'd spent every Saturday afternoon since we came to America watching all of the karate movies I could find on TV. I had studied Bruce Lee, then *Five Deadly Venoms, Drunken Master, The Kid With the Golden Arm*—all of the greats. I saw myself as a master of the martial arts from the time I was a small child and I told my brothers and sister that I was a descendant of the Shaolin. There was a tall white building that we could see from the highway every time our parents drove us to visit our grandmother and when we passed it I would bow.

"What are you doing, Nel?" Melky would ask.

"I am bowing to the Temple of Shaolin."

We later learned that it was a juvenile home.

The weekend before this confrontation with Walter I had watched *Five Deadly Venoms*, so I thought I could take him with a combination of my favorite styles from the film. I saw myself as a union of Toad, the best defense, combined with Snake, the best offense. Walter was big, so I went right after him, attacking him Snake style and landing a few blows. I backed up and took a flying Snake kick at his head, at which point Walter grabbed my legs in midair and body-slammed me into the pavement. Then he sat on me and started punching.

I blacked out, because Walter was no joke. Then I came around to the sound of my sister Melky yelling, "Get off my brother!"

I was dazed, in a semiconscious state, but when I heard her voice, my instinct was that my sister was being attacked. Like the Hulk, I got an adrenaline rush, picked myself up, and started swinging wildly. I connected, a fist connected back with me, and as I became aware of my surroundings again, I realized that Melky and I were single-handedly fighting off a mob of boys and girls that had circled around to watch. Once I got my bearings, she and I went back to back and proceeded to punch and kick our way home. From time to time we would falter: she would get thrown into the bushes or I would fall down, but we picked each other up and kept going. The entire time our brothers, Sam and Sedek, were across the street watching but not helping us at all.

When we got home, Melky and I were pretty jacked up. My eyes were blacked, her lip was bleeding, and we had bruises forming all over our bodies. Once we caught our breaths, we turned to our brothers in disgust.

"Why you didn't help us?" I asked them. Melky just stared at them; her face said it all.

"You let us fight all of them alone," I said. "You just walked home across the street like you wasn't even part of the Jean family."

"All of us couldn't fight," Sam said.

"Why not, Sam?"

"If you two got killed someone had to report it to Mom and Dad."

The next day I went to school determined to slap-box myself some respect. I found myself a fight and in front of everyone I won it. Slowly, day by day, week by week, I challenged every bully I thought I could take, and every time I beat one down, I won a little bit of ground for the Jean family. It wasn't some huge coup, but just like those girls in Marlboro, the kids in school got the message that we weren't going to back down.

My campaign to stop getting harassed got a boost when I caught the eye of a guy named Hasade, who was the most feared kid in school. He had been clocking me and he respected my courage for taking on the bullies. Somehow he became my best friend.

"I like the way you be slap-boxing those fools," he said to me one day out of the blue. "You ain't scared at all."

"Nah, I'm not."

"There's more of them than there is of you."

"Yeah I know. But what else I'm supposed to do?"

"Hang with me, man. You'll be alright. My name's Hasade."

Hasade wasn't like anyone else in school. He was my age but he seemed years older. We were only in elementary school, but Hasade had his own moped, and no one fucked with it. Some days he was picked up in a white Mercedes-Benz. He was the man and nobody messed with him.

At recess he held down his own area of the playground, and in that area he did gymnastics, which was a big part of the street culture at the time. It was an extension of break dancing, so being able to backflip was something all the kids wanted to do. It was dangerous, because we were doing it right there on the concrete. So those of us who could do it stood out. Hasade was the best at it and he taught me how, which earned me more respect, especially with the girls.

Nassau Elementary was a rude awakening in every way. Not only did I realize that being Haitian made me different from every other black kid, but I also learned that getting girls took more than a smile.

I had learned about love back in Brooklyn, in the Marlboro Houses the day I met Magdelena. We were just little kids, but when I kissed her on the cheek by the elevator I understood what love was. I didn't see her before we moved, so I never got a chance to say good-bye. I thought about her all the time, and I developed a crush on a girl in my class because she looked like Magdelena. It felt like I was getting a second chance.

The girl sat next to me in homeroom. The first thing I noticed about her was that she carried a raggedy bag. She lived with her mom and they were on welfare and her mom was on drugs, so this girl was taking care of both of them. She couldn't afford a new bag or new clothes or anything like that.

"You are too beautiful to carry a bag like that," I told her one day. "You look like a bag lady."

I was always asking her to spend time with me because I liked her, but she always pushed me away. I had to find a way to make her like me.

"If there's one thing I could do for you, what would it be?"

"Bring me a bag," she said.

"If I do that will you spend time with me?"

"If you want me to spend time with you, bring everyone in class a bag. If you can do that, I'll walk you home every day."

I was in love. She was the one for me, not only because she was beautiful and made it hard to get her attention, but also because she wasn't just thinking of herself; she was thinking of everybody. I went back to the house daydreaming about her and wondering where I could get that many bags.

Then fate stepped in and set me on the path toward learning a lesson. At that time one of my aunts' daughters was living with us and she had bought a bunch of fake Louis Vuitton bags that she was going to sell for triple in the 'hood. I'd say she had about two hundred of these things, all stacked up along the walls of her room. I didn't know what a knockoff was at that age, so to me, these were the real deal, just about the best bags money could buy.

Here was the answer to my problem.

I waited until she left the house and then I went to her room and tossed twenty of the bags out the window into the garden, where they landed without making a sound. *The Lord has answered my prayers*, I thought. *I have enough bags for the entire class.*

The next morning I fetched all the bags out of the garden and brought them into school. I gave my entire third-grade class, including the teacher, a Louis Vuitton bag.

My teacher knew something was wrong with this picture.

"Where did you get these bags, Nel?"

"Well, my mom is a missionary and she brought them back from a trip. She believes that everyone should be living equally so she told me to bring enough of them to school that everyone could have one."

It was a pretty good day in class that day. Everyone left happy with a Louis Vuitton bag and the girl I liked became my girlfriend. She gave me a kiss before we walked home from school together and when we stopped at the corner store she bought me a lollipop. Life couldn't have been any sweeter for me: my girlfriend had a Louis Vuitton bag, I was sucking on a lollipop, and everything was good because it looked like I'd gotten away with robbery.

I was wrong, of course. My teacher had already called my parents and asked them about the bags. I was walking home feeling like Robin Hood, but the Sheriff of Nottingham was there waiting for me. This was the start of a theme in my life: whenever I see people who need stuff that I know other people have in excess, I get it for them. In my mind, if someone isn't living off of something that someone else is desperate for, I try to bring it to the less fortunate. In my mind, by taking those bags, I was following my father's orders and obeying his morals as I understood them from his sermons.

I rolled into the house that evening, sucking on my lollipop like I was the king of the world, to find my mother standing there waiting for me.

"Where are the bags?"

"Uh . . . what bags?"

There was no hesitation: out came the slapping and the hair pulling. My father relied on his belt; my mother used a wrestling slap that started way back behind her shoulder and came at you in slow motion. That never mattered, because there was no way to avoid it. This time she caught me in midair trying to move, and hit me so hard that she threw my entire body backward onto the floor.

"You will get those bags back."

That really was the hardest part of all. I would have taken ten more beatings to avoid that. I was the man one day and the next I was a beggar. It didn't go over well, either: most of the kids returned them, but all the kids who lived in the projects on Walnut Street looked at me like I was crazy.

"You can go fuck yourself, man; we're keeping these bags," was pretty much what they said.

Worst of all, my girlfriend gave hers back. The one person I had done all of it for was so sweet that she understood the kind of trouble I'd gotten myself into for her. Still, she didn't feel any obligation to remain my girlfriend once she'd returned her bag. In the end, my mother had to pay my aunt's daughter for the bags I couldn't get back, and I paid my mother in chores for months and months.

When I was about twelve, I started getting into all kinds of trouble, mostly for shoplifting. My cousin Nason and I had these down parkas like so many street kids in Brooklyn, and besides keeping us warm, those coats were great for stealing all kinds of shit. Our biggest heist was foiled though. We planned on lifting a few cases of army men to sell to the kids in school. We were like drug dealers, buying a large amount of what was in demand, with a plan to break it into smaller numbers and sell each one. In our instance, it would be pure profit because we'd stolen the shit in the first place.

Those parkas were big, but you put two cases of plastic army men under one and it sure don't look right. But we didn't see that; we were too close to victory to be sensible.

"Where do you think you're going?"

It was the security guard, one hand on each of our shoulders, right as we got within sight of the door.

"What have you got under there?"

"Nothin'," I said. "My stomach just hurts. I'm sick."

He reached into my coat and grabbed the boxes of toy soldiers.

"This is nothing, huh? What do you want me to do, call the police or call your mom?"

I wanted them to call the police, but Nason told them to call our parents.

My mom came and got me and whipped me all the way back to the house. Then she sent me to my room. When I walked in, something was different: there was a red blanket on my bed. I turned around and she was standing there.

"Do you know why this red blanket is on your bed?"

"No."

"Because I'm going to chop you up and I'm going to put your body parts under this blanket. The red will hide the blood. By the time the detective shows up, they won't be able to tell which parts are the bed and which parts are your organs."

This wasn't a very logical plan, but to a twelve-year-old it made sense. I was terrified.

"Your father did not sacrifice everything he did to get you to this country to raise a shoplifter. Do not leave this room. I will be back."

My mother left me there in silence and closed the door. I started pacing around, my brain going wild, trying to decide if I should run or if she'd just catch me and start slashing me with her butcher knife. I was a wreck for the whole night, and my mother didn't talk to me until the next day. She didn't kill me either. But she did make her point. Until then I had never thought about any sacrifices she or my father had made for us. I had only thought of myself.

MY FATHER HAD DECIDED to move us to New Jersey back in 1985 because of a vision he had. He told us that one day, while driving in the car, he passed a WELCOME TO THE GARDEN STATE sign on the highway and he knew that would be our home.

"New Jersey—the 'Garden State,'" he said to himself. "This is where I will build my garden of Eden."

From all the stories I've read, the Garden of Eden was never as crowded as our house. My father was a proud homeowner, but after a short amount of time, he realized that he'd gotten in over his head. My parents couldn't afford their mortgage, so they were forced to rent the top two floors and move our family into the rooms on the first floor, which also served as the church. They also got us out of the public school system after Nassau Elementary by enrolling us at Our Lady Help of Christian, the local Catholic school.

It was partly my age, but the Catholic school environment inspired me to investigate my true nature. I am named after a holy man and a rebel and in that holy environment, the rebel came out. I began to test the boundaries of what I could get away with in every possible way. My first year there, the nuns and the priests decided to raise money by giving each student a certain amount of candy to sell in the neighborhood. Whether we wanted to sell these chocolates or not, each kid had to take boxes of them home and had to return with the money to fund whatever program they were supporting that year.

The total dollar amount the school would receive per student if we sold all of the chocolates was, like, $242.50, which was a lot of money to me. I got the boxes up to my room, saw how much all of it was worth, and decided to see for myself. I opened a box and took out a chocolate.

Let me see what these things taste like if I'm going to sell them, right? I thought.

Eating one chocolate from the box meant I had to pay for the whole thing because the school hadn't given me the chocolate so I could eat it. This exact moment was when I fell in love with chocolate, and I'm still crazy for it. I opened the foil wrapper and ate one—and it was incredible.

In the course of two weeks, I went through most of my supply, a whole $250 worth. The problem was that I didn't have $250 for my teacher when she asked for it, so the school sent a letter to my mom asking for the money.

My mom went to the school to ask why she owed them $250 dollars and they told her, "These chocolates were to be sold, and your son took them home but brought nothing back. We assume he ate all of them, so you owe the school this money or we'll kick your kids out."

I ended up getting a West Indian beating at the time for being a glutton to the tune of $250 dollars' worth of church chocolate. I still had a few boxes under my bed, so my mom took those and returned them. Still, she had to pay $200 and she wasn't happy about that. I hadn't even wanted to take those chocolates home, so I was not liking my school too much.

As time went by, another incident added to my negative opinion. We had a priest at school named Father Sheen who taught my Bible class. By that time I had my own concept of the Bible and knew all of the stories from hearing them in my dad's church. When somebody told me something about the Bible I didn't agree with, I didn't care who it was, I would debate him. It's what I believed my father would do.

One day in Father Sheen's class, he was preaching that the devil is bad and that God is good.

My hand shot up from my desk.

"Yes?"

"But at one time the devil was good," I said.

"What?" Father Sheen said, glaring at me. "What are you saying?"

"Yeah, Father, at one time, the devil was good, wasn't he?"

I was right; the devil was an angel in heaven before he fell. I was just telling the truth. But it cost me my ears getting pulled by Father Sheen because this was a very hard-core school. I yelped like a kicked dog when he did it. In any other situation like that, kids would laugh at the guy in my position, but in Our Lady of Help, the students knew better than to do that if they didn't want to be next.

Still bending my ear, Father Sheen walked me out of class and down to the principal's office where I expected a beating followed by a blessing with holy water to exorcise the evil spirits. I sat in the hallway while Father talked to the principal. Then they brought me into the office and we sat in silence. More nuns and priests filed in, called down to make sure I wasn't Damien or some shit. Once a crowd of our teachers was assembled, Father Sheen asked me to repeat what I had said in his class.

"Um . . . I said that . . . well, the devil . . . he was good at one time . . . wasn't he?"

As soon as I said it, the nuns crossed themselves and no one answered my question.

They held me in the principal's office until my mom and dad came to pick me up. With my parents now in the room, the principal asked me to repeat what I'd said one more time.

"Did you hear that, Mr. and Mrs. Jean? Your son said that the devil was good at one time."

As an adult man, I understand why this was such a big deal in that Catholic school. They didn't want me spreading the idea to the other kids that the devil was ever good, even though, according to the Bible, I was correct. He was an angel that was led astray, who fell from heaven. If that idea was misinterpreted, they would have a riot on their hands.

My parents stood on either side of me, looking at me, while across the desk my teachers stared at the three of us.

"Son, is that what you said?" my mother asked.

"Yeah," I said. Then I turned to my teachers. "Father Sheen, wasn't the devil once an angel of light who lived in the heavens with God until God cast him out? Until that happened and he decided he wanted to do his own reign, he was just like any other angel. So, he wasn't bad at that time. He wasn't born bad; he got bad later."

It was so quiet in that room. I looked up at my dad for approval and though he didn't come out and agree with me, because he couldn't, I know I saw a smile in the corner of his mouth. He never told me so, but I think he was proud that his son had interpreted the Bible for himself and told these Catholics how he saw things. I was taking after my namesake John Wycliffe.

I ended up getting suspended from school for a week and I took that shit *mad personally*. I mean, look, I was right. My Bible knowledge was correct, and they knew it, too. But they couldn't admit it, so they punished me. That wasn't right, so I decided—and my brother Samuel Jean agreed to help me—that I should blow up the school. We would take this Catholic school out so it wouldn't teach any more lies. Father Sheen was not telling the kids the truth, so this school shouldn't be there—simple as that. I was intense as a child; my life could have gone in any direction.

To commit this act of terrorism, Sam and I started preparing a bomb. We were taking science at the time and we'd learned a little bit. We knew we should start with some light bulbs, and that we'd need gas, fire, a torch and everything. We'd learned how a battery cell makes electricity spark through copper wire, so we came up with our version of how that could be translated into a spark that would ignite our bomb. Our flawed logic was basically this: the battery cell makes light, so let's apply that light to this gas and use a small torch to make it burn. We put this all together in a paint can, planning to start a fire that would destroy the school.

The only problem was that it didn't go off. It didn't work at all. It didn't even light up. It smelled like a gas station but that was as far as it went. We took it to school on a weekend and tried to light it and throw it down a stairwell into the basement, but nothing happened so we left it in a dumpster and went home. In spite of the teachings of Christ at home and in school, I was turning into a serious troublemaker. Thank God I found rap. It became my faith and my calling. Like my father before me, that calling put me on my path and delivered me from trouble—though my love of it got me into trouble, too.

. . . .

IN 1985, RAP WAS exploding and the sound of it could be heard all over the streets of our neighborhood. It was the start of the golden age: the Run-DMC's, the L.L. Cool J's, the Jeeps, and the big radios all booming. I couldn't let my dad ever know, but I wanted to be a part of that. I loved the rhythm and I loved the music; I just had to hide it and listen to it on my Walkman when I knew he wasn't around. What I wanted to do was blast my music while I walked down the street.

We always had two lodgers at any given time in the upstairs rooms on South Clinton Avenue, and for a while one of them was a nice lady named Fifi who worked as a secretary or something like that. She was cool: she had a job and she made a nice little home for herself on our top floor. Her home got a lot nicer the day she brought home a big 1980s Sony radio to give the place some swagger. I saw her walk in with it, and every day after that all I dreamed of was taking it down to my room and playing the music my dad didn't want me listening to.

Radios like that were a status symbol on the streets; they made you fresher than any sneaker known to man. I had to have this thing. When she went to work, I snuck up to her room and there it was: it had the light-up equalizer, the two tape decks, the "loudness" button, all that shit. It took about fifteen batteries and it weighed like fifty pounds. That radio had no business hiding out up in that lady's room. It belonged on the street, on my shoulder, so I could roll up to recess like some Catholic school version of Radio Raheem.

My father had been raised in the hill country of Haiti and had a green thumb unlike anyone I've ever met. I've seen him turn the filthiest back lot into a garden bursting with vegetables. No matter how barren the soil, he would coax tomatoes and string beans from the concrete. In our small yard in East Orange, he grew a field of corn. There were thugs on the block out front, but behind our house it looked like Indiana. That was where I planned to hide the radio.

The next day after the lady left for work, I snuck up to Fifi's room and destroyed everything. I broke her mirror, her picture frames, dumped out her drawers, all of that. I wanted it to look like a burglar had come through the window and robbed her. I took the radio and carefully tossed it out the window into my dad's field of corn where the tall plants cushioned the fall. Then I went back to my room, got ready for school, and went downstairs.

Before we left for the day, my mother always gave us an inspection: she'd check our bags, make sure our uniforms were straight and that our homework was done, and then we were off. After that I ducked into the backyard, got the radio, and caught up to my brothers and sister. Boom! I snapped my music on—"Sucker MC's" by Run-DMC. And it was on.

I walked along and dudes were like, "Damn, homie, that's a big radio!" I was living the dream. All day long I was the man at school, but come three o'clock, I had a problem: I couldn't bring the radio back home. I didn't want to leave it outside in the corn overnight, so I took it to Hasade's house on Walnut Street. He was the only guy I could trust not to keep it, because he already had one.

When I got home, my crime had been discovered. Fifi was there, screaming that she'd been robbed, that her stuff had been broken, and that her radio was gone. My mother is a wise woman, so she'd already figured her kids were behind it. How could we not be? What kind of thief breaks into a top floor room through the window without being caught and doesn't steal from any other room in the house?

My mother's intuition was strong, and she had her methods to keep us in line. She made us believe that she could read our minds, and since we believed her, we allowed her to. We would tell her what she wanted to know by squirming to the right or left under her gaze. She read into every bit of body language when we were lined up being questioned by her, and always got her answer because she translated what her intuition told her into the movements of her magic broom.

When one of us had done something wrong and she wanted to find out who it was, she would line us up in the kitchen and walk back and forth, asking questions. If she didn't scare us into admission that way, we knew what was coming. "If you do not tell me, I will get my broom," she'd say. "The broom knows the truth. The broom finds the one who lies."

Mom had us brainwashed with this magic broom. It was never used for cleaning; its purpose was to learn the truth when her children had done something wrong and were lying about it. Whomever the broom pointed to was the guilty one.

But before she went to the broom, Mom always gave us one last chance to step forward from the line if we were guilty of the crime. Eight times out of ten that would do it, because we were so scared of the broom coming out that one of us would confess even if we hadn't done it. The mere mention of the broom set us squirming like worms in the rain.

Stealing the radio wasn't something I was ready to go down for, though, because that was a big crime. So I prepared myself for the broom and kept my face straight.

"Mrs. Fifi was robbed today," my mom said, glaring at us. "I am going to ask you all only one time if you had anything to do with it."

No one said anything.

"If I don't get the truth right now . . . you know what will happen."

My brother Sam started crying.

"She's gonna get the broom," he whispered through his sobs. "She's gonna get . . . the . . . broom!"

My brothers and sister started looking at each other, wondering who was going to squeal. Then they all started talking at once, all of it nonsense. I remained silent, not only because I was guilty but also because I knew the broom would choose me anyway. It always did, because my mom's instinct, which was usually right, told her that I had something to do with it.

That moment was pandemonium: all four kids pleading their cases, half crying and half shouting nonsense until my mother silenced us.

"Does anybody want to tell me where is the radio?"

We all shut up.

"Yo," I said. "I don't know anything about no radio."

She looked me straight in the face and then walked to the broom closet.

As soon as she opened that door my brother Sam turned green. He is incapable of lying and always has been, which is terrible because today he is a lawyer. Every time the broom came out, if Sam knew anything about the crime committed, he'd throw up. He started doing that now.

Once the broom was out, my mother would work her way down the line, asking each of us questions to determine who was guilty and who was innocent. She was a master trickster whose show began the moment the broom appeared. My mother was a very beautiful woman who always dressed very properly, with perfect manners. It took a lot for her to take steps this dramatic to enforce her rules. When she got the broom she was no longer the mom we knew—which made it that much scarier for us kids.

She'd make circles around that broom with her hands while looking us in the eye, distracting us from the fact that she was using her feet to make the thing move. If she decided you were guilty, she'd let the broom lean toward you. We learned her method a few years later when my sister caught her at the store testing new brooms with her feet. Even after that it didn't matter. When we saw that broom we all knew someone was going down for something.

Most of the time my mother's convictions were just, but sometimes her judgment was off, which still meant the belt and extra chores for the innocent. Our fear of this broom was real.

Years later I used the memory of that tension to create a piece of music for the first film score I ever wrote. It was for *Life*, a comedy starring Eddie Murphy and Martin Lawrence, directed by Ted Demme. I was having trouble finding the right emotion for a scene. The music needed more intensity and danger, so Ted Demme told me to think of something that brought those feelings to mind. Something that made me scared and nervous. That was easy: the broom. I thought of my brother Sam and how he'd start shaking, and wrote what I imagined that felt like.

My other brother Sedek wasn't much better that night: he was so scared he couldn't even answer my mother's questions, which meant he would be convicted. If any of us started wigging out, usually my mom would just let the broom fall on us. But he was so confused and scared that she let him off that time. My brother Sam was passed over, too; then came my sister Melky.

My mom stared at her a long time. She knew what she was doing. My little sister was like Tootie on *The Facts of Life*; she always got her older brothers in trouble because she couldn't keep her mouth shut.

"What do you know about a radio, Melky?" my mother said.

"Well," she said, looking at the floor, "Nel went to school with a radio. I've seen him with one."

My mother and the broom moved down the line to me.

"What do you know about a radio?" she said.

"Oh, the radio my friend gave me?" I said. I kept my eye on the broom handle.

It didn't move—but my mom's hand did.

Slap! She smacked me across the face. "Go to your room and wait for your father to come home! You are lying!" I was in for it.

A few hours later my dad came home and a few minutes after that he burst into my room.

"Where is the radio?" he said. There was no way a lie was getting me out of this.

"I don't have it here," I said. "A friend of mine has it."

"Okay then, wait here."

My father had a few belts he used to discipline us, but this time he got the shocker, his thick leather cowboy belt. He gave me a few slaps with it then he stopped.

"You and I are going to find the radio."

We started walking through the hood, my dad behind me wearing his flip-flops, carrying his big-ass belt. Every few steps— *pow!*—he struck me. All the kids on the block stopped what they were doing to watch this.

"Damn, homie!" someone yelled. "Your dad crazy!"

The blows hurt, but the embarrassment stung more. We walked all the way down Walnut Street, the thugs and dealers staring at us, to Hasade's house. Hasade opened the door, took one look at my father, and started shaking his head.

"I see you got caught, homie. Minister, I had nothing to do with it and I want nothing to do with it. Nel, get the radio yourself; it's right over there."

With the radio at my side I prepared to walk back home, expecting a beating the whole way.

"What are you doing?" my father asked me.

"Returning the radio?"

"I want you to hold it the way you did this morning when you were proud of yourself. How did you hold it while you showed off to your brothers and sisters? Did you hold it down at your side like it was your schoolbooks?"

"No."

"Show me how you did it."

I put the radio on my shoulder.

"Now turn it on. I want you to walk home just the way you walked to school today."

I turned on Run-DMC and started walking, with my father a few steps behind, whipping me the whole way.

"Turn it up louder, so they all turn to see you. I want the whole neighborhood to know you're a thief. You will wear these marks I give you so that they will know you are a thief."

I was like a hip-hop Jesus carrying his cross up the mountain.

That wasn't the end of it either. My father borrowed the radio from our tenant that weekend so that he and I could visit my grandmother. He made me put it on my shoulder and turn it up real loud as we walked to her door.

My father dealt swift justice and you knew it was coming. My grandmother was more like the wolf in *Little Red Riding Hood*. She would ask innocent questions in her loving grandmother voice and then pounce on you and eat you up.

"Where did you get the radio, Nel?"

"Oh . . . this radio? The radio . . . I stole it, Grandma."

"What? We didn't raise no thieves in this family! Get over here!"

Then the wolf came out, in the form of her belt. Then she went to her desk and got out a Swiss Army knife.

"Thieves must pay for what they do, Nel. You must pay. Come here and take off your shirt. When I'm done with you, you will know that your grandma don't raise thieves."

My grandmother cut me across the back with her knife. She left a series of small scars that healed quickly but left marks that I didn't forget. Every time she lay into me, she made me repeat after her: "Grandma don't raise no thieves." She gave me a Passion of the Christ beating. Then she brought me into the kitchen, sat me down, and fed me.

And that was how justice was dished out in my family.

My grandmother knew how to keep kids in line, and our parents relied on her to do it, too. She was daycare for the extended Jean family: all of my cousins and I spent our afternoons there together pretty often. She would watch television and we would play in the other room, but she had ears like an owl and eyes in the back of her head. My grandmother loved television and watched it all the time, but she didn't understand English or any of the shows very well. That didn't matter; if it was on, all those pictures going by made her happy. The one thing she really paid attention to and took interest in was Lucha Libre—the Mexican wrestling where they wear masks. She'd turn the volume up real loud on it and knew all the wrestlers by name. She loved it so much that if you tried to argue with her that it was fake, you were in for a long, serious debate that you were not going to win. You might get beat up, too. As if to prove it was real, my grandmother liked to slap Lucha Libre nonbelievers upside the head while arguing with them. I'm serious; she was obsessed—to the point that she body slammed one of our cousins when he kept insisting it was all bullshit. Then she put him in a headlock down on the floor until he cried mercy. Grandma was fit and she was no joke.

She had to be; she had raised a lot of kids and survived a lot of tough times. Her oldest son, Jean, was a real tough kid who ended up becoming a marine. Then later he disappeared after he served his time. No one in the family really talks about what happened to him because I don't think anyone knows for sure. I'm pretty sure he got killed. He started rolling with a Jamaican crew in Brooklyn, doing crimes, and the next thing we knew he was gone. His last name was Jean just like mine, and his path could have been mine, too. We were a lot alike, because there were exactly four trouble-makers in the family: him, me, my brother Sam, and my cousin Nason. Any of us could have gone down that road.

They called my cousin Nason and me the Twins because we got in trouble together all the time. We did stupid shit—holding up grocery stores, stealing car radios—just about every petty crime that takes place on the street. Mostly my cousin and I went into cribs and took what we could within three minutes. That was my rule. Three minutes was all we had. That's why they started calling me Speedy, and later, Spidey, like Spider-Man. Nason and I got good at it, too. We did most of this when we were thirteen, fourteen; we were those kids you didn't want to run into out there in Brooklyn. And during those years, my grandmother was the one in charge of looking after us most afternoons until it was time for us to go home to our parents.

During one of those afternoons we realized that my uncle was not nearly as pious and God-fearing as his brother Gesner. His tastes were much more earthly, judging by his porn collection. To my teenage eyes, watching people have sex on video was the craziest, most incredible thing I'd ever seen. These films were pretty innocent, now that I've gotten older and seen real hardcore porn, but back then, my eyes bugged right out of my head. Like new devotees of any religion, we began to study these sacred documents, behind closed doors, every afternoon, until my grandmother caught us. She whipped us to high heaven, and after that my uncle's door had a lock on it. Only a woman as tough as my grandmother could have kept us in line, despite our numbers: on any one afternoon she might be looking after as many as fourteen kids—all of my father's siblings' kids, plus us, his kids. She ran a tight ship, keeping us off the streets while our parents were at work and keeping us quiet enough for her to be able to watch Lucha Libre. To do that she behaved like a drill sergeant, shouting at us to keep quiet, get in line, whatever had to be done. The oldest four of us, being headstrong teenagers who thought they were thugs, eventually decided that we'd had enough of taking orders.

We held a kid group meeting and I decided that there was only one thing to do about Grandma holding us down: we had to get rid of her. My little sisters were there, and like I said before, they were like Tootie from *The Facts of Life*, just snitches all the way. My younger sister Rose was growing up to be just like my sister Melky in that regard.

"You can't do that! I'm gonna tell Mom!"

I didn't care. I had a plan.

"Listen to me," I told everyone. "The old lady always asks for her milk at four o'clock. One of us warms it up for her every day."

I looked at my older cousin Jean. "You and I are going to be in charge of warming up her milk today," I said. "And we're going to put Ajax in it."

"What?" asked my brother Sam.

"I saw this on television," I said. "It is the quickest way to kill someone."

All of them looked at me in silence.

"We will have approximately one minute before she recognizes that there is Ajax in her milk because it will turn a different color. But if we put it in first she will get enough of it down to put her out and then I will pour the rest of it into her mouth. This will work. Everyone who is for this raise your hand."

Everyone except my sisters raised their hands.

"Why you didn't raise your hand?" I asked them.

"She's our grandmother," Melky said. Grandma had never laid a hand on them, so they didn't see it the way we did. They never did anything bad, either.

"Listen, you've got no part of this," I said to them. "You stay back while we handle it, okay? You've got nothing to do with it."

"Okay," they said. They didn't look very happy about it.

When four o'clock came around, right on time, Grandma asked for her warm milk. I went and warmed it up, stirred the Ajax in, and when it looked somewhat white again, I brought it to her. I don't know who I was trying to fool; this shit smelled horrible. I can't even believe I once wanted to do this to my grandmother.

My grandmother was the wisest woman, and a shark. She took the cup like it was nothing and started singing a song to me.

"Come sing with me, Wyclef," she said. And she started singing a song she made up as she went along that went something like this: "Sun up gets nice, sun up gets nice, but you're a snake, you're a snake. I don't trust you . . . sun up, gets nice."

"Yes, I am," I sang along halfheartedly with her. "Sun up gets nice." I had no idea where this thing was going.

My grandmother usually took her milk in the kitchen, leaving us kids in front of the television for a while. This day she brought her milk with her into the family room and sat down with all of us.

"What are we going to watch today?" she said. None of us could stop staring at her milk, which she hadn't even come close to sipping.

Yo, just drink that milk, Grandma, I kept thinking.

Grandma sat there for close to an hour, knowing damn well what she was doing. She ignored the fact that the more time went by, the more us kids began to act like we had ants in our pants. We were shifting in our seats like waterdrops on a hot frying pan.

"Line!" Grandma shouted all of a sudden. Like my mother, when she had something to say and wanted our complete attention, she'd say "line" and we'd have to all get in line.

Except when Grandmother told us to get in line, it was even worse than when my mother told us to get in line. My younger siblings had the same reactions, but much worse. My brother Sam had his hand over his mouth to keep from throwing up before he even got in line. My sisters were babbling and whining and blaming us for things that hadn't even happened, while my cousins Nason, Jean, and I stood there stoically, insisting we hadn't done anything at all.

"No one is in trouble," Grandma said. "No one is in trouble, children."

Everyone got quiet, because now she had us. We were really lost. She didn't even need a broom to get us into the palm of her hand.

"You see, today I was thinking," she said. "It is not nice of me to keep my milk all to myself every afternoon. So I decided that we should share this milk. Together we will choose one of you to drink the milk each day, starting this afternoon. So, children, who is going to be the lucky one?"

No one made a move.

"If no one comes forward then I suppose we must choose," she said. "How about . . . Stephen—he will drink the milk."

Stephen was one of our youngest cousins and probably the only one who was too little to understand what we'd done to it and what was going on. He would drink it just because Grandma asked him to and she knew this.

"Yes, that is what we will do. Stephen will drink the milk, then George, then the girls." She named all the youngest kids. We couldn't let that happen, but before Nason and I could figure a way out of it, our cousin George gave us up.

"Clef and Nason put Ajax in the milk, Grandma," he said. "They want to poison you. Don't make me drink that!"

Grandma knew we were up to something, because we were stupid to think that Ajax—which is green and white—wouldn't change the color of the milk. You could see all the particles swirling around in there, and with the heat and all that, it turned completely funky. She knew we put something in it because you could smell it, too. But hearing the truth really shocked her. She got quiet and stared at us intensely for a long moment. Then she got up and walked out of the room. We could hear her talking to herself in the kitchen.

"I can't believe this," she said. "These children want to kill me! What am I doing wrong? My own grandchildren . . ."

By the time my mother showed up after work to get us, my grandmother's sadness had turned to anger and disgust.

"Your little rats tried to kill me," she said to my mother. "They put Ajax in my milk and tried to poison me."

My mother looked horrified.

"These things that came from your womb," my grandmother said. "They tried to kill me today."

When we got home, my dad got his belt and started swinging

at whichever one of us was closest, and then he kept on going. He chased us into our bedrooms and one by one gave us the most vicious of all the beatings we ever experienced. Then he threw my brother and me into a cold shower so the water made our skin tight and the wounds hurt more. Who could blame him for it? We had tried to poison his mother. He never forgot it, and neither did she.

My parents were strict, but how they raised us is what kept us out of trouble and in my case it probably kept me alive. Just like dozens of kids in the neighborhood, many of them my friends, I started staying out late, doing petty crimes, on my way down a path that would lead to prison or death. Most of what I got into was burglary, but some of my friends were killing and selling drugs before we were even in high school. As a young man I didn't think anything could touch me, but as I started seeing kids I knew get shot left and right, I began to change my mind.

My mother, more than anyone else, also had a lot to do with it. When she felt me slipping down the wrong slope, she sat me down and told me all about her life so that how my parents had lived and all they'd done to get to America would be in my thoughts. She told me about giving birth to me and all of the pain she went through, she told me how my father had run from immigration and worked in sweatshops, and she told me something I never forgot.

"You have purpose, son; there is a reason that you are here," she said. "This is something you do not see now, but it is the truth. There is a reason we named you after John Wycliffe. We did not give you this name for you to run wild in the streets and end up deported back to Haiti."

I didn't know what my purpose was yet, but she was right. I knew I'd end up dead or in prison, just like all the kids around me, if I didn't change my ways. Sitting here today in my house with my wife and little girl, I'm glad for those punishments, because if I hadn't learned those lessons, I wouldn't have all of this. My parents are why I'm alive and thriving while six of my best friends from school died before they were twenty.

One of them was named Gene Swarrow, whose father was a minister, just like mine. We were inseparable, and he was my right-hand man. We cut school together, we went on double dates, we did it all. Both of us loved music and both of us rapped and both of our fathers forbade us from hanging out together, because they saw we were two of a kind. It didn't matter that we weren't supposed to be friends anymore; we spent all our time together anyway. What happened to Gene was exactly what my mother foresaw for me if I didn't change my ways.

When we were both about nineteen, Gene robbed somebody with a shotgun. I wasn't with him then, because I'd thrown myself into music, which got me off the streets. After that incident his family sent Gene down to Florida to live with some relatives and make a new start, but I talked to him all the time.

"I'm getting my life straight down here, man," he'd say. "You have the right idea with music; I'm doing that, too. I'm working with some local dudes. We're getting a group together."

"You being good? You sure you're not into that crazy stuff, man?"

"Nah, nah, everything is good."

That very well could have been me, because my parents were definitely the type who might send me away to get myself together. My mother felt that the surroundings were the problem, not her son. But sometimes getting away doesn't solve the problem.

Gene wasn't staying out of trouble, and some boys he had a beef with down in Florida ended up chasing him down the highway. He tried to outrun them, but he couldn't. They shot him, and his car went off the road and into a tree.

I wish I had been more strong-willed as a young man and more intent on my purpose to not go down that path. Gene was like a brother to me, and he was as strong-minded as I, but maybe I could have pulled him onto my side. He had such potential that I wish he could have shown to the world.

MY REAL SAVING GRACE was music, and in junior high, I met a few characters who guided my development and changed my life. The first was Robert Frazier, who came to be known as the rapper Chill Rob G in the late eighties. Rob released a classic album called *Ride the Rhythm* that got a lot of attention when the German group Snap! sampled his song "Let the Words Flow" without permission in their song "The Power." That song was such a huge hit that Rob did a version of it himself, which gave his career a nice jump-off. He had skills and an incredible flow, and things were looking up for him, but a few incidents in his personal life caused him to drop out of the game at the height of things and he's never really returned to it.

Long before that, Rob and I became friends at Our Lady Help of Christians. Like most Catholic schools, we had to wear our uniforms, which were blue pants and Oxford shoes with black socks and plaid ties. We were definitely the only kids for a three-mile radius wearing hard-bottom shoes. There was nothing fresh about us at all.

Rob was a rock star at school though, because he got around that rule by bringing a change of clothes with him. At recess he would put on his street gear and that was coolest thing to me. He was the coolest guy I'd ever met and he taught me how to rap. I was in sixth grade, about twelve years old, when we started talking on the playground, me in my uniform, and him in some Pumas and a tracksuit.

"Hey man, how come you don't have a uniform?"

"Yo, this is lunch period. The playground. You could wear what you want. Then you go back and change."

"What's your name, man?" I asked him.

"Rob G, man. What's your name?"

"My name is Nel."

"Oh yeah? From now on, you know what your name is gonna be?"

"No."

"Nelly Nel."

Man, I ran with the name Nelly Nel for a good five or six years. People would call me Nel and I'd say, "Nah. I'm Nelly Nel, ya hear me?"

At recess every day Rob would rap with a whole bunch of people surrounding him and hanging on every word. He was cool, he could rhyme, he had the pretty girls. I wanted to be just like him.

"Man, how do you know how to rap?"

"You know, just poetry, man. Just poetry."

"Could you teach it to me?"

Rob G was my first rap teacher. He was my guide into hip-hop, at recess. He taught me that rap was more than just rhyming to be fresh and clever. He taught me to tell a story; he laid out what our songs would be and we started practicing routines. Rapping with Rob directed my energy toward something positive and away from wanting to pull the fire alarm and argue with the priests and blow up the school. I stopped thinking about throwing egg bombs because I thought rap was cool and wanted to concentrate on that instead. I was an egg-bomb expert by the way. I would boil six eggs, cut them open, and let them sit in a bag for three weeks. Then I'd bring it to school, open the door to a classroom, throw it in there, and run.

Rob naming me Nelly Nel was one thing, but I had to do something about my clothes, because I was making the dude look bad.

"Girls need to see that you take off that uniform and put on something fly, my man," he said.

That was a risky proposition for someone like me. Stashing clothes in my bag, with my mom searching us like the secret police every morning, wasn't a good idea.

Every other weekend we'd go to see my grandmother out in Brooklyn where she lived with my uncle and cousins, and that's when I'd hang out with my cousin Nason. He was just like me: always starting trouble, always the center of attention, always running a scheme. On those weekends, if Nason got a beating, I'd get one, too, because you could be sure that we were both to blame.

When we visited next I said to him, "Nason, yo dude, I need some clothes." Nason always had great clothes—where and how he got them, nobody had to know.

"I got you."

He gave me three sets of Pumas, a gold chain, and two Adidas tracksuits. I was chillin', dude.

It was a risk, but I took it: on Monday I snuck the clothes out in my bag, underneath my books, and at lunch period I dressed up cool, like Rob G. And that day began the first official Rob G and Wyclef cipher there on the playground of Our Lady Help of Christians. My name was Nelly Nel, and I had come correct, but I had a problem: I didn't know what to rap about.

"Rap about whatever it is that's inside of you, whatever it is you want people to know," Rob G said. "But at the same time, you've got to keep it fly so that the girls don't get bored."

With that in mind, the first line I ever came up with was "Back in the Bronx, where I came from, MCs danced to the beat that went ah-rum-pa-pum-pum."

Rob G said, "Nelly Nel is the place to be, grab the microphone because you visciously!"

And then I came out with my line.

Rob G stopped the cipher right there and pulled me aside.

"Back in the Bronx? You wasn't in the Bronx. You lived in Brooklyn, man."

"Yeah, but you said to say what naturally came out of my head, but to say it so the girls wouldn't think it was boring."

Rob just shook his head.

We developed it from there, mostly because Rob kept us up on the best rappers around.

"Yo, we got to check out the Start Us Crew."

The Start Us Crew were the best; everyone knew it. They were older than us, in East Orange High School. They had Mike C, Sergio—all these guys Rob and I learned from just by watching them.

They had taken Rob G in like a son, and he had taken me in as his little brother, and one day while they were rapping they sang a chorus together: "This is the way we harm-on-ize."

"Yo, Rob, that's cool. They singing," I said.

"No, man, they harmonizing."

Rob didn't realize that I'd learned all about singing in church. In his world of hip-hop, they called it harmonizing.

"Listen man, these dudes get elevated. That's how they come up with all this stuff," he said to me one day.

"What's that mean?"

"They be smoking the ganja."

"What's that?"

"I'm gonna show you."

Rob got some ganja from a dude over on Walnut Street and he rolled it up.

"Yo dude, this looks like tea, man."

"It ain't tea."

I did not want to smoke this stuff because my mom didn't want me to do drugs. She said if I ever did drugs I'd end up on Walnut Street with the thieves and the fiends.

"I can't do no drugs, man," I said. "My momma will kill me."

"Nah, nah, nah, man, this ain't drugs. It's sensi. Sensi ain't drugs."

I started to feel a little bit better about it, because this shit looked harmless, just like tea. And if I was smoking tea, well that wasn't so bad.

"It looks like tea. My momma can't get mad at me for that."

"Your call, man," Rob G said.

"I got an idea."

Next day I got home and took a tea bag and brought it to school. In the afternoon we went to Rob's house and I took my tea bag out, took the tea out of it, and rolled it up in the joint paper. I lit it, took two pulls off of it, and I don't know what happened, but I went unconscious. I passed right out and hit the floor of Rob's room.

"Yo Nel! Yo Nel! Yo Nel!"

I woke up when he poured water on my face.

"You see, motherfucka! If you would just smoke the sensi, this shit wouldn't have happened!"

That was my first encounter with marijuana. Rather than smoke weed, I smoked a tea bag. After that I wouldn't smoke shit. I thought I'd die if I smoked anything, if something as simple as tea could make me pass out. I got over that fear later, of course.

Our Lady Help of Christians had a talent show right before graduation, and that was the first performance of Nelly Nel and Rob G in all their glory. That is what I consider my first hip-hop experience, onstage, in that little gym at school. The kids loved it, because they thought we were cool: Rob was the star and I was his sidekick. We had them clapping, all their hands in the air, and as I looked out at the crowd I thought to myself, *This is what I want to be doing for the rest of my life.*

I felt like I had a purpose and that was to make people feel good no matter what they were going through. I could provide them with something they didn't have: an escape from their reality. Through my music, I wanted to bring them to a world, at least for a little while, where everything was going to be okay.

And you know what? At that talent show and whenever Rob and I ciphered, I always started with my line about the Bronx. To me, taking a bad line and making it work was a skill. Rob G realized it, too. He said that line was my secret weapon when we battle rapped other crews, even though it was mad corny.

"That line is the first one you wrote and it's terrible," he said. "If you come out with that, the other rapper will underestimate you, and once he do that, you come back and whup him."

Rob G was my mentor at school, while at home my music was developing thanks to some very different teachers. By that time, my dad had replaced our *Muppet Show* instruments with real ones and our little band began to sound really good. Guitar had become my main instrument and I learned everything from two people. The first was Jerry Duplessis's brother, Renel. He taught me my first four chords and a bunch of Flamenco progressions. I was happy to learn them but I didn't want to play flamenco; I wanted to play something that sounded cool. I wanted to make my guitar sound like what I was doing with Rob. Slowly I tried to figure that out on my own.

I couldn't have done it without a man named Omexis who rented a room from us for a short time. That was his name as far as we knew, but he went by more aliases than Ol' Dirty Bastard. His name changed with the seasons: some people called him Commissioner. Some called him Max. Some called him by what we thought was his real name, Omexis, and others called him Joseph. He had to be the biggest hustler in town. I don't know his real name. He played guitar, so for the months he lived with us, I'd go upstairs to his room and listen to him play. His style was Western: it sounded like the soundtrack to *The Good, the Bad and the Ugly*.

"Omexis, that is so cool, man. Will you teach me?"

He squinted at me like a cowboy in the sun.

"Go get your guitar."

When I'd sit up there and get lessons I'd notice passport photos all over the floor with his face on it, under six different names. He had false Social Security cards, driver's licenses, everything. Whatever this dude was into, it was serious. He was an outlaw, playing real outlaw music.

I don't know what Omexis was doing, but he always came home super late. I have always been an night owl, so I was up, usually listening to forbidden music on my Walkman. To get upstairs, he'd have to pass by my room and usually he'd stick his head in.

"Hey, what's an A scale?" And then I'd have to play it.

"You remember the G minor?" And then I'd have to play it.

"Okay, good job, I'll see you later."

He was always on the run, that guy.

Between Omexis and Jerry's brother, I developed a style all my own and I learned how many zones of sound the guitar was capable of. I had started with the accordion, then the trombone. All I wanted was an instrument that I could play as a lead singer of the church band that would cause the girls to notice me. Neither of those was gonna do it. But the guitar did.

The only problem with learning all of these scales and becoming capable of playing whatever I heard was that it caused a war to start in my house. My brothers and sister Melky and I would rehearse every evening, and as we got better, I tried to sneak some of the music we liked into rehearsal. The minute we even tried to, my dad would interrupt us.

It didn't matter how softly we played or how far away from us he was; the man had superhuman ears. The moment he heard a note of music that didn't sound right to him, there he was.

"What is this you are playing?"

"We're trying something new just to practice, Dad. We won't—"

"You won't play it at all. There will only be church music played in this house. Do you hear me?"

"Yes."

The man wasn't going to hear any kind of music or talk or anything else that didn't pertain to Jesus Christ. If he did, he'd pull off his belt and administer a round of whuppings. The one radio station my father played, both in his car and in our house, was called Family Radio, which is a listener-supported twenty-four-hour-a-day Christian radio station.

In reality, all of us kids listened to pop music on our Walkmans

like every other kid—just more secretly. We fell in love with rock
and roll, hip-hop, reggae, and eighties music and we'd sneak downstairs to catch music videos on a show called *New York Hot Tracks*
that was on Friday nights on channel 7. The hosts would be in
nightclubs and musicians like Boy George or David Bowie or the
Beastie Boys would come through and the hosts would show their
videos. We loved it, because we saw musicians doing their thing
on television every week. It was very hard for us when they'd show
Michael Jackson videos, because what kid at that age can sit still
when they hear Michael Jackson? We'd have to keep each other
from singing and dancing, because if we made any noise, our father
would come out of his room and kill us.

One night we were gathered around the TV with the volume
turned down low, sneaking a peak at *Hot Tracks* when Eddie Van
Halen came on. And I just about lost my mind. I had never seen
anyone play guitar like that. I had never heard a guitar sound like
that and suddenly all that I knew meant nothing.

"What the hell is this?" I whispered.

All of us were motionless, just staring at this guy play. "We've
got to learn how to do that."

There was no way we could ever play rock and roll outright as
the church band, but once again a visitor to our home showed us
the way. My parents always had Nazarene missionaries from all over
the country and the world coming through to stay with us, and one
of them who saw me practicing my guitar gave me a tape of a band
called Petra. Their name is the Greek word for "rock" and they were
the originators of Christian rock, starting all the way back in 1972.
They made us realize that religious rock could be cool to play. I have
to thank them for that, because Petra allowed us to play music in
church that wasn't corny, that we could never have gotten away with
otherwise. My dad would accept it as long as it was about the Lord
and had Jesus's name in it. Petra sounded like Bon Jovi, but instead
of "shot through the heart," the lyrics would be "shot to the devil."

Petra gave me an even better idea, which I shared with my siblings while we were practicing one day.

"Listen, we can play whatever we want."

"No we can't, Nel. You know that," my brother said.

"Yes we can. So long as we put Jesus's name in it. Y'all gotta trust me."

This plan worked. We'd learn funk songs and rock songs and change the words so they were all about Jesus, the Lord, and heaven. My father, who never listened to pop music, thought we had written all of it. He had no idea we were borrowing from artists like James Brown, the Police, and Pink Floyd, who didn't speak about Jesus in any way he would have approved of.

We developed a sound by blending all of the music we liked into our own groove, with lyrics inspired by Bible stories that we knew by heart because we'd heard them all our lives. We became the main attraction on Sundays, especially to all of the kids. Their parents liked it, too, because we were more entertaining and different than the same old hymns done the same old way every week. We were a cover band, just playing in church, but no one realized that because most of the adults in the congregation were Haitian immigrants with no knowledge of American pop music. This new style inspired us creatively, because we were getting our way without displeasing our dad.

Every form of rock record that came out in the eighties made its way into our set at one time or another. We did Yes, Steve Miller Band, Asia, Van Halen, Aerosmith, Metallica, Black Sabbath, you name it. The one thing we couldn't do was hip-hop, because my dad knew hip-hop. It was the sound of Walnut Street: all the thugs walking by with their radios, all the drug dealers' Jeeps bumpin' so loud it shook the front windows of our house. He knew that rhythm and all it represented to him too well. He called it bum music.

My mother listened to a lot of country music, so we made sure to include a lot of it. To her, the soulful singing and harmonies sounded like the Christian music the missionaries brought with them to Haiti. She didn't always hear some of the more secular stories about tears and beers and all of that in there. To her those voices and guitars sounded like the Nazarene missionaries from churches in Kansas City and Texas. She loved Crystal Gayle and Kenny Rogers and when she really wanted to get down my mom would blast Charlie Daniels's "Devil Went Down to Georgia" as loud as her record player would go.

Through my mom I learned to love Johnny Cash. When I was given the honor of playing at the tribute to Johnny Cash in 1999, with him present, I covered "Delia's Gone," my very favorite song of his. I don't think anyone expected me to play a faithful version of it on acoustic guitar with just a bass accompanying me. I've always been good at imitations and I did my version of Johnny. I freestyled a verse, too, and I was worried that the Man in Black might not like it, but when I saw him later that night, he told me he loved it and he was happy to see me make the song my own.

"That's what real folk music is about," he said. "Making a song your song."

I LISTENED TO EVERYTHING I could get my hands on that was rock and pop at the time—but never any R&B. I didn't know the Stylistics, the Four Tops, Marvin Gaye, Berry Gordy, the Temptations, none of that. My parents had never heard it because in the seventies when that stuff was going on, they were migrating to the States within the church, so they weren't exposed to it. Put it this way: I didn't even know that that Michael Jackson came from the Jackson 5; that's how much all of that music passed me by.

We were exposed to reggae, which found its way into our church band, thanks to my cousin Jerry Duplessis. He had just come from Haiti and he brought records that had been played on Radio of Light, which was a Christian reggae station in Haiti. In the same way that we were influenced by the pop music we saw on TV and heard on the radio but made it Christian, these Haitian groups took reggae and made it Christian. They put Christian lyrics over music inspired by Jimmy Cliff and Bob Marley, who were coming out of Jamaica.

There, one artist who influenced us more than any other was Riguard Divarnere because Jerry was his bass player. He was just twelve years old at the time and his bass was much too big for him, so he was nicknamed Little Bass. Jerry fell in love with the reggae groove and he brought a lot of his records with him when he moved in with us. This Riguard Divarnere was heavily influenced by Jimmy Cliff and Bob Marley and when I first heard him, I knew I wanted to sound like him. I wanted to be that kind of singer in the church.

Jerry was having a great time playing that music down in Haiti—maybe a little too much. I remember hearing that he had been hospitalized down there because he had overdosed on drugs. The truth was that Jerry's dad had left the family in Haiti and come to America to live with us and set up shop the way my father and so many others had. Once he was gone, Jerry's family home basically turned into a marijuana farm, and one day Jerry smoked so much that he ended up in the hospital. Little Bass got that high—so high that he needed medical attention. You've got to really try hard to do that.

Jerry's father, my uncle, the one who later sponsored our musical careers by providing a space where we could record without my dad knowing about it, sent for Jerry via a visa through the church. He showed up with his big bass, already a rock star to us.

I was excited because I thought Jerry would start playing in our band. He was five years older so I figured he could really teach us some stuff. That didn't happen right away, because we were forbidden to hang out with him at first. My mother ordered us to keep an eye on him and tell her if he was doing drugs. He was clearly the black sheep, which I loved. It was nice to no longer be the only one.

One day Jerry brought me a cassette, and at the time he couldn't even speak English.

"Listen to this stuff, man," he said in Creole.

He had a tape of a sound system from Jamaica called Stone Love. Sound systems are a vital part of the musical history of all Caribbean cultures. They are collections of DJs, MCs, and engineers who travel around the country in a truck or bus outfitted with a generator and huge speakers to throw street parties. This was how reggae, rocksteady, and other forms of music were spread to the people all over the island. This is where the DJs of the South Bronx drew their inspiration to throw parties in the parks in the summer time, and this is how hip-hop was born.

Stone Love was started by a guy named Winston "Wee Pow" Powell and has been going strong for almost forty years. I pushed Play on the tape and heard this guy speaking in an accent unlike anything I'd ever heard in my life. He was saying, "Dis tune is a tune straight outta England, a number one tune, dis one." The first thing I started doing was imitating that accent all day long because I thought it was cool and funny. That tape changed my life and got me hooked on dance hall, reggae, and all of that.

Jerry introduced me to other great reggae records, like King Yellowman, Gregory Isaacs's "Night Nurse," songs that I've loved all of my life since the first time I heard them.

One night, all of us were in bed going to sleep, when I smelled something unusual. It was a smell I knew right away we weren't supposed to be smelling in our house. I heard my mom wake up and come down the hall. She started banging on the door, which was locked, with Jerry inside of course.

"Open this door right now," she said to him in Creole.

"I'm using the bathroom. I am peeing!"

"No you're not. Open up. Now!"

By then all of us were standing behind my mom. Jerry opened up and a cloud of smoke came out and engulfed all of us. I tried not to crack a smile. It was going to be the first time someone would catch a beating besides me.

Jerry's dad had found his own place by then so my mom brought the phone with her before she started interrogating. She told Jerry his dad was on the phone but she didn't let him say hello. She held the mouthpiece to his mouth and started asking questions.

"What were you doing in there, Jerry?"

"Nothing. I was going to the bathroom."

"Why is there all this smoke in here, Jerry? Have you been smoking?"

"No, I haven't been smoking."

She took the phone back and smelled it.

"You haven't been smoking? Well why does this phone smell like smoke? No one smokes in this house."

"Uh . . . I don't know."

"I'm going to keep this phone and let your dad smell it, Jerry, because I know you were smoking in there and now he will, too."

That did it, and Jerry broke down on the spot.

"Yeah, I've been smoking. But I haven't been smoking weed. I was only smoking a cigar."

The truth was he wanted to smoke weed, but he didn't know where to get it. His English wasn't very good either, so he couldn't even ask anybody. So he smoked a cigar instead, trying to get a bit of a buzz. He had to get a fix. It was a step up from smoking weed, but getting caught smoking a cigar in the minister's house didn't go too well for him. It didn't matter that he was eighteen years old; he was treated like a misbehaving child that day.

3

TO THE BEAT OF
MY OWN DRUM

We lived at 107 South Clinton Street in East Orange for four years, from the end of my elementary through junior high school. When we moved out, my grandmother and Uncle Renaud—Jerry and Renel's father—moved in there, relocating from Brooklyn. In that house my father had forbidden hip-hop, but in the basement just a few years later, we built the recording studio, the Booga Basement, and in that studio *The Score* was recorded. It makes complete sense when you look at the history of the men in my family: my father did his best work as a preacher, but he only did so after he went against his father's Vodou beliefs. And in that little home, I did my best work recording music my dad considered immoral poison, one floor below the room where he used to preach. It was a circle of life.

My father made a church out of every place we lived, but he was always looking for a proper building for his flock, and he had never had that in America. One day in 1985, he had the entire family in the car and we were driving down South Clinton Street, toward Newark. It's about fifteen minutes away from where we lived. It was just a regular day. I think it was early winter and kind of rainy, and I don't remember where we were going, but that day changed everything for our family. We passed 1108 South Orange Avenue, and there it was: the Garden of Eden my father had been looking for in the Garden State. It was an abandoned funeral home that had been condemned and was halfway burnt to the ground. He slammed on the brakes and the LTD station wagon came to a halt slowly and clumsily.

"This is it!"

"What is it, Gesner?" my mom asked.

"This is what we have been looking for!"

"What is? What do you mean?"

"This is what I mean: I have found the church. I have found our home."

At that point all of us kids began turning our heads around like we were in *The Exorcist* because there was no way in hell that he could be talking about that burnt-up, ashy building.

"Dad! Where is it?"

"There it is. We will rebuild. We will call it home."

The building at 1108 South Orange Avenue had been burned almost to the foundation. It was a skeleton with a half-intact roof and walls so charred that you couldn't tell what color they used to be. This is where my father was convinced that we should be and where he believed he could have the church he'd been searching for.

The family thought my father had finally gone crazy. This place, even to us, wasn't a place to call home. The dead didn't have a choice by the time they got there, but we still did. I saw what was going to happen: we were going to become the Haitian Addams Family living in this place. I wasn't about to go to a new high school with kids knowing my family lived in a burnt-out funeral home. To the right side of the funeral home were a big parking lot and an Irish pub. Across the street was a run-down supermarket, and on the left side was an Italian social club: one of those joints where they drank coffee and ran numbers and had late-night illegal card games.

Family portrait from Haiti sent to Reverend Gesner Jean in Brooklyn, New York. Picture taken in Port-au-Prince, Haiti. From left to right: Jean-Guillame Innocent (cousin), Yolande Jean (mother), Samuel Jean (brother), Elianna Duthil (standing, grandmother), and Wyclef.

Clef's first birthday:
Port-au-Prince, Haiti.

Port-au-Prince, Haiti. From left to right, back row: Paulette (cousin), Idalie Bonny (grandmother). Front row: Samuel Jean, Wyclef.

Reverend Jean writes a letter home
to his wife and kids in Haiti:
Brooklyn, New York.

Reverend Jean (left) with his siblings
Marie Rose Theophile (center)
and Fresnel Innocent (right):
Brooklyn, New York.

Proud parents at the airport to
pick up their sons:
Port-au-Prince, Haiti.

Wyclef's mother (left), with
Philomene Duplessis, the aunt who
raised him in Haiti:
East Orange, New Jersey.

Wyclef (left) and
Samuel Jean,
newly arrived in
America, wearing
outfits made by
Reverend Jean:
Brooklyn, New York.

Wyclef Jean, in an
elementary-school picture:
Brooklyn, New York.

Clef (right) enjoying Christmas toys with his cousin
George Theophile (left): Brooklyn, New York.

Sunday breakfast: East Orange, New Jersey. From left to right:
Farel G. "Sedeck" Jean (brother), Samuel Jean, Melky Jean (sister),
Wyclef, Yolande Jean, Reverend Gesner Jean (father).

Family portrait after church: Newark, New Jersey.
From left to right: Wyclef, Samuel Jean,
Sedeck Jean, Melky Jean, Yolande Jean,
Reverend Gesner Jean.

Wyclef and Sam, proudly showing
their middle-school diplomas:
East Orange, New Jersey.

Middle-school graduation, Our Lady Help of Christians:
East Orange, New Jersey. Left to right: Wyclef,
Reverend Gesner Jean, Samuel Jean.

Church portrait, Wollaston, Church of the Nazarene:
Quincy, Massachusetts. Left to right, back row: Wyclef Jean,
Melky Jean, Sedeck Jean, Samuel Jean. Seated: Reverend Gesner Jean,
Rose Jean (sister), Yolande Jean.

Clef singing at a wedding: Newark, New Jersey.
Left to right: Joel Servilus, Wyclef, Jerry "Wonda" Duplessis, Khalil, and Jackson Servilus (obscured) on drums.

Wyclef singing at a gospel concert: Newark, New Jersey.

Reverend Gesner Jean with his trademark cowboy hat: Boston, Massachusetts.

Sedeck (left) and Melky (right) with Reverend Gesner Jean (center): Brooklyn, New York.

Ordination day for Reverend Gesner Jean (seen here with Yolanda Jean), Denville Church of the Nazarene: Denville, New Jersey.

Reverend Gesner Jean's graduation day from seminary: Port-au-Prince, Haiti.

Wedding picture: Gesner Jean and Yolande Jean: Port-au-Prince, Haiti.

Before a family trip to France: Teterboro, New Jersey.
From left to right: Claudinette, Angelina, and Wyclef.

Wyclef, c. 1997; outtake from
a photo shoot in support of
The Carnival.

Wyclef (center) with Angelina Jolie
(left) and Brad Pitt (right) in Haiti
supporting humanitarian relief
efforts after the 2010 earthquake.

My father would not be stopped, so he went ahead and bought it.

"God sent me a vision," he said in his Sunday-sermon voice when we asked him why we had to move to a destroyed funeral home from a very nice house we liked. "It will become a great church that this community needs. From the ashes we will rebuild. When God speaks you must listen. This will be a great church."

My father had a great idea, but let me tell you, that place was never quite right. He was doing improvements on it from the day we moved in until the day he died, and even by then it was still a work in progress. The neighborhood wasn't any better: while we lived there, there were more carjackings and automobile-related thefts on that block than any other block in New Jersey. To this day the sound of two-bit car alarms going off at night is almost peaceful to me. Those were the crickets that put me to sleep at night when I was a kid; now they just remind me of home wherever I hear them.

As I said, this building was fried. Most of the roof was there and all of the walls were there, but it looked like a house of cards painted black with soot. We never learned what caused it, but it didn't take the Fire Department to figure out that the blaze had started in the attic and made its way down. The third floor was destroyed, half of the second floor was fine, and most of the first floor was intact. The basement held the rooms where they had prepared the bodies. There were drains in the floor and all of the equipment—embalming fluid machines, leftover chemicals and supplies—was still there. There were coffins in the freight elevator, too.

This place was eerie. You could feel the spirits of the dead there. Even if you don't believe in that kind of thing, our home when we moved in would have changed your mind. The charred walls didn't help us feel less like we were in a horror movie.

My brothers and sisters and I adapted pretty quick coming from Brooklyn, but we already got teased because we were a preacher's kids. If they saw us coming out of the funeral home every day, that would have been too much for any of us. So every morning, we'd have a lookout: one of us would sneak a look from the window, and when no other kids were coming down the block, we'd run out the back door and down the side of the house to the street. We didn't tell anyone where we lived. We also had to keep this from our mother and just act like we preferred the back door as our exit of choice. She would not have been happy with us at all if she knew that we were not proud of our home.

The coffins in the basement and the big freight elevator where they brought the bodies in and out were just scary. Next to that was a room with the metal table where they sucked the blood out and dressed the bodies for the funeral. The day we moved in we found the big knife they used to break bones sitting there on the floor. That was our new home. The basement, of all places, was where my father decided Bible study would take place. He walked around that room like it was as grand as St. Patrick's Cathedral.

"This is where we will bring in the chairs!" he said beaming this huge grin. "We will sit here and do our study. The next room will be for services."

I know I wasn't the only one in the family who thought that this was a little bit crazy, but my dad wasn't the kind of leader who failed. He wasn't the kind who listened either, so we knew that this was how it was going to be. He spent the first few months we lived there walking through the house praying in every room, every day. That didn't do much to convince us kids that the place wasn't haunted, and we had reasons for that, too.

At first I thought it was a joke my little brother was playing on me, or my parents' version of the monster's claw that got us to pray back in the village in Haiti. But it wasn't either of those: there were ghosts in the funeral home, and they liked to steal our blankets when we were sleeping. It was scary, but it wasn't *Poltergeist*; some invisible hand would pull the blankets off of us some nights. It happened to my younger brother, my sisters, and me. We would wake up and the blankets would be on the floor at the end of our beds. All of us had experiences where we woke up, saw the blankets moving, and were frozen with fear.

It happened a lot, because those ghosts liked taking blankets. I always knew when they were coming, too, because I could hear them. There would be a creak in the hall and then the whistling of a breeze through a drafty attic. I'd feel that cold wind pass over my skin, and then a feeling of dread would grip me. The moment I heard that sound in the middle of the night I was paralyzed. I'd try, but I couldn't yell; whatever that energy was would keep me from crying out.

After it happened to me a few times, I knew it wasn't just a bad dream. After it happened to my brother and sisters, I knew I wasn't crazy or special. I asked my father about it because I knew it was real. I wanted to know if he believed in spirits the way he believed in Jesus Christ. I wanted to know if he was as Haitian as me, because Haitians believe in ghosts.

"Nel, there are spirits all around us in this world," he said. "They live alongside us, all of the time. The dead are a part of our world."

I nodded, hanging on his every word.

"Most of them mean us no harm, but some are mischievous, and others can be dangerous."

"Why do they like to take my blankets?"

"I don't know."

"Well, what can I do when I hear them coming to take my blankets?"

"There is only one thing you can do to turn them away."

"What is it?"

"Recite Psalm 23."

Let me tell you, whatever you believe in as far as God and religion, I don't care what you say, I recited the psalm when the ghosts came back, and it worked, each and every time. They never bothered me again.

. . . .

MY FATHER OBTAINED SOME funding from the Nazarene Church and some more through donations from his congregation and promises from all of them they'd volunteer their time on the weekends to help us rebuild, and that was how it went. We lived on the second floor, and my father started doing church in the basement every Sunday.

He also put up a sign in the parking lot that said it was for the church only. Between the supermarket, the pub, and the Italian joint, there were always cars in there, during the day and all night long. Eventually he taught people: usually by walking outside every few minutes for the first few weeks we were there, to ask them to leave. You couldn't blame people; the funeral home had been abandoned for years.

The only ones who didn't take any of that seriously were the Italian dudes. After we'd been there a while, my father decided he'd had enough of it. One night, he looked out the window and saw the lot full of cars. I knew it was all the Italian guys because every other car was a Cadillac Eldorado. It was hot that night and my father was wearing shorts and sandals as he went out the door to go talk to these guys. I was worried, so I ran behind him to watch what happened in case I had to report it to the police.

My father walked right up to the door and knocked on it like it was nothing. This huge guy straight out of *The Sopranos* opened it.

"Preacher, how you doin'?"

"You must move all of these cars. They are *not* to park in the church parking lot."

"Take it easy, Preacher," he said slowly. "Don't worry about it; we'll take care of you."

"I want these cars moved. I will call the police."

I saw a look of confusion cross the guy's face briefly, and then that calm came back—which is the sign of a man you need to be careful with. Real gangsters and killers never lose their cool.

"Preacher," he said, "we *are* the police."

It was the only time I saw my father flinch, realizing that he'd walked into something he'd not counted on: a situation he could do nothing about. He wasn't afraid, but it was the first time I'd seen him pause. In situations like this, he either got his way or kept talking, making his point. He stood there for a moment and for once he didn't stand his ground.

"Okay then," he said. "Good night."

"Good night, Preacher."

The next day, we were rehearsing the church band with my father when we heard a knock at the back door. I went up to see who it was. It was the Italian guy from the night before.

"Get your father."

"Hello again," my father said.

"Preacher, this is for you." He handed my father an envelope full of cash. It was thick, half-opened, and I could see the bills.

"This is to help with your repairs, Preacher. Looks like you've got a lot of work to do here." The guy smiled at him in that way that mobbed-up Italians do: he was friendly but you knew he meant business. "We're gonna park there, Preacher, but we'll be donating to the church. We may even come by for confession one of these days."

The Italians did what they said they'd do and their donations really helped us out. They were definitely made men, because nobody fucked with their cars, and on that block, back then, a parking lot full of Eldorados was like a stack of money left on the street in Times Square: it was unlikely to be untouched the next day. If nobody was pinching a parking lot full of Eldorados in Newark, New Jersey, in the middle of the night, something was up.

Our new house was never quite right, to tell you the truth: it was haunted and it never looked good. By the time my father died in 2001, it finally looked alright inside thanks to the missionaries from Kansas, Texas, and all over the world who came to stay with us and help rebuild. The church was moved out of the basement and onto the first floor by then, but the outside still needed work. It always seemed to need a paint job, and we never got around to any kind of landscaping in the front yard. Only after I had made enough money did I take care of things. My father wasn't going to let me buy him a new church outright or move him out of the place he had chosen. I helped him the only way that he would find acceptable: I contributed to the church fund.

Living in the burnt old funeral home had one advantage: people thought we were weird, and that can be a good thing when people want to intimidate you. Across the street and down the block from us was a deli owned by a Chinese guy. And as there are outside every deli owned by an Asian guy in any bad neighborhood, a pack of dudes always hung out on that corner, and claimed it for themselves. They weren't the toughest on the block, but they were a pack of bullies capable of doing some damage. One day my little brother Sedek went in the store after school and when he came out one of the thugs slapped him across the face just to humiliate him. I got home a little while later and I found Sedek sitting in the window by the door waiting for me.

"Clef, these thugs smacked me," he said. He looked scared and sad. "I was coming out the Chinese store and they smacked me. I've been waiting for you to come home so you can go get me my respect back."

"What now? Are you okay?"

"No, I'm not. I need you to get me my respect back."

I'm not the kind to back down, but this was a lot of pressure to put on me. I knew these guys: there were four of them, and they were all bigger than me. They looked like ballplayers and I looked like a mouse.

"Okay brother, I will do this for you," I said slowly, narrowing my eyes at him. "I will get you your respect back."

I had no chance of outpowering these guys. I had to rely on something else. I thought about what everyone in the neighborhood said about Haitians: they all thought we practiced Vodou. And that scared them. They thought we could put curses on them and steal their souls. I thought about how I could adapt this myth into a method of survival, how I could reimagine my roots to fit in on the block.

I went to my parents' room and into my mother's closet to get her squirrel-fur scarf. It was a string of squirrel bodies, with the heads on each end. It was one of those scarves that you see and you say to yourself, *That motherfucker is wearing ten squirrels.* I wrapped that around my neck. Then I went into my father's closet, all the way to the back, where I knew he had a machete. I took it out of its sheath and put it on the floor. Then I grabbed his raincoat and put it on.

I knew I'd need some sort of Vodou powder to scare them with so I went to the kitchen and filled the pockets of the coat with salt. I hid the machete under the coat, tucked the squirrels inside the collar, and stood by the front door with Sedek.

"Listen to me," I said to him. "I am going to get you your respect back. I want you to sit here by this window and watch the street. I am going to bring that guy over here and I want you to come outside and smack him just the way he smacked you. That is how you get your respect on this corner. They have got to respect us, so we are going to make them fear us."

Sedek kept looking out the window and back at me. "Okay," he said.

I looked strange, man: raincoat, squirrel scarf, and something long hidden under the coat. In broad daylight I was wearing squirrels around my neck, with a machete hanging down the side of my leg. I wasn't something you saw every day, even on South Orange Avenue.

I walked across the street toward them slowly, kind of dragging the leg I held the machete against as if I had a slight limp. As I got closer I opened my eyes wide, like some crazy Zulu witch doctor.

"What the fuck you lookin' at?" one of them said.

"I am looking at four dead men," I said. I was still too far away for them to get the full impact of the squirrel scarf, so I pushed the coat back to let the heads show.

"He has dead fucking squirrels around his fucking neck, man!" These guys were in their teens, but they were tough. I was two or three years older than they were, but there was no way I could take them. I might as well have been five years their junior.

"Yo, what the fuck is that shit?"

That's what I wanted to hear, so then I went in for the kill: I reached into the pocket and threw a fistful of salt into the air at them.

"What the fuck, man?" They backed up and started to separate.

"That is the voodoo shit I been telling you niggas about!" one of them said. "Them niggas is witches, man! Fuck this motherfucker!"

The moment I heard that, I pulled the machete out, opened my eyes even wider, and held it over my head, still walking toward them.

"Yo, what the fuck! He got a fucking sword, man!"

They started to scatter in every direction, and like a lion, I pounced on my prey, the tall one who had smacked Sedek. I got him in a headlock and, with the knife at his throat, began to drag him across the street toward our house. I got to the door and looked up to the second floor and saw Sedek sitting in the window, sucking his thumb. That's what he used to do when he was worried: sit in the window and suck his thumb, even as a teenager.

"Dek, get down here, now," I said.

"What the fuck, nigga? Let me go!" I tightened my grip and put the knife closer to the dude's throat.

"I will cut you like a goat if you don't shut up, motherfucker. You will not disrespect my brother or my family. You will apologize to him!"

Dek came outside, business as usual, looking like we hadn't just talked about me doing this.

"Dek!" I yelled. "Smack this motherfucker right now like he did to you."

Dek just looked at me, confused.

"Smack him!"

"I don't want to smack him," he said.

"You what?"

"I don't want to smack him." He half-smiled. "I just wanted my respect back."

Sedek is my brother and we are very close, but as you can see by this story, we are very different also. We share the same blood, but he was raised in America and I am an immigrant. From being born in the village, it was already my nature to get him his respect by any means necessary, and respect to me meant an eye for an eye. But to Sedek it was a little bit different. We learned a lot about each other that day. His perspective was that of a Haitian American, whereas mine was that of an immigrant, someone used to fighting for everything he'd ever have. I was upset with him: I did not understand how he could just stand there when I had risked my life for him.

"I could have gotten locked up, Dek. Why the hell you didn't do anything when I did that so you could get your respect back?" I asked him.

"I just wanted my respect."

"And how did you get it? You didn't slap that kid!"

"I didn't need to."

"That is bullshit, man."

I was mad at Sedek, but I learned something from him that day because in his heart he was like Martin Luther King Jr. He didn't have to slap that guy to get his respect; violence wasn't going to solve anything. He was taking the Christlike stance, but I didn't understand that at all at the time. I thought there was something wrong with him then, but I know that there was nothing wrong with him now.

OUR NEW HIGH SCHOOL, Vailsburg, in Newark, was as much of an eye-opener as the new neighborhood. Every morning before we left the house, we'd wait until every kid on the block had walked by. We didn't want to stick out; we just wanted to become part of the crowd. But our parents made sure that didn't happen, and it had nothing to do with the funeral home. As they had since we were kids, they sent us to school on the first day in our Sunday best, which is not the best way to fit in at public school. This was a tough school, too; because of its location, kids from some of the worst parts of Newark were bussed in. Showing up the first day like that, I really stuck out. But I decided to run with that, and make the suit my thing. I didn't want to say that my parents had made me wear it, so the next day I wore a suit again, making it mine, but I spun it a bit. I was a big fan of house music and Culture Club at the time, so I did my take on Boy George's sense of style. I threw on an oversized trench coat and a hat with my jacket and tie, and I looked fly. My parents loved it that I was wearing proper clothes like that to school, and I turned something that made me stand out in a bad way into something that made me stand out in a good way.

Vailsburg was very different from my last school. There was more of a variety of kids than at my Catholic junior high school, but the same segregation between Haitians and black American kids was there. It was even worse. In the cafeteria, the Haitians had a section and no Haitian would ever sit outside of that. Those lines were never crossed. I, of course, wanted to cross them.

There was only one way to do this: I had to learn to battle rap, because it was all that the black American kids cared about. This wasn't Rob G and me on the playground, running things while the girls looked on. These kids were serious. The ciphers were bigger, the audience was bigger, and the rappers were better. The whole school would skip class if they heard two good rappers were going to square off.

My entrance into that world came through a guy I met named Robin Andre, who was a Guyanese Muslim kid. He was a great musician who played piano and loved Stevie Wonder. He could do anything in his catalog. We started hanging out, bonding over music, and becoming friends. We had the religion thing in common, too, because even though I didn't believe as strongly as my father, it was a big part of my life. Robin even taught me the Lord's Prayer in Arabic. Another friend I made through music was named Rodney. He was a freshman like me and he was really into the battle rap scene at school.

I wanted to gain acceptance in school by doing what the American kids did, but better, so when I got into the game I decided to come packing. My dad had gotten himself a gold microphone that he used on Sundays in church. It just sat in the pulpit the rest of the week, so Monday through Friday I brought it to school with me in an old briefcase. I'd take it in the morning and return it at night. The briefcase and mic really completed my Culture Club look.

I waited for the right time, which was one day when this dude Shamu was freestyling in a cipher at lunch. He was very clean-cut, with wavy hair swayed up on the side. I was eating lunch with my friends Robin and Rodney, watching this guy, who'd got the whole crowd going. He was rhyming and looking around the room, and when I caught his eye, he started making fun of my outfit. He started taunting me.

"Funny derby on his head like the Pet Shop Boys," he said. And then, "He's so black he's blue; he need to go back to Timbuktu." All the kids were laughing.

Shamu was the dopest, most swaggered kid in school, and every time he started rhyming, a crowd of girls, guys—everyone from all grades—formed. And there was I, this skinny Haitian kid looking like he just came from a Culture Club concert.

I didn't care. I popped the combination on the briefcase and got out my gold microphone. I jumped on the cafeteria table and my first line was: "Back in the Bronx, where came from, I danced to the beat that goes par-um-pa-pa-pum-pum."

That was just tradition; then I got to work. "I may be from Timbuktu, but even if I point it out on a map, he still don't know where Africa's at." The rest of my rhymes were about him underestimating me and how I was going to take his girlfriends and chew him up and spit him out. What I didn't realize is that I was taking out the best rapper in school, and I was just a freshman.

Battle rapping is a face-off between two individuals. It's like a one-on-one basketball game, except an audience decides who wins, so it's more like a dunk contest than a one-on-one game. When you dropped a dope line on someone, all the kids watching would scream, and the loudest cheer won the day. Their approval was like they were saying, "He just slammed that ball in your face!"

My plan worked; pretty soon word got around that Nelly Nel was something else. Shamu, of course, didn't like the way it went down, so he asked his friend Rah Ski, this junior who really was the best rapper in school, to go against this Haitian freshman and take him out.

Whenever there was going to be a rap battle that everyone wanted to see, it would be organized in school and it would go down during one of the two lunch periods that day. Then every kid would spread the word and people would cut class to check it out. Word would spread down the hallways like wildfire. Dudes would just open the doors to classrooms and say, "Second period lunch, Rah Ski gonna battle!" and run off before they got in trouble. Our school was like a combination of the schools in *Fame*, *Beat Street*, and *Breakin'*, all mixed together—intellect, poetry, and the streets. When kids caught wind of a battle like that going on, half the school would cut class to see what went down.

I walked into that lunch period with my gold microphone, and

Rah Ski was already there. He had his boys with him and I had mine with me. The second he saw me he started in.

"In Spanish today I learned 'yente yente,' you look like the man they call Kunta Kinte."

I saw my opening there and I took it and made fun of the fact that he only knew two words in Spanish. "Let me teach you something about it," and then I insulted him in Spanish. Most people in school didn't even know I knew Spanish.

The kids went ballistic. It took him literally ten minutes to even get a line out because they were screaming so loud. After that we went toe-to-toe for the next hour, all through lunch. It got to the point that the principal came down to see what was going on.

Later on I put this all in song with the line, "The principal said, 'who is responsible is due for detention' because in this school I got a rap education." That is really what happened. The principal came in and said that if he ever saw Rah Ski or me rapping again in the cafeteria we would be suspended. That is how big of a disturbance it was.

I was much younger than Rah Ski, but I earned his respect the only way you can in rap battles: through rhymes and vocabulary. I wanted that respect, because it wasn't about impressing girls on the playground anymore; it was about earning a place of equality for all of my Haitian brothers and sisters in school. Playing guitar, singing in church, writing songs—that was my natural element. Rapping was something I had to work hard at. So this was a real victory to me. English wasn't my first language either—Creole was—but I had just proved to every kid in my neighborhood that I could do it as well as any black American kid in our school.

I became the Kobe Bryant of the cafeteria and school yard, and guys began to step to me. One of them was named Abdullah, and to me he was a rookie, so I didn't pay him no mind. He was the only kid I battled who actually hit my Achilles heel, though. Abdullah knew something that I had managed to keep hidden all that time:

he knew I lived in a funeral home. Like any cocky champion might, I didn't see it coming. My first line even set him up.

"Spit your verse, because I'm about to put you in a hearse."

The dude looked right at me and said, "Oh yeah? You always acting like you in the zone, but I'm gonna pop your secret out today. You live in a funeral home."

That hurt. It was personal and I wasn't expecting it. The crowd started laughing like hyenas, running in all directions, holding their stomachs. I had to think fast.

"Why you all running? Where you going, come back. Y'all know I didn't start the drama. Yesterday I was sleepin' with his mama."

It was a pretty good line, but it wasn't good enough. His line was so strong he had left this gladiator bleeding in the sand and set Rome on fire before I even tried to get up and strike back.

Battle raps are wordplays that go 16 bars, 48 bars, 64 bars—whatever it takes. They are always spur-of-the-moment and they are always focused on your opponent. But the best battle rappers always come prepared. The best ones have a lot of rhymes memorized that they can spit back at any given time. That was usually my strength, but Abdullah burst my bubble when he built off of my hearse metaphor.

The battle-rap circuit extended beyond our school, too. It was real underground, and you have to remember this was years before anything like the Internet was there to connect people. By word of mouth, kids in school would talk to other kids in other schools about the best rappers they'd seen at lunch or in the school yard. Reputations would be built, and just like any competitive sport, the athletes and the audience would want to see who was best. There was a circuit, and kids would set up these battles. They would meet outside each other's schools and sneak each other in to watch a battle royale between the school champions. It was just like football or anything else—it would be Newark versus East Orange—just in rap.

. . . .

SOMETHING I NEVER GOT used to in my American inner-city school experience was that tradition called Haitian Day. The Haitian population was definitely set apart: we sat at our own tables in the lunchroom; we walked home together; we hung out together. And one day a year, we defended ourselves from the rest of the student body together. My first year at Vailsburg High School, the other students really pulled out the stops, too. They let it be known that as soon as the school bell rang at the end of the day, it was on. The Haitians knew it was coming, and word went out that we were going to fight back as hard as we had to, no matter what they did. I figured this was going to be some stupid school prank shit: some roughhousing, stealing our books, just typical stuff. I was wrong. As the clock ticked those last few minutes off, the school courtyard began to look like the end of *Do the Right Thing*: two sides just staring each other down. Kids had brought pieces of pipe and tire irons: this was serious. It was the day the Haitian kids said, collectively, "We ain't gonna have it."

Then the bell rang.

The fighting broke out and it was such a mob scene that it spread onto the street. I wasn't even getting messed with because by then I fit in so well; all my American friends didn't think of me as one of the Haitians. I didn't like what was happening to my Haitian people though, so out in front of the school I jumped on the hood of some car and broke the windshield.

"Nel, I thought you was on our side!" this American kid yelled at me. "What are you doing man?"

"No, I'm Haitian, man! And you can't be messing with these people like this!" Then I got off the car and kicked in the headlights.

The fighting became a small riot. People got pipes, bats, garbage can lids, whatever they could find to beat on each other. Kids were breaking into cars, looting school property, and destroying a lot of innocent people's front yards. A few people got stabbed and were taken off in ambulances.

The next day, things were different. There was a mutual respect, or maybe it was mutual fear, because no one wanted to see that happen again. There was too much violence and it was too widespread for the school to even try to pin the fighting on anyone in particular. A few kids got suspended just to make a point, but they had probably already been in trouble anyway. That day was the sound of an entire school exploding.

I was cool with the black Americans, so some of my friends asked me to talk to some of the Haitian kids, just to make peace, since I was accepted in both groups. And after that day, I made a point to start rapping about being Haitian whenever I got involved in a cipher or a battle in school. Through my art, I began to represent my people in a different way, which helped to calm the tension and prevent any further violence. The anger between the two groups wasn't over, but because of hip-hop, I became a mediator and negotiator in my school. Before things could escalate between these very big groups, I would be able to go back and forth and keep anything bad from happening. The school didn't have someone like that before I started going there. And the language I used to do it all was hip-hop.

At the same time that I was using this new American language of rap that I'd learned, I was expanding my horizons musically. I remember sitting at the piano in the music room freshman year and playing it when no one was in there between classes. The choir teacher, Miss Price, heard me from down the hall and came in.

"Did someone teach you what you're playing?" she asked.

"No, I just learned how to play."

"Can you read music?"

"No, I play by ear."

"You are very good," she said. "You really have an amazing ability. You should join the choir."

"Aw, hell no!" I said to myself. If I joined the choir, dudes wouldn't think I was street anymore. I already had to cope with everyone knowing I was in my dad's church band; being in choir in school would be too much. I wanted anything but that at school: I wanted to explore other areas of music I couldn't do at home.

"I don't know about that, Miss Price," I said. "That's not really what I want to do with music. I'm already in my dad's church band and that's enough. The kids here all know me as Nelly Nel. And Nelly Nel wouldn't be in no choir."

Eventually she convinced me otherwise by asking me to sing a song or two with the choir whenever they performed. I enjoyed it more than I thought I would, so I became a full-time member. Through choir, I got to know Mr. Hayes, another music teacher, who convinced me to join the jazz band. The two of them were my mentors.

One afternoon before choir practice, Miss Price came over to me at the piano, where I was playing, waiting for all the other kids to arrive.

"You should learn to read music, Nel," she said.

"Do I need to? I can play what I want by listening," I said.

"You write songs, don't you?"

"Yes."

"Well if you ever want your songs to be used in a movie or have an orchestra play them, then you'll have to pay someone else to write out the music, so you might as well learn to do it yourself."

I stopped playing. "People get paid to listen to music and write it out?" I asked. "How much do they get paid?"

"Sometimes they get up to fifty thousand dollars," she said. Miss Price knew how to motivate her students.

"Where do I start?" I said.

Miss Price taught me to read and write music and once I did, I really began to love her class. We were doing renditions of "Birdland" by Joe Zawinul in both the choir and the jazz band, so I began to play the upright bass in both bands. Mr. Hayes taught me everything about playing that instrument, as well some guitar. He was all about technique. If he taught you to play "Take the A Train" by Billy Strayhorn you had to play it back for him exactly as it was written on the sheet music. He wasn't a fan of improvisation in class because his job was to make sure we mastered the basics. Once I started getting good at bass, I decided to make my performance more exciting by spinning the bass around while I played. Mr. Hayes stopped us cold.

"Nel, what were you doing?"

"I was playing. Did I make a mistake?"

"This is not a circus show, Nel. This is serious business. This is jazz. You have to pay attention. You have to focus. You can't distract the audience from this piece of music with flashy showmanship. This piece of music was created to be played at a standard that is expected. Do not do that again."

I didn't do that in class again, but I tried to funk up the jazz band with my playing style as much as I could. I also liked to get to the music room early to warm up and as I played my scales, I made sure to spin my bass.

I learned technique from Mr. Hayes, but Miss Price expanded my musical mind intellectually. "If it's music, you have to know a piece of it," she'd tell us. She'd teach us everything from Bach to Beethoven to Art Blakey, some country, standards, and everything in between.

All of this was the first formal training I had, because music to me was something that came naturally. It was something I had figured out with my brothers and sisters and learned from the villagers back in Haiti. I'm not saying it wasn't something I didn't take seriously, but it wasn't something I ever thought could be taught with a pen and paper, the way we learned math and English. It was more than a hobby for me, but it sure wasn't school. My two teachers changed it all for me and I began to see music as a discipline, as something as important to learn properly as a language.

I studied it hard, and my efforts paid off my sophomore year, when our jazz band qualified for a national competition to be held in Pasadena, California. I thought I'd made the big time, because I hadn't been on a plane since the one that brought me over from Haiti. We rehearsed a ton, we had everything ready, and I thought to myself, *We're gonna rock this*. Though I'd not spun my bass in his presence since that day in class, Mr. Hayes knew me by then, so he kept reminding me to stay focused during the weeks leading up to the competition.

"I know, Mr. Hayes. I won't spin my bass."

Landing in California, I felt like I was in Hollywood. It was sunny compared to home; every block looked like a movie set. I couldn't believe a place that shiny and new was even a part of the same country. We got to our hotel, which was incredible to me. There was soap and shampoo in little bottles for us here and we didn't have to pay for them? I put as many as I could find in my bag to take home. We had chaperones and all that, but I felt like a grown-up taking a plane to California and staying in a real hotel room. I guess in a way I was.

We got to the competition and I saw right away that these other bands meant business. Every band was going to play the same number, and there was some sick playing by some really, really good players. I took it upon myself to figure out how we could stand out, because in my mind, if we didn't take home the trophy, we shouldn't have come. There was only one thing to do: spin my bass and do my thing when we got out there. Mr. Hayes would thank me when we won.

Finally it was our turn. Just as the other teachers had done, Miss Price and Mr. Hayes helped us set up and introduced each of us. Then they announced what we would be playing, and took their seats.

I stayed cool for the first few moments of the song, but then I had to show my character. I smiled at the judges, I spun my bass, and I did every single thing Mr. Hayes had told me not to do. I had to give them something special; this was Hollywood.

He was fuming when we got off the stage. He took me outside of the auditorium and practically knocked me out.

"This could cost us the competition! Do you know how selfish that was?"

"I'm sorry Mr. Hayes . . . I was just trying to make us stand out."

"You did that alright. You looked like a fool. You were showboating while everyone else playing with you took it seriously. You need to apologize to them!"

Mr. Hayes was right. We played very well and we ended up in the top three, but we didn't win. And it probably was my fault.

AT AROUND THE SAME time that I understood music as something to be learned and studied at an academic level, I got my first experience with it as a legitimate career. And from the get I learned how everyone surrounding that career could be. I'm not the first to say this, but musicians are the meat in the shark tank. You know what I'm sayin'? The people who make their money from music are always circling, looking for their next meal.

I had a gym teacher, Mr. Wendall, who got obsessed with this rap group that I started to be in. We were called Exact Change. Exact Change featured me, Robin André, who was the Muslim guy who taught me the Lord's Prayer in Arabic, this kid named Chris, a kid named Todd, and this other kid named David.

In Jersey, just the way they do it all over America, there were high school talent shows that were a regional thing. People from other schools could enter, and if you had a music group of any kind, that is how you did some kind of little tour when you were still a kid and your group wasn't shit. You'd compete and you'd meet other kids who did music from other schools; it was like a social network for hip-hop.

Mr. Wendall saw us perform regularly at these talent shows and he realized that we had some chemistry. Robin and I always did vibe like that and onstage we flowed tight because we had each other's backs. The other guys fit in well with us, too. For a bunch of very different kids, we were a cohesive unit.

Mr. Wendall came at us hard; he wanted to manage us and he promised us all that fame and fortune if we signed a contract with him, which we didn't.

We had another big figure influencing us at the time too—a woman named Jan Berger who worked for RCA Records. Robin and I, who were inseparable at the time, met her through an internship program that her company did as an outreach to schools from rough areas in the New York metropolitan area. She was in charge of this program that got internships in the music industry for kids who were musically inclined. It really was a scouting program for business and creative talent.

Jan approached Robin and me at some talent show and asked us if we wanted to be in the program. Of course we did; it would give us a way to be in New York City working at a record company. It didn't pay, but it got us there and that was good enough. Jan became our manager because she was connected in New York. She did have to sell my father on the idea, though.

Jan was good at selling, and once I told her how my father felt about hip-hop, she figured out how to make it all work. She told my dad how the program was focused on the business end of music. She made it sound like I would be assisting music executives and learning how to make music my day job, rather than to be an artist. I remember so clearly the afternoon she came to our house. I'd told her about my father, but nothing could prepare her. Regardless, she knew what to say right away.

"He will start working in Manhattan in the record industry," she said. "I know the hours are long, but it's a competitive field. It's good to start young."

That's what my dad needed to hear. He looked at her long and hard. "Okay," he said. "As long as I know where he is 24/7 and I can call you any time, this job is okay with me."

I did have a real internship in Jan's office, but it didn't involve anything that would help me get a real job as a music executive or anything else. I was just an intern. I did what needed to be done, whether that meant getting coffee or taking papers to someone or picking up dry cleaning. What it did was get me into the city, and get me in and around the industry. It also got me away from my house and offered me plenty of time to work with the rest of Exact Change under Jan's leadership, in an effort to get us a record deal. Jan was a pro: when she spoke to my dad, she made it sound like she was running a school-sponsored program and we were going on a field trip.

What we were really doing was going into the studio with Kurtis Blow. Yeah, that's right, Kurtis Blow produced our demo. At the time, in the late eighties, Kurtis was the most high. And I don't know how he was connected to Jan, but she got him to record us and he tried to shape us a little bit. No one we knew could even think about being able to do that for real. On the East Coast at that time, Kurtis Blow was our Dr. Dre.

While that was happening, Mr. Wendall was trying to push us to perform his way, which was at a more local level, and involved a hokey concept. He demanded just as much of our time as Jan, who had much better connections, and a very different idea of what we should become.

Jan put us together based on looks. She had me, and she thought Chris would be the next Michael Jackson, and each one of us was a specific type of dude: I was the Caribbean kid, Chris was MJ, Robin was our serious-minded Muslim type, and the other two were fly B-boys. I wrote almost all of the rhymes for the group, but she had me handing out parts to everyone else. I had written a song called "Rap Translator" that was multilingual, and that did something to her. After hearing the possibilities in that, she made sure we had a

Spanish dude, a black dude, a white dude, and she gave each part to one of us based on how closely we looked to be natives of that language. I could have done all of them myself because I'd written all of them. I thought it was bullshit that she was handing them out. I was sacrificing my art, for what? I wanted credit for my talent as the cornerstone of this act. I was feeling like this was some bullshit.

Jan had come along first, before Mr. Wendall, but once he saw us perform, he wanted to manage us, too. And so a power struggle began. Mr. Wendall was more focused on managing me however. He saw me as a talent and also as his retirement fund, if he played my cards right. Mr. Wendall had seen every single show we ever did in school, and he saw how people reacted to us, which was unilateral: everyone loved us.

We trusted him, too, because we'd known him for years. He was our gym teacher—and every member of Exact Change spent more time in gym than most of our other classes. Mr. Wendall wanted us to stand out, so here's what he came up with: he thought we should wear tuxedos and carry canes at all times. I guess he saw us as Boyz II Men at a junior prom. How he thought this would give us cred, I don't know. None of us were old enough to sign away our rights, so Jan and Wendall were vying for some kind of future return and hoping to get us to devote ourselves to their own visions and not the other's.

Their ideas couldn't have been more different: Jan had us doing straight hip-hop and Wendall had us doing this overdressed young talent thing. But the songs were the same, and they were a mix of languages, styles, delivery—all that. Exact Change wasn't exact at all. Depending on the day, we might be $2.50 or we might be $.75, you know what I'm sayin'? It all depended on who was counting.

The truth is that Jan met us first and was molding us, and Mr. Wendall got involved once he saw there was something there. Aside from his very strong ideas about what we should wear and how we should present ourselves, he also tried to poach me from the group.

He was real cool to me in gym class and it started from there. Once he saw my musical talent, right away he told me he wanted to manage me. And once he saw Exact Change, it seemed like he tried to drive a stake through the group by pulling me out of it. I guess he saw me as his money-maker and wanted me all to himself. He was driving the group apart and making a play to grab it, all at the same time. He would constantly tell me that I was the only one who had a future and that I didn't need the other guys. At the same time he was telling the other guys shit about me to get them to want to leave the group. He was playing puppet master all around.

Wendall was smart to know that I was the talent in that group, and he began to take me out apart from the rest of them to show me that there was a world beyond Exact Change and whatever Jan Berger had lined up for us. He acted like a college scout courting a top high school point guard, and the way a good scout would, he tempted me with the perks. The best of them was the night he took me to Amiri Baraka's house.

Amiri is a poet, a writer, a college professor, and one of the most controversial minds of our generation. He had parties a few times a month where people would get high and read their poetry, and he'd have a jazz band playing. Live poetry with jazz was the sickest performance and knowledge I'd ever seen, and it made an impression on me. Wendall might not have had the right intentions, but he did know that I needed to see beyond my world and for that I thank him.

These two sharks were swimming around us hard, waiting until we were old enough to be able to actually promise them something. I was seventeen, and would be eighteen soon, and as that date came closer, they began fighting. They couldn't help it; they'd start yelling in front of us. It was verbal sparring over who would get the group when we turned legal. Each one of them pleaded their case to my family, hoping that they would sway me to sign their way. My dad realized that I wouldn't be signing up for a business job if

I signed a contract with Jan. Once he heard that loud and clear, he had no interest in whatever else she had to say. As for Mr. Wendall, well that went even worse. Wendall was not a businessman; he was a gym teacher, so his brand of negotiation was aggression. His whole pitch to my dad was that I'd never do better than what he was offering, which was based on commitment to his team and some kind of management contract for life. I don't remember the details of it; I just remember what my dad said to him.

"Get out of my house now, devil!" he shouted. "You will not do this to my son. I turn you to sand!"

That pretty much ended Wendall's campaign to be my manager and to break up Exact Change.

The funny thing is, man, even once we were dedicated completely to Jan Berger, we didn't get any further with our band. We'd play gigs in Hoboken, at all these small clubs, and even though I was underage, I'd be let into the bars with my little tuxedo on. That was the funny thing, too: even after Wendall was out of the picture, we kept the tuxedos, which was always the thing I hated the most. Who raps in tuxedos? It would have made sense if we were R&B, but this was hip-hop. We'd sneak into poetry festivals to perform and try to get into clubs with fake IDs, hoping our outfits made us look older. That was the only advantage of them. We got a regular gig in Hoboken after a while because the owner of that spot thought we were over twenty-one.

The other side of my music life was a community church band I was in, called Helping Hands, which got big enough that we played other churches besides my dad's, and then I was in the jazz and choir bands at school. With those two bands I played all kinds of talent shows, either in high schools or in churches and gospel competitions all over the Eastern Seaboard.

This was my triple life: one was the two church bands, both of which I had to do because of my father and my family; the second was truly musical, in the jazz and choir; and the third was hip-hop—my education in what I thought was the coolest form of music because I identified with it. Within hip-hop, I had to hide the fact that I loved and played the other two, because I thought they'd think I wasn't cool anymore for listening to jazz and classical music—not to mention playing Christian music for my father. There was nothing cool about that from a hip-hop standpoint. I had the church band going on Monday through Sunday, and Wednesday through Saturday I rehearsed with Exact Change. Before I expanded my horizons, all I wanted was for Exact Change to get me somewhere. If only Exact Change had been as big as the church band; every kid in the neighborhood wanted to be in that band, and none of them gave a shit about Exact Change. I'm telling you, we were the Beatles of the church bands in New Jersey.

That was my week-to-week life in high school. Most days I stayed after school late on purpose because by the time I was fifteen, I didn't like being home that much. I'd do the jazz and choir practice thing after school, then go practice with the church band and get home as late as I was allowed to. The later I stayed at school the less a chance there was of anyone in my class knowing where I lived.

The first album I ever recorded was a church album with Helping Hands. We did it in a studio in a few days when I was seventeen, thanks to Joe Servelis, who was our teacher and guide, the way Mr. Hayes was in the jazz band. He helped us record an album of church music done our way, which was like a cross between reggae, rock and roll, and traditional gospel music.

Joe became our manager in a way, the one who got us booked into playing other churches, for which we were paid, too. Joe was there watching every show, giving us tips. Usually he'd tell me to tone it down. He usually said I was jumping too high or performing too much. He was right, too, because I was doing backflips in church. I can see now that it was a little bit much. Your performance should be directed by your location and your audience, and there I was acting like I was headlining Madison Square Garden in a place were people came to worship. Jesus was the main attraction, not me, but I didn't see that at the time.

"You can't do that in church," Joe would say.

"Yeah I know. But yo, church got to be lively when we play because the rest of it is boring."

I was the youngest one in that band. Jerry Duplessis was in that band on bass, because he'd become the adopted brother. His brother Renel Duplessis was in the band, too, on guitar. I played with this band when they'd go do gigs, and I also ran the band with my brothers and sister in my dad's church.

Helping Hands was a hot band and Joe knew it. He sold copies of that album and he started getting good money for booking us. It didn't take me long to realize that everyone was coming to see me, the little skinny kid who did backflips and led the band.

I was jumping in the name of the Lord. I was the main attraction: I was the James Brown of the church band. People would show up and be like, "Where he at?" I realized I had power in this band. I saw him charging people for tickets, but we got nothing. I began to go to maestro Joe Servelis and ask for the money we'd made. He always had an excuse.

"I had to rent you a PA. That cost me, so here's twenty dollars. That's all that's left."

Every time I asked about it, that twenty dollar cost went up slightly. It became forty dollars, then sixty dollars.

"Those PAs getting more expensive?" I'd ask him. We kept drawing bigger and bigger crowds, but the size of our PA stayed the same. That opened my eyes.

In high school, I really started to clash with my father because of the rebellious nature of what I wanted to do with my life. His thing was education and he had a specific plan of how he wanted my life to go. He had a plan for Sam, too; he became a lawyer. Sam and Sedek were both on that path because in high school, they were both on the debate team, while I did music. Their grades were always better than mine because you have to be good at school to even think about doing debate club.

I wasn't terrible at school when I put my mind to it. One time when we took some national achievement test, I got a very high grade because my mom asked me to try. I studied hard and I did it for her.

"You can do this if you want to, you see?" she said when she saw my grade. "Why don't you score well on your tests all the time? You just need to try."

"Because my brain is thinking of other stuff," I said. "This stuff is done already, Mom. It's easy because I know how to do it."

I put myself out there on that test for my mother. I did not do the same for my father, who demanded that I come home each night by a certain time. This became the reason why we clashed day and night once I was a teenager. At a certain hour it was lights out, and he locked the doors and everyone was in bed—no questions asked. As I began to participate in all of these musical groups, I'd still be out at rehearsal with Helping Hands by lights-out most days of the week. Even if I were spending all my time rehearsing with Helping Hands, playing nothing but church music, my father would have wanted me home by then. It was one of the rules he lived by, and he demanded his children did, too.

My father would bolt the doors, but that didn't worry me because I knew the door wasn't the only way in. Sometimes there was a basement window open and if all else failed, I knew I could climb up the drainpipe that led to my room and crawl in my window. My friends in Helping Hands started calling me Spiderman. They'd walk me all the way home just to see me do it. That is why I started wearing Spiderman gear when I started performing hip-hop outside of Exact Change. Not a mask and all that, but there was always a spider reference somewhere in my outfit. It was partly an inside joke, partly a rap alter-ego.

If I was any kind of Spiderman, I was the one in the black suit—because I didn't stop crimes. If anything, I gave in to my impulsive nature and committed them. I'm ashamed to say it now, but the theft I did most was to steal from my family—namely the money from my father's church funds. I took a little here, a little there, and after a few times without getting caught, I got out of control. The thing was that I didn't think I was doing anything wrong or anything selfish because I never even used the money for my own good. I usually gave it out to friends and kids who needed it more than I or my family did. I guess I thought I was Robin Hood. It got to the point where it had to stop, and I definitely put an end to all that with a bang. At the time I did that last burglary of my own house—which was the last petty crime I ever did in my life—I was fighting with my dad so much I didn't care how mad he got. I figured he'd throw me out once he found out I did it, and that was fine because I was ready to live somewhere else anyway. I didn't know where and I didn't know how, but I knew that all I cared about was doing hip-hop, and that sure as hell wasn't going to happen under my father's roof.

At the time I had a hooptie old Datsun that I used to get around in. And that day I had my cousin Nason and my brothers, Sam and Sedek, in the car waiting for me as I went into the church safe and put all the money in a bag. Then I went out to the car to drive us all to the Burger King where we worked. I didn't tell them what I was doing, but as soon as I put this brown bag of money stuffed to the top with about a thousand dollars in small bills back there with them, they knew something was up.

"Clef, what you doing?" my brother asked me.

"Don't you worry about it."

"Dad gonna kill you."

"Only if he finds out." I turned around and stared him down.

We got on the highway, heading toward Burger King. My plan was to drop them off, and then go buy some food for the really poor kids and homeless people who were always hanging around in the parking lot begging for scraps. I was going to give the rest of the money to the kids we worked with, because we worked hard and deserved more than minimum wage. To me it was as simple as this: those kids needed money and the church, which was doing fine, had money. In my mind, this was following my dad's lessons. If there was money in the church and God said to give, I was going to give the congregation's money to my hardworking brothers and sisters at Burger King that day.

We were on the highway in the left lane and it was so hot we had all the windows open. All of a sudden this Porsche cut me off and I slammed the brakes, which started us skidding until we slammed into the median and, *Dukes of Hazzard*–style, went up on two wheels for a hot minute. Then we slammed down on the median and skidded sideways to a stop. We're lucky the car behind us didn't smash right into the side of us because that hooptie Datsun's doors were paper-thin.

No one got hurt from the accident, but something was lost, alright. While the car was up on two wheels, the bag of money opened up and got sucked out the window by the wind. As I got my wits about me, I looked out the cracked windshield and saw all this green paper flying behind us, most of it now on the other side of the highway, getting slapped all over the oncoming traffic. It was all gone.

The accident distracted my father from realizing that the money was missing for a while, maybe a week. He and my mother were too happy that we were okay to notice, but eventually he figured out it was missing so I had to admit to it. I had no story to cover it up and deep down I felt like I didn't deserve to get away with it, even if I could have. So I got a beating worthy of St. Peter for that. Christ was crucified facing forward but St. Peter was crucified backward. A St. Peter's beating is when they hang your ass in the air backward and beat you to death. That's what I got, and I could barely sit down for a week.

There was no getting around that one, but it's a good thing my dad didn't know about half the shit I was getting into. If he had known, I probably wouldn't be here today. My whole life then was like *Porky's*. How I spent my school days and school afternoons would have ruffled his feathers like nothing else in his world. I don't think he would have understood why and how I'd managed to get into the local strip club at least once a week.

That started during my sophomore year when my friends and I discovered that we could sneak out of Vailsburg High School pretty easily after checking in first period, and not be noticed as missing if we got back by lunch. A three minutes' walk away from school was a place called Go-Go that we passed a million times on our way to the deli next door to buy some candy and lunch. That little neon sign with the blacked-out windows had always made me wonder.

"What that mean, 'Go-Go'?" I asked my American friend.

"There's naked women dancing in there."

"What? In there?"

"Yeah."

"We gotta find a way to go up in there."

The next time we cut out, I led the charge and we just walked in. And for the five seconds I was inside, oh my God, I thought I'd found heaven: there were women everywhere in just bras and G-strings. It even smelled like heaven to me. Then a big dude blocked our path and pushed us outside.

"What y'all want?" He was a mean-lookin' dude.

"We wanna see the women."

The guy started laughing. "Shouldn't you be in school right now, little man?"

"Yeah, we're going back there . . . But we want to see the women."

This guy was smirking at us now. "Little man, you know you ain't old enough. I can't let you in there, but here's what I can do for you: You give me ten dollars. I give you ten minutes."

"Okay, thank you, man!"

That guy was cool, because he wasn't worried about the cops showing up or if it was morally wrong for high school kids to be in a go-go bar; he was just being human. He knew what it was like to be a young man and to want to see naked women. So every Friday we'd visit him and get our ten minutes in Go-Go.

I loved watching the girls dance and once they got used to seeing me there, they'd talk to me and I'd ask them all about their lives. I was a kid. I didn't even know enough to ask for a lap dance.

I'd ask questions like: "What makes you do this stuff?" "You're dancing naked, why?" "Does your man know you're doing this?" I was coming from a curious, sensitive spot, but I just didn't understand that I was probably offending them.

They were cool women. They'd be honest with me. They'd say, "You know, I've got three kids at home and I have to do this to make money. You've got a mom at home and if she didn't have your dad, she'd have to do this to support your family." I thought that was incredible.

There was one question that was always answered the same way: "No." And that question was: "Can I get a dance?"

Once I understood what that meant, I asked it all the time. They would put their hands on my cheek and tell me I was cute, but that was as far as I got. I didn't care. Sneaking out of school for forty minutes to go to a strip club was the most forbidden, coolest experience ever for me.

In high school, besides Burger King, I also had a job in Manhattan, so I'd take the train in a couple of afternoons a week and do my internship at CBS/RCA records with Jan Berger. To make some extra money I got a job as an assistant security guard two nights a week for Donna Karan in downtown Newark. I liked having that uniform, and I'd tell my little sisters I was a police officer.

That job didn't end up so well, though. I was doing so much stuff between work and all my bands that getting enough sleep became a problem for me. Donna Karan's showroom front desk had a real nice office chair for me to sit in, too, so a lot of nights I fell asleep. On one of those nights, some dudes broke in the back door and stole a whole rack of clothes that were bound for Manhattan to be in her fashion show. I lost my job over that incident, and I should have, too. I felt worse, though, because there was some one-of-a-kind shit in there and Donna probably had to get something made real quick to fill that hole and get her show up on time.

Years later, after I'd become famous, I met Donna at fashion week in New York and she was telling me how much she liked the Fugees.

"Donna, I have to tell you something. You might not know this but I owe you a check."

She looked at me like I was crazy.

"You see, a long time ago I was your night security guard in Newark," I said. "And I fell asleep on the job and a whole rack of clothes for your show was stolen. I still feel bad about that. And now that I've met you I feel even worse!"

"Wait, that was you?" she said, smiling. "You do owe me a check then!"

I REALLY DID START to become a problem once I became a teenager. Like I said, my dad didn't like me staying out, so I became skilled at sneaking in. I even hid a butter knife in the bushes so those nights he locked my window, knowing that's how I got inside, I could still get in. Then he started listening for me, so it would be this race to see if he got to my room faster than I could get under the covers. The only time I got caught was when I wasn't fast enough to get my shoes off. Sneakers on, under the covers? That's being caught red-handed.

He knew I was doing music outside of what I did in church and he knew that some of it had to be hip-hop. I never admitted it and he never heard it, but we both knew what was going on, and that threw gas on the fire. He wanted me in church Wednesday, Friday, Saturday, and Sunday, and when I couldn't oblige that, he started coming down on me. Keeping to his schedule was just the first step in a larger plan that he had in mind for me, which included Eastern Nazarene State College, the same as he planned for my brother Sam. My brother followed that path, but when I didn't respond, my dad pushed me away, and it all came to head in the middle of winter my senior year in high school. He threw me out of the house and left me no other choice than going to live with Shoe Man.

Shoe Man was one of those characters who only exist in poor neighborhoods: he had no real job; he just made money by hustling to fulfill whatever need his community had. People like Shoe Man are like Muppets in a way, just cartoon characters that you never know much about, but they serve the one function that everybody knows about in your neighborhood. Shoe Man was the guy who got sneakers off of some truck and sold them at a huge discount. He was the guy you asked to get you the new Jordans, so among the kids, this guy had power. Sneakers are like cars to teenagers in the 'hood: they determine how flush you're rolling. Shoe Man didn't even have a shoe store, but he didn't have to; people just came by his apartment to buy their shoes.

He had other hustles going, too, the biggest one being getting kids to stand on line at the DMV to register cars or get government ID cards for illegal immigrants. Shoe Man would walk the neighborhood recruiting kids he met on corners. He had a number of aliases and passports and a stack of Social Security cards. He had a whole system going for getting Haitian immigrants registered in the US government system with green cards, visas, all that. I knew I could go there and live with Shoe Man because he was always looking for kids like me to do his work for him. All the parents in the church told their kids to stay away from Shoe Man because he was shady. They'd say that the kind of work he did got a lot of kids arrested. But nothing could stop Shoe Man; he was always able to recruit teenagers when their parents' backs were turned. He'd tried to recruit me many times, so I knew he'd let me in.

I knocked on the door and a few moments later Shoe Man opened it a crack.

"What's going on?" he asked.

"I want to work for you, Shoe Man," I said. "My dad kicked me out and I have nowhere to stay. Can I stay here and work for you?"

He turned around and looked back into the room. "Who's at the door?" I heard his woman say.

"Nobody," he said over his shoulder. "Listen, you can't stay in here tonight. She's crazy. You got to stay in my car."

"Alright, then."

It was winter in New Jersey at the time, and global warming wasn't really helping me out any. I spent four freezing nights sleeping in Shoe Man's Toyota during a blizzard. Independence from my father's house rules was not all it was cracked up to be.

The fifth night, after the snow had stopped, Shoe Man told me it was cool to come into the house and sleep on the couch. He and his girl had been fighting but they'd figured it all out, he said. Until about 2:00 AM when I woke to the sound of her screaming.

"Fuck you, motherfucker!" she yelled. "Fuck you! I'm going to kill you, you piece of shit!"

I looked toward the bedroom and saw Shoe Man running, barefoot, toward the front door. She was right behind him and she wasn't kidding: she had a knife in her hand. Before I could even sit up, she sunk it into Shoe Man's back. He started yelling as blood started squirting everywhere. She didn't let up, either; she cut him two more times before he fell to the ground. The living room was a blood bath, and I ran for my life through the kitchen and out the back door.

It was snowing hard that night and the cold blinded me when it hit my face. I had nowhere else to go but home, and I knew I'd have to make amends. I crept into the church through the back door and went to sleep in one of the storage rooms. I slept there soundly until the morning, and didn't wake up until Sunday service was already under way. My father was in the middle of his sermon when I opened the door and walked right into the room. He didn't stop speaking, but he didn't take his eyes off me. There was only one thing for me to do: repent in a very big way.

I went down the aisle and dropped to my knees in front of him.

"Forgive me, Lord, for I have sinned. I repent!"

My father kept his eye on me but otherwise ignored me kneeling there and continued with his sermon. I held my hands up to the heavens.

"I repent!"

He still didn't acknowledge me. Then I felt a hand tap my shoulder. It was my mother.

"My son, do you need prayer? Do you want to pray for forgiveness?"

"Yes, Ma, I need prayer. I want the Lord's forgiveness. Please pray with me!"

"Bow your head, my son," she said. My father looked at us skeptically, and then slowly came down the aisle and joined us.

"He is a sinner, Gesner. He needs our prayer," my mother said, as the whole congregation looked on.

"Please, pray for my soul," I said, looking up as pitifully as I could. I kept thinking about how cold it was outside and what sleeping in Shoe Man's car would be like that night.

My mom turned to the congregation. "What shall we do? Will all of you pray for our son and his sins?"

"Yes," they replied together.

"Well, then," my father said, "let us pray for his soul."

My dad beckoned me to the front of the church, made me kneel, and then put his hand on my head.

"Son, do you repent of your sins?" he said in a booming, dramatic voice.

I earned an Oscar that day, because I didn't feel that I had sinned, but I convinced everyone. "Yes, Father!" I yelled. "I repent! I am a sinner! I praise God and I repent!"

All I cared about was that I was inside, somewhere warm. And for the first time in a week I'd gotten a decent night's sleep. I was happy to go and take a seat in the back of the church. I had earned it. It was so warm that I fell asleep in a matter of minutes.

After services were over, I took my mom aside for a minute.

"You know, Mama, I'm sorry I ran away for a while, but I have to tell you something," I said.

"What is it?"

"I love music, and I am going to continue doing it. It is what I want to do with my life. I know that Dad doesn't like to hear what I'm doing, but my music doesn't come from the devil."

My mother looked at me long and hard. "Well, Nelust, I am fine with that because you are going to do as you see fit. But I have to ask you to do something for me and for yourself."

"What is it, Ma?"

"You cannot tell your father about what you are doing outside of the house with your music. You must play in the church and that is all he should know. Do we understand each other?"

"Yes."

It was as if my mother understood that music was like religion in Haiti: whether a Haitian practiced Vodou or Christianity didn't matter, it was all a relationship with a higher power. The details don't make as much of a difference as people make them out to do. If you make music and communicate a message, you are speaking a universal language that goes beyond God's or the devil's music. But not everyone sees things that way, and my father was among them.

I honored my mother's request and I kept hip-hop out of our house—or at least away from anywhere my dad could hear it. We didn't practice it in the house and I didn't work on rhymes out loud there, but that didn't mean I'd stopped writing ciphers. The irony was that as much as my father hated hip-hop in every form, his brother did not. My uncle Renauld loved rap, R&B, and all the music my father thought was evil, so he let me, his nephew, set up a studio in his basement. It wasn't even his basement; it was my grandmother's. But it was his workroom—a room no one else could go into. It became the Booga Basement once I devoted myself to making a life of this. Once we founded the Fugees, that place was our refuge. But that couldn't happen until I ran away from home.

I was in my last year of high school, and my brother Sam had already gone off to Eastern Nazarene College, just like my father wanted. In Gesner's eyes, I was next. Of course I'd have to graduate first, and there was one little problem with that: algebra. I think the biggest issue I had with algebra was that it was first period in the school day. I was already spending my nights in recording studios laying down music and rhymes all night, so I was tired. But besides that, I've just never liked to get up in the morning. I still don't. If all of the music stuff I was doing outside of school was happening between six and nine in the morning, I don't think I would be a musician today. That is how much I hate getting up. Becoming a father has changed all that for me, because once you're a father, your mornings are no longer your own. I wouldn't change it for the world, but back when I was a teenager, I wasn't having the early morning bell. I never made my first period class, so by the end of the year, I was failing algebra. And if I didn't pass it, I wouldn't have enough credits to graduate or walk in my robe to get my diploma.

There wasn't time enough left in the year to turn that grade around. I think we only had one or two more tests and even perfect grades weren't going to push my average above the failure line. There was only one thing to do: beg and charm my teacher into letting me slide. Her name was Miss Serato, and she was a pretty nice lady, so I figured I had a chance. I had to do something special, though, so I got my guitar out and wrote a song for her. Then I waited in school until she walked out and sang it to her. All I needed was a D-, so a serenade had to count for some kind of extra credit, right? If I didn't graduate, my father was going to kill me, and put me in one of those old burnt-out coffins down in our basement.

"Oh, Miss Serato," I sang to her in the hallway outside her class, "you gotta let me go. It's not my fault that I be waking up late. I be in the studio the night before, I can envision myself in Madison Square Garden, I beg your pardon, Miss Serato. Oh, Miss Serato, please let me go." The song was a nice, humble ballad. And it didn't do a damn thing to melt her. That woman was tougher than nails.

"So you're asking me to pass you, Mr. Jean?"

"Yes, Miss Serato. I know I'm not close to a pass, but maybe you could just this once?"

"And why do you deserve this?"

"I just want to graduate, Miss Serato. My father will kill me if I don't."

I started playing the song again, and finally she smiled.

"I'm not going to pass you, Mr. Jean," she said. "But I will give you summer school and if you pass summer school you will graduate. That's a great song, and you're a very talented kid. So I'll give you this chance instead of failing you."

I blew through summer school and I got my diploma, but there was no way I was going to college, so instead I ran away for good. I slept on couches and lived with friends and different people from around the neighborhood until I finally landed at the Booga Basement, and that became my home.

Uncle Renauld let me live there and let us record there, but I had no way to survive. My cousin Renel got a little bit of recording equipment, and I learned how to use it, and I started charging people from around the 'hood for recording time. Everybody thought they were a rapper or a singer, so I'd make them a beat, record their song, and charge them for it. It was easy money for me, and that was my hustle. They'd come see me at the Booga, I'd make the beat, record and engineer everything, and give them a DAT of their song. It didn't take long for word to get around that all anybody had to do was come see me.

We started out with a little 6-track Akai digital recording machine that Renel bought. He made that initial investment of a couple hundred dollars, and I always say that if there hadn't been a Renel Duplessis there would be no Booga Basement, no Fugees, no Wyclef, none of it. So thank you again, Renel.

I could mix and record on that tiny Akai board, which would dump it all to a memory cassette that would be spit back out to a DAT or a regular cassette tape, whichever you had available. It didn't take me long to master all the knobs on that little box, and soon I was turning out tracks like a fiend. The first thing I ever recorded for real on that machine, and got paid for, was for my future wife, Claudinette. She paid me to record her singing a gospel song. I liked her a lot, but I was always about the money.

Renel saw that I was serious and that I spent the time it took to learn to use everything, so he kept buying what he could and slowly our little studio grew. Every time I could afford to, I'd take some of the money I made recording demos and buy more, too. We got a VFX keyboard, then an Akai S900 sampler. Anyone who knows about hip-hop production knows that these pieces of gear are the classics that defined the beats we know so well today. Later on, after I met Khalis Bayyan and watched him use his Linn 9000 drum machine, I was all about that piece of gear. It's so easy to get a very real, analog-sounding drum track going in no time with one of those. I still love a Linn. The beats never sound like a machine made them. I started adding guitar effects, too, which was a whole new world to me. I got the Big Muff distortion pedal and the Wah-Wah, and things got interesting. Those two are very basic, but they're all you need to get a whole range of sounds.

It's a good thing I got all of that gear, because things were about to change for me real quick. You never can see those moments coming in your life, when someone walks through your open door and everything you've been looking for is right there. It all starts falling in line without you even trying, and it's natural because it's meant to be. It's easy to say you have to be ready for it, but how can you ever be, really? Life is not some plan laid down by man.

4

THREE BECOME ONE

The first time I met Pras Michel was in my father's church. The Jean Family band was like the Beatles in our little corner of the 'hood and Pras, being a Haitian like myself, knew all about us. He came down one time when we were rehearsing to try out. The only thing we didn't have in our band was a horn player and Pras, seeing an opening there, came through with a trombone.

Now that I know him, this story is even funnier. Pras is a great rapper and has a good ear, but trombone is just not something that vibes with his style. And let me tell you something: he was the worst trombone player I have ever heard in my life. But he was the funniest guy we'd ever had around, so we let him stay and hang out at rehearsals. He started coming by every day and was like a little cousin who kept us laughing and made every practice better for that reason. Soon he and I became really good friends. He is a unique guy; he really sees the world his own way. He's not like anyone else I've ever met in my life.

Pras has always had a few hustles in music going on and still does to this day. By the time I was all moved out and living in the Booga, scraping by, making beats for the thugs in the 'hood, he was talking about this group with these two girls that he said were as beautiful as they were talented. I always took what my man said with a grain of salt, but he was right about this. Somehow he had charmed his way into the working in the studio of Khalis Bayyan, one of the founding members of Kool and the Gang, who is a musical genius in his own way. Khalis had seen potential in Pras, and he was working with him to put something together.

Pras called me one afternoon and said he needed me to come down to this studio to lay down some vocals. "I'm here with those two girls I told you about in this group we callin' Tyme. We doin' a track," he said. "I need you to come sing some of that reggae stuff you're so good at." He played it cool. I don't think he even mentioned that he was being produced by Khalis.

The two girls were named Marcy and Lauryn, and the minute I saw Lauryn Hill, I couldn't believe my eyes. She was in the vocal booth, and when she came through the door to say hello I experienced that feeling when everything stops for a second. It's a moment I'll never forget.

"Damn, she's beautiful," I said to Pras when I got him alone.

"Oh no. No, no, no. You can't go there. I know you, man. I'm friends with her brother; you can't go there."

I slowly took my eyes off of her and looked at him. "Okay, man. I feel you." I respected his request—at first—and only fooled around with Marcy a little bit in the early days. She was a little older, after all.

That day in the studio I did what any teenage boy does when he sees two fly girls: I started showing off. I ran around, picking up every instrument in sight, playing little riffs, singing hooks, soloing on guitar. Those girls weren't going to let me go nowhere from this group after they saw what I could do. Then I went into the vocal booth.

"Okay, what do you need?" I asked them.

"We need a vocal part and a rap."

"Okay, just turn the mic on."

I didn't have a notepad, no lyrics, nothing. I just did what I'd learned to do battle rapping, just flow straight off the top of my head about whatever was on my mind. I started going off, and I have no idea what most of it was but I do remember coming up with a hook, which was this: "The enforcer, the enforcer, the enforcer, the enforcer." Don't be too impressed. It was probably the worst Fugees demo ever made. The only thing that saved it at all was that I did it entirely in Jamaican-style patois, which was easy for me because reggae is my favorite kind of music. The girls didn't even realize I was Haitian until later; they thought I was from Jamaica. Unlike Haitians raised in Haiti, who listen to kompa (which is a derivative of Haitian merengue or zouk—or Caribbean soca, which came from calypso and was influenced by DJ culture), I grew up on Bob Marley and everything brought out of Jamaica to the rest of the world by Chris Blackwell and other British record labels in the 1970s.

That day we recorded a song called "Ride, Little Boy, Ride," which had a reggae flavor, with Pras and me rapping and Marcy and Lauryn singing. Marcy had a multioctave range like Mariah Carey, and Lauryn was a natural-born soul singer. She really was, right from the start. She learned to rap—all that came later—but from the moment I first heard her, that voice was pure blues and soul unlike anyone else I'd ever heard. And as everyone knows, she is beautiful, just a natural beauty, with a glow that no one can take their eyes off of.

When we were on the road, years later after we'd sold millions of records, we'd joke on the tour bus about the great lost Fugees songs—which should remain forever lost. That was our name for the worst tracks we'd ever recorded, and "Ride, Little Boy, Ride" was definitely in our top five: one of the best of the worst. Those early songs were the sound of raw talent getting acquainted, and it only takes one visionary to see the potential there. That was Khalis Bayyan, which is the Arabic name he assumed after he converted to Islam. He was born Ronald Bell, and along with his brother

Robert, founded Kool and the Gang. Ronald played saxophone in that band, and after they broke up, he became a skilled record producer. Khalis was the one who saw our future.

"There is some form of magic going on here," he said. We looked at him in disbelief. I knew I was fly and we thought we were good together, but when Khalis Bayyan tells you so, suddenly what you're doing becomes real.

"Yo, I'm serious. There is something interesting going on here. You all should stay together and keep working."

Khalis was the Fugees' Obi-Wan Kenobi from that day forward.

When we all met, I was a senior in high school, Lauryn was a freshman, and Pras was a sophomore. I had been doing the Exact Change thing before that. It was incredible to work with Kurtis and I spent most of my time watching him carefully, trying to pick up what I could from how he handled himself in the studio. He was focused, he had a great ear, he knew what he wanted, and he knew how to make it happen. He gave us direction, he defined the sound we should have been going for, and he knew how to get us there. Exact Change wasn't the right group for me, but it wasn't a bad one. We sounded like Arrested Development: a hip-hop world beat sound and a little bit of the consciousness.

After that came to an end, I was signed as a solo artist, just after I turned eighteen. People think my first record deal was with the Fugees, but it wasn't. I got one as a solo artist signed to a major label called Big Beat Records. A guy by the name of Craig Kalman signed me, who later went on to develop T.I. and Flo Rida. I released a house music record on that label called *Out of the Jungle*, and I dedicated it to Nelson Mandela because it came out in 1990, the year he was released from prison. People might not realize that I was definitely into house music growing up; all the hip-hop kids from Jersey were, because we would all go dancing on the weekends and in the clubs they played a lot of house music as well as hip-hop. We hit up places like Club 88 and Club Zanzibar in New Jersey, all weekend and a few nights during the week. Zanzibar was a legendary spot in Newark. It opened in 1979, and was a huge two-level building with disco on one floor, and house and hip-hop on another. It had legendary DJs like Larry Levan and Tony Humphries. The place had an amazing sound system and was a huge cavernous space inside a kind of futuristic-looking yellow building. The style at the time for club kids was to wear a backpack, and I had a Batman sticker on mine. Everyone wore big boots and baggy pants, whether they liked rap or house, and everyone danced in circles and showed off their moves. My track was a combination of both styles, so it got a lot of play in the clubs because it was the perfect transition track for DJs. It was produced by a guy named Trevor Nelson, who created the beat, and I wrote the rest of the song and the lyrics.

I was working on my solo stuff while the Fugees were getting our thing together, and I felt that the Fugees were much cooler, because I wanted to be part of a group. Being in a group was like joining a vibe: you had partners to play off of, you had a groove, and you had something bigger than yourself to develop together. I liked how Lauryn, Pras, and I played off of each other. It was just the three of us, and it felt that way almost from the start. Even though she didn't leave the group for about two years, it never felt like Marcy shared the same do-or-die mentality when it came to the group. She gave it a try but she was thinking about other things, and eventually she went and did those things. The three of us saw no other option—and we didn't want one—other than our music. Good thing we felt that way, because it was going to be a long road to the top.

MARCY CAME FROM A good family from the suburbs and even when she still believed, they didn't see this rap thing working out ever, so they pressured her to quit the group from the start. They wanted her to go to college and pursue a career on Broadway, which she eventually did. If she had stayed, the Fugees would have been two guys and two girls, because the musical chemistry was there. Lauryn sang the soulful stuff, Marcy sang the high notes, Pras rapped, and I did more Caribbean-flavored rapping and singing. I think about what that formula would have been like, what *The Score* would have sounded like with all four of us. It would have been incredible and Marcy would have been lethal on those songs. She was the most vocally talented of all of us, no doubt. And that's saying quite a bit because all of us could act, sing, and dance. We could show up and do dance routines and pass as a dance troupe if we wanted to. That version of the Fugees would have been a four-person powerhouse. That wasn't meant to be, but it didn't slow us down. After Marcy left, the rest of us kept at it and pushed each other even harder than before. One thing I know is that we would never have gotten further on our own than we did together, because the music we made as a unit was so much more than the sum of its parts.

I'm not sure how I can explain to all of you who were young kids when the Fugees came out just how much different the times were. When we were coming up, if you wanted to make it in music you had to be a complete entertainer. You had to be able to rhyme, sing, break-dance, act, play instruments—all of it. You had to know how to entertain people on every level and have the musical skills to boot. The movie *Breakin'* was just in theaters and if you couldn't spin on your head you weren't shit. Pras, Lauryn, and I were just teenagers, but we weren't going to settle for anything less than being a supergroup, and we were willing to put in the work.

We rehearsed three to four times a week, and we didn't just go through our songs. We'd get in front of a big mirror in a dance studio and work out our stage routines, down to the smallest gesture. We went through it all over and over until we anticipated each other's moves so well that we weren't even thinking anymore. We spent about six hours rehearsing, three nights a week.

Lauryn's mom respected her daughter's dedication to music,

because she was willing to drive her across town from the suburbs of South Orange to the 'hood to practice with Pras and me—two Haitian kids with nothing to our names. Mrs. Hill didn't judge; she picked us all up and dropped us all off each day. Our guide through all this was Khalis Bayyan of course, who came down to help us work on our dance moves, and had us in the studio writing new songs every night we weren't rehearsing.

I've always been the leader of the bands I'm in, because I'm a born ringleader, basically a P. T. Barnum. In the Fugees, that was my role. I was also the big brother to both Pras and Lauryn, not only because I was older, but also because I always had a plan and got us where we needed to go. At least that's how it started.

My relationship with Lauryn was that of a mentor at first. She didn't know how to rap and I taught her. Lauryn's gift is her voice, and I've never heard a more beautiful soul singer in my life. She is among the greats: Roberta Flack, Aretha Franklin, Nina Simone, and anyone you want to compare her to. She's a natural, and those notes and that passion just come out of her.

She didn't understand rhyming, though, and for months, Pras and I did all the rapping while she and Marcy sang the hooks. I felt like something was missing though, so one day I asked her if she would ever rhyme.

"Sure."

"You ever done it before?"

"No. If you two can do it I know I can."

"Okay, little sister, alright."

I wrote down a few verses for her, some I had been working on, and added a few lines I made up on the spot. She looked at the paper for a few minutes, and then told me to put on a beat. And when I did she tore through them like a pro, not even looking at the words. If she could memorize lyrics that quickly, I knew she'd be one hell of an MC.

I gave her a stack of MC Lyte and Queen Latifah CDs and told her to listen carefully and learn the rhymes she heard. She took to that like a pyro to matches and had the rhymes down in two or three days. She was incredible, an artist who had found a new inspiration. Soon I was rhyming lines to her that she would memorize on the spot and spit back at me better than I had expected.

I was her mentor, and I wrote rhymes for her starting then and for a while to come. I taught her all about rhyming, showing her the swag and style, just the way Chill Rob G had shown me years before. It didn't take Lauryn long to make her style her own, though. She's a very gifted woman.

As she, Pras, Marcy, and I kept working on our group, we got tighter musically and personally, and soon I was asking Lauryn to come down to the Booga to sing hooks on the little demos I was producing to make some cash. I didn't do it for every track, but for the ones that were worth it, I'd say, "Yo, you want this to be really good? Chill for a minute. I'll get this girl down here to sing you a hook you will not believe." Lauryn would leave her parents' house in the suburbs on the good side of the tracks and come down to the 'hood in East Orange and I tell you, her participation put me in a position to increase my prices. That voice won everybody over, every time. I was moving her into getting some street cred, and giving her a chance to expose her craft—her voice—which is every bit as beautiful as she is as a person. She is intelligent, compassionate, talented, and beautiful. That is how things started between us, working together on all levels, two artists who fell in love.

As I've said, Lauryn's parents supported her pursuit of the arts, and around this time, after we'd been practicing as the Fugees under Khalis Bayyan's management, she got cast in the Whoopi Goldberg film *Sister Act 2* because she was pursuing acting full-time as well. She went to LA to try out, and that distance brought us even closer together. She'd call me every night and we'd stay on the phone for hours while she told me every detail of her day, and I told her every detail of mine. She was in LA, hanging with Whoopi, telling her about her group back home, the Fugees. Sometimes distance like that and hours on the phone can bring you closer than seeing each other every day.

She went on that trip with Robin Bask, my other best friend growing up, who was, for a while, the fifth Fugee. Robin, as well as Gene Swarrow, were my closest friends and I would have done anything for them. Robin was a talented kid, and we wanted to make this a supergroup, so I brought him in when things got rolling. He could sing, he could dance, and he could play all styles of piano like a pro. He was able to bring a lot to the demos we were working on and he fit in well with us musically and otherwise. Now when he went to California with Lauryn, he made a mistake that cost him his place in the group. Apparently there were a lot of crazy charges on Lauryn's credit card, and Lauryn's dad was not happy about that at all. He gave us an ultimatum: either Robin goes or Lauryn goes. Unfortunately that credit card mistake cost Robin his career with us. It was fucked up, because he was my best friend, but I did what I had to do. Robin and I are still cool and we're still close to this day and he still calls himself the fifth Fugee.

After that Hollywood trip, Lauryn got cast in an off-Broadway play called *Club XII* that was a hip-hop interpretation of Shakespeare's *Twelfth Night*, with his language translated into modern slang and song. It was produced by Quincy Jones and it was a touchstone for the culture, because the entire cast was made up of stars and stars-to-be from our generation. Everybody with talent from our little scene was cast in this play in some way, either as an actor or a crew member. Lauryn was in it and I was in it. I wrote a good portion of the music for it. MC Lyte was in it, as was Lisa Carson, who became a star on *ER*. I only tried out because Lauryn was trying out. That's how we rolled: if either of us was doing something, the other one would be, too. The play wasn't a huge commercial success, but it got everyone noticed. After that, Lauryn got more roles, including one on *As the World Turns*.

Like I said, acting, music, dancing—all of it was part of entertainment to us, and we didn't care which one we used to get ahead. We wanted to do all of them, so if acting came first and was the way to music, that was cool. If we got a job dancing somewhere, that was fine, because it would probably lead to something else. We were on the hustle, individually and together, always looking out and always looking for our next stepping stone. At the time, Lauryn and I were doing it all, so we went for this play, and we got it. Whether the acting or the music came first, it didn't matter to us. We were just grinding. If she was auditioning, I was auditioning. She got it, I got it, and we were in it together. At the time, I was almost out of high school, heading into the last months of my last year. I threw myself into the play with everything I had. I ended up rewriting all of my lines and for every part where the director didn't have any music, I wrote some. It really was the first off-Broadway hip-hop musical.

The play was incredible. While I was working on it, I also met Quincy Jones for the first time. He told me something I never forgot. After our first performance, after I'd written half the music for the play, he said this: "I've been watching you this whole time, young blood. I will see you again, because you've got what it takes."

THE FUGEES KEPT ON going. We hit the studio, practiced our dance moves, and by then we were under Khalis Bayyan's umbrella. We were signed to his Le Jam production company for a development deal, which means they were investing in developing us, in hopes of getting a record deal, so we would record with him at House of Music in West Orange. Khalis was a great teacher, but something became clear to me: he did not have his finger on the pulse of the times. He had us focusing on our live show, which was the right thing to do, but he did not realize that what we were putting together was too far outside the sound of the day for us to get anywhere. Khalis was a great mentor artistically, but he had no business savvy when it came to the industry.

We discovered this the moment we started doing showcases for record label executives. We would go to their offices and perform. I played guitar and rapped, Lauryn and Marcy sang soul songs, and Pras hyped everything up like a rock star. It made no sense to them at all and we could see it in their eyes. Absolutely no one was interested in us. They wanted what was already out there, which at the time was hard shit like Onyx, conscious stuff like De La Soul, R&B like New Edition and Boyz II Men. We'd come in and they'd see two girls and two guys: me with a guitar, rapping and singing, Lauryn doing incredible diva-like soul, and Marcy singing with the power and range of Mariah Carey. No wonder they were confused. There was way too much going on for these people.

We also started looking for a manager, and most of them turned us down, too. One of the last meetings we got that showed any kind of promise was with David Sonenberg, a famous manager who had Meat Loaf and a bunch of other people at the time. We went to audition for him in his office in Midtown Manhattan and I'll never forget that day. We played a few songs and at the end of our show I jumped up on his desk. My pants were too loose, so they fell down. But I wasn't going to quit rapping, so I just kept on going right there in my boxers with my jeans around my ankles.

"I don't know what you kids are going to be," he said when we were done. "But you're going to be something."

David signed us and David believed in us, and that is when things started finally moving forward. All those labels had said the same thing—that our formula wouldn't work, that we had a rapper playing guitar and a soul singer and another rapper who wanted to be a rock star. There was no mold we fit into, so all of those A&R guys had no place to put us. There's not much of a music industry left to speak of, but what there was, back then, wasn't willing to take risks. If you were different, like us, you would be passed over. Executives wanted songs that fit on the radio and fit video concepts that BET would like. We were daring, and the labels were not daring. They were taking no chances because everyone wanted to keep their jobs. Something fresh had to break through on its own before the label guys would go out and sign a handful of acts just like it. They'd never be the first to jump.

Lucky for us, once we signed with David, he got our demo to a very small label out of Philadelphia called Ruffhouse Records, who had a joint venture deal with Columbia. Ruffhouse was run by Chris Schwartz and Joe Nicolo and they loved our music. At the time they had groups like Cypress Hill, the Goats, and Kris Kross. While the big labels were doing their thing, these two were doing something else, and it was working. We auditioned for Joe Nicolo and Chris Schwartz in our manager's office, which wasn't the typical thing to do. Usually artists auditioned in rehearsal studios on small stages.

We didn't do our usual songs either; we took a different route. Lauryn sang the Beatles' "Let It Be," and then we broke into one of our songs, with me on guitar along with a backing musical track. We did everything without microphones. We got into it, and by the end, there I was on the conference table going for it so hard that my pants ended up around my ankles again.

When the music stopped, Chris Schwartz stared at us like we were crazy. "I don't like it," he said.

The room was dead silent, and all I kept thinking was, *We're fucked*.

"I don't like it," he said again. "I love it!"

That was it. We signed a contract on the spot, and through our production deal with Khalis Bayyan's Le Jam Productions, we got to work on our first record, *Blunted on Reality*. During that time, Lauryn and I became much closer and we started to see each other seriously. We were together 24/7, working on our music with this amazing artistic synergy going on. I fell in love not only with her, but also with the art, and everything we were doing, because it was all tied up together. She was so young, so beautiful, and so talented, I felt like she was a being straight from the source, straight from God and all that it is to be creative and beautiful on earth.

I feel like people think of Wyclef and Lauryn when they think of the Fugees, but nobody should underestimate Pras. He was the visionary who saw the talent coming together; he is the one who called me in and thought it would be a good match. People also underestimate his ear. In the studio he added so many small ideas that made the music what it is. He also brought a rock element to what we did. He listened to Metallica and Guns N' Roses and had that swagger to what he wanted to do. One time he made us stop everything to listen to an Eagles song that had a sound or string treatment we were looking for. The Eagles aren't something you hear pumped from a hip-hop studio regularly, but he was right. He always wanted to make things bigger; he wanted them to sound like Queen. When we were able to control our own production, Pras was a real genius with that—using the engineering to get a bigger, full sound, while keeping it raw.

Blunted didn't sell very well, but it did get our name out there. And since we were on Columbia through Ruffhouse, we got some tour support and had a team booking gigs for us across the country and in Europe. We played colleges, high schools, wherever, and we'd sell copies of our album out of the trunks of our cars wherever we went.

Blunted is not a bad album, but it had one problem that could not be overlooked: it didn't sound anything like what we did live. It captured our talent, but it sounded out of touch with who we were as performers. We were taking orders from our production company and couldn't get the sounds we heard in our heads onto the record. They wanted loud reggae-style choruses, Pras and me to rap hard with a rock-and-roll spirit, and Lauryn to calm things down vocally. She would subdue the energy and then pick it back up. It wasn't consistent, because I was out there rapping hard like Onyx did, just all rugged street energy. The music on the album sounds smooth, if anything because Khalis's production style came from that Kool and the Gang kind of vibe. There are twenty-four or so music tracks coming at you on most of the songs on *Blunted*. We envisioned the whole thing as simple and stripped down, but what we got was the opposite of that.

Lauryn had, in just a few months, become a better rapper than me, Pras, and half the females in the industry at the time put together. She would take a few bars from rhymes I wrote and build off of those. We wrote most of the songs on the album that way. It was our first album, and we were finding our voice as a group. We had so much talent we could have done anything: I have a five-octave-range voice, and Lauryn—forget about it—she can take you into any realm. We voiced our opinion throughout the process, and even though we did it their way for the most part, they did give us each our own songs, which was cool. The only song on that record that was entirely my idea and executed the way I heard it was "Vocab," which is just me on acoustic guitar with all of us rapping. Lauryn got one of hers on there, too. She had a jazzy beat by a producer named Rashad who worked with Khalis, and she had Khalis arrange something very simple around it. The song ended up being "Some Seek Stardom." I wrote the hook and she wrote the verses. Pras got one of his on, too, because I think the production company looked at us like teenagers, and for at least those three tracks they let us do what we wanted. His is called "Giggles." I wrote the hooks on most of the songs and we all envisioned the interludes. The Fugees never had ghostwriters; we really did, from the start, come up with all of the rhymes and song concepts.

When people came to see us live, they could not believe it was the same band. We would blow the headliners off the stage wherever we went, and we started to get a reputation for that. Our live show was so full of energy that it was hard for anyone to follow us. We had no restrictions in the live show. We had a drummer, a bass player, a DJ, a keyboardist, Lauryn on vocals, me, and Pras. For shows, I could create a new arrangement for each song, like Amadeus or any composer would, and that's just what I did. Nothing sounded the way it did on the album, because we made all of those arrangements harder and more dynamic live. I would jump from guitar to keys, Lauryn would command the stage, and the audience always connected with us. Even if they didn't know the music, they felt like they were part of what was going on, because they connected with the emotion. So we were the number one hip-hop performers around when it came to playing live, but we had an album that was completely forgettable.

There is no way we could fail live, because we'd been practicing that side of our act for years. I'm a show orchestrator—that is what I do—and when you put me on a stage, it's like you've just wound up a top. I will smash them every time until I die; that's who I am. Back then when we didn't have any hits and we were opening for bigger acts, but we had nothing to lose, so you'd better understand that I did everything in my power to make sure no audience forgot our name. I would have lit myself on fire if I had to: they weren't going to forget the Fugees. Even if they didn't like the record, audiences were leaving there thinking that even if we brought 5 percent of that live energy into the studio next time around, our album would be bangin'.

I was always thinking of ways to promote us, to get the word around, and to catch people's attention. One of my ideas none of us will ever forget. In 1994, we released a single called "Boof Baf," which was on *Blunted on Reality*, and we started getting all kinds of club gigs for established artists. I was always thinking of ways to command that time, and I became convinced that we needed a visual prop that everyone would remember. I had no idea what it should be. Pras and Lauryn didn't either; they just thought I was crazy. I'd go on for hours about this mysterious thing that I couldn't figure out, and how we needed it onstage with us. To me, this element would make us or break us. The Fugees needed a symbol.

By this time I had moved out of my parent's house completely and moved into the Booga Basement studio. There was a small room upstairs on the landing before the main door to the house, and in there I had a mattress and not much else because that's about all that would fit. One afternoon I was napping in there and woke up to a Bud Light commercial. It was an old one, when Bud Light had Spuds MacKenzie as their mascot. Spuds wasn't anything new by then, but he was still the most famous dog on television. He had nothing to do with beer, but this crazy-looking dog that wore Hawaiian shirts and sunglasses was the face of Bud Light. No one outside of dog breeders knew what kind of dog he was before those commercials, but everyone knew Spuds—and they knew Bud Light because of him.

"That is what we need, man!" I said out loud. "We need a Spuds MacKenzie."

America is an amazing place, I thought. In this country a dog that looks like Spuds can become more famous than most actors in Hollywood and just about every politician other than the president. There had to be some way to make an animal like him work for us. They would remember us if we had a mascot.

Our next gig was opening up for Jodeci, who at that time were the coolest R&B group going, and one of my favorites of all time. We had just gotten ourselves a booking agent and this was the first date they landed for us. We were all excited because Jodeci were like the continuation of the Jackson 5, and were right there in the boy-band tradition on the R&B side. In the early nineties they were as big as the Backstreet Boys, 'N Sync, and the rest of them. This was a big chance for us and an opportunity to be exposed to a well-established audience. I had to find us a mascot.

I started going over the facts. The show was in a big club in Manhattan, so we needed something that everyone would be able to see. A dog like Spuds wasn't very tall, so that wasn't going to work. Besides, I couldn't just take the Bud Light dog and put a Fugees shirt on him. I had to be original.

I got into my hooptie ride, which was a busted-up blue Honda, and drove to a livestock store in the middle of the 'hood in Newark. This place had live animals that you could buy to take with you, or they would butcher them if that's what you were after. It was definitely an immigrant-run store that was operating outside of the health codes, put it that way. On the drive over I figured out what would be the right size to catch people's attention and be different enough from the norm.

"Yo, I'm here to buy a cow," I told the guy.

He looked at me over his glasses. "You need to buy a cow?"

"Yeah."

In my mind, all cows were like the ones we had in my village growing up. They were small, and whenever someone went off to buy one for their family, they always came back with a young baby cow. That is what I expected to take home. It would fit in my car, it would be cute, and between shows we could use it for milk.

"Right this way," he said.

He took me out back into a barn full of huge cows in stalls. "I can sell you any of these. This one over here . . ."

"Yo, man, these cows are enormous," I said. "They're too big. I need to take this cow home in my car. Don't you have no baby cows?"

"We don't. These cows people buy for butchering. We can do that if you want."

"Oh no, man, let me explain. I'm in a music group and we're doing a show tonight. We want an animal that will get the crowd's attention. Something small I can take with me, but something they'll remember."

He cocked his head to one side and looked into the distance for a minute.

"A show . . . I think I have something for you. Come with me."

He led me past more stalls to the very back of the huge barn. He opened up a door and lead out the craziest looking goat I have ever seen. It was white and shaggy with a long curled horn sticking straight up on each side of its head. It had red eyes, and it looked stoned and pissed off. It kinda had its shoulders up and looked like it was about to rumble. Now that I'm thinking about it, that goat was kinda a thug.

"What the fuck is this shit, man?"

"This is special," he said. "This is a rare Mexican goat. You have this at your show and your crowd will go nuts."

I had never seen anything that looked like this thing, so maybe he knew what he was talking about. This goat wasn't cute like Spuds, but he was scrappy and no one was going to forget that face.

"Alright. How much is the goat, man?"

"Two fifty."

"What? Come on, man. You gotta help me out. You can't be hustling me over this ugly fucking goat."

"You don't understand. This is a rare breed Mexican goat. You never see goats like this out here. Best I can do is two hundred."

It took a little while, but I got the guy down to $150. The three of us walked to the front of the warehouse, to the little office with the front counter. The dude started to lead the goat around back.

"I'll be right out with this for you."

I know I hadn't known this goat for long, but in that short time, in my mind, he'd become the Fugees' mascot. I had forgotten that they butchered animals at this place. My reaction to what the man said was very innocent at first: I figured he was going to wash the goat and make him presentable. Then I realized what he meant.

I ran around back and caught him just in time. He had the goat's neck over a butcher block and was about to pick up the axe.

"Hold on, man. I don't want to eat that goat. I want that goat alive!"

"You want him alive?"

"I want him alive. I want to bring him onstage with my band. He's gonna be our mascot."

"This goat is not the dinner for the people coming to your show? I thought you were buying him to impress these people. This isn't an animal you want for a pet."

"We're gonna put him to work," I said. "But we don't want to eat him."

The guy looked at me for what felt like a very long time. "So you want to take this goat with you right now, and you want to make him part of your group?"

"Yeah, that's it, man. This goat is the guy. This goat is coming onstage."

At that point I had nothing to lose.

"Let me ask you something, my man," I said. "If we're not eating him, and you don't need to butcher him, does he cost less?"

Dude was disgusted.

"No. He is exactly the same price."

It wasn't until I got the goat into my car that I realized how bad he smelled. His size wasn't the problem: being Mexican, he wasn't a tall goat. But let me tell you, he smelled like nothing I had ever known before that moment. When you're on a farm or surrounded by livestock the way it was in that place, you don't realize how one animal smells with so many around. With a Mexican goat in my hooptie Honda it was a whole other story.

That Mexican goat smelled like a pile of wet straw, dirt, and the shit pond back in Haiti all put together. This creature wasn't of the earth. It wasn't natural. Smells trigger memories and I'm still able to go back to that drive in my car too easily. It's a smell I wish I could forget, but I can't. That day, I put the windows down, I held my breath, and I still couldn't stand it. I thought about turning around, but just then I looked at the goat and saw him with a Fugees shirt, some glasses, just being our Spuds. That's when I remembered that I was right. Fuck the smell; this goat was our ticket.

At first this Mexican goat was well behaved. He just sat in the backseat looking out the window, eyeing me sometimes. He'd turn his head from side to side, real relaxed, taking in the scenery. He seemed real mellow.

When I got back to the 'hood, I ran back behind the house to the Booga Basement, which was really the garage under the house. As usual there was a collection of neighborhood dudes playing ball in courtyard between our house and the crack house.

"Yo! Come on out to my car. Y'all got to see this," I said. I was real excited because this was the thing. I'd finally found it.

About twenty feet away, the pack of homies stopped dead in their tracks.

"What the fuck is that, man?" I don't even know who said it. They all felt the same.

"Yo nigga, you smell that shit? What the fuck is that, Clef?"

"Hey yo, easy, man!" I said. "That is a rare Mexican goat. He's coming onstage tonight."

"Mexican what? That thing smells like shit, man."

"Help me, we gotta hose him off and get him ready for the show. We gonna put a Fugees shirt on him and some glasses and he gonna be our Spuds MacKenzie." I meant it.

They all just kinda looked at me funny.

"You crazy, Clef. That ugly motherfucker ain't no Spuds MacKenzie!"

"Come on, man. We got to get this goat in the basement. I can't let my aunt see this goat. She'll kick us out."

We led the goat to the basement and I washed him. I didn't think that once you wet down a goat, all the stench in it would really come out. But I did learn that washing a goat makes everything about a goat worse.

My rare Mexican goat started stinking so strong that his odor rose up through the ventilation system in the garage into my aunt's house. When we heard her start coming down the stairs, we ran the goat outside into the garage, still soaking wet, then took our places in the basement as cool as could be.

"What's going on down here?" she asked.

"Just working on some music," I said.

"What's that smell?"

"What smell?"

"Don't you lie to me, Nel. It smells down here."

"I think a few of the guys have gas, Auntie. Really, I'm sorry but that's it."

I don't think she believed us but she left. We went to the garage and the goat—he was still chill—now smelled worse than hell because he was damp. We toweled him dry, and then we got my aunt's blow-dryer to help dry his fur. But none of that got the stink off. By this point it was getting toward showtime and I wasn't going to be discouraged, so I made him look fly by putting a green Fugees "Boof Baf" shirt on him, along with some sunglasses. He was ready to roll as far as I was concerned.

This was a big show for us so I'd asked one of the heavy dudes in the 'hood whose name was Chop Chop if he'd drive us to the club in Manhattan. He had a chop shop where he ran stolen cars and drove this fly Jeep. He didn't figure that he'd show up and have to make room for a "rare" Mexican goat.

"You gonna be big after tonight, man, right?" he said. "Don't you forget me. I'll get you where you're going, but don't forget me. We family. We a team."

"Yeah, man," I said. "I got you. When I win my first Grammy I'll thank you, man. I'll never forget you. But I got one more favor to ask tonight, man."

"What's that?"

"We got to bring my goat in the Jeep with us."

"Your goat?"

"Yeah, man, I'll get him. He's real small; he's real cool."

Like I said, washing and drying the rare Mexican goat didn't do much for the stink.

"What the fuck, man?" Chop Chop yelled. "It smells like shit, man! You can't bring that thing in my car! Do you smell this thing, Clef? Do you? It smells like shit, man!"

"Nah, it's cool, man. This thing is our promotion. This thing is our ticket, man. People see us with this goat they will not forget it. This guy right here, he is the new member of our band."

Somehow I convinced this dude to put the goat in his car. I don't remember what else I said to convince him.

Everyone I knew thought I'd completely lost my mind. The thing was, I was like Alexander the Great in my circle: my decisions were never to be questioned. But, still, I could hear the rumblings of mutiny.

The whole way to the club I heard them rumbling, but I didn't care. We were going to steal the show, and I felt justified when we rolled up to the club and saw Jodeci coming out of their limo and one of them had a pit bull.

"You see what I'm saying?" I said to my car of people. "He got a pit bull! Every group has a pet. You need an animal if people are gonna remember you. How can any of you question me on this goat, man?"

It was quiet for maybe ten seconds.

"Yeah, he's got a dog, dude. This thing in this car is a fucking goat, man."

They had a point. I definitely agree with them now.

Getting the goat inside the club was waging a war. The promoters were not having it, talking about safety and health regulations, but the truth was the smell. We had these conversations outside in the wind and they were already too overwhelmed by the Mexican goat. To be honest with you, we rolled with some pretty heavy dudes back then and I'm not sure how it all got worked out, but despite the club and the promoter's better judgment, they let us bring our stinky little dude into the club.

All of this took so long that by the time we got inside, it was time for us to go on. We stood in the wings with our goat, waiting as the emcee for the night, Big Cat, introduced us.

"Ayo," he said. "Before we bring Jodeci out, we got this little group for you. All the way from New Jersey, it's the *Fudgies!*"

The motherfucking Fudgies, man. He pronounced it like we were the topping on an ice-cream sundae.

"That don't matter," I said to Pras and Lauryn. "After tonight, they'll remember the Fugees. We are the motherfucking Refugees! One and only."

I must have looked ridiculous saying that, but who cares. When you have nothing else but confidence you'd might as well oversell your shit. I was wearing a black-and-yellow rubber fireman's coat that night. I was obsessed with wearing something noticeable and I'd wear that or some kind of oversized leather Spiderman bomber jacket to every show.

"This is our moment, y'all. They gonna remember who we are," I told Pras and Lauryn. They agreed, I think.

And then we took the stage.

Pras went out first as he always did, and got the crowd going.

"Yes, yes y'all! Lauryn, where you at?"

Then Lauryn went out and started singing and freestyling.

"Yeah! Clef where you at?" she asked.

It was my turn and I had my prop. I'd found my mascot, I had my Spuds, and he was a stinky Mexican goat in a t-shirt and sunglasses. I'd gotten a big chain for him, too. It was around his neck and I was going to lead him onstage, all thug. The only problem was, at the moment when we needed that Mexican goat to be chill and just roll with the program, he didn't. The minute I led him toward the lights of the stage, he dug his hooves in. He wouldn't budge.

I don't know if it was because this was the first time that goat had ever heard music or seen strobe lights, but this dude started trippin'. I hadn't thought this could be a problem until that moment. I didn't know what else to do, so I started talking to him. I don't even know if it was a him or a her.

"Yo, goat, just calm down, man. It's cool, we gonna go onstage now. I got you, goat."

That didn't do much.

"Come on. They gonna love you, man! You just got to come with me right now." That fucking goat wouldn't move.

I was standing on the side of the stage, looking at Lauryn Hill out there smiling, getting them all hyped up. "Here we go! Here we go! Yo, Clef, where you at?"

"Yeah, yeah!" I said into the mic, still hoping this goat would start moving so I could join my group and play my part. Damn, had I misplanned this? No, man, I hadn't. This goat and I had an understanding. He was just having stage fright. I'd talk him through this. He had to trust me: I had delivered him from the slaughterhouse to the club. I was literally planning a conversation with this goat. Then I realized something had to be done quick.

So I picked him up and carried his ass onstage with me.

I put him down on my side, by my microphone, thinking that this Mexican goat and I had a bond. It was clearly a one-way relationship; that goat was lying to me from the start. I hadn't found us a mascot or a symbol or a cheerleader that believed in us. All I'd done is find a round-horned, stinky, cheap, mud-sucking Mexican goat who had no desire for a career in the entertainment industry. I'd bought the cheapest mascot money could buy, literally and morally. And as if to send the point home, it was clear to me, real fast, that dude wanted nothing more than some peace, some quiet, and a stall to call his own far away from me and this stage. Like every smooth R&B act does, Jodeci had a huge female fan base and that night the first ten rows were nothing but hot, fly girls all dressed up in their best. I had told everyone, from the security to the promoter that this goat was all good, but he wasn't.

I came on with the goat and put him down next to me on my side of the stage. He stopped freaking out and just stood there, so I thought maybe we were in the clear. Our DJ dropped the beat to our single, "Boof Baf" because what else were we gonna do? I had grown somewhat immune to the stench of this goat, but the minute I brought him out, I watched all those fly girls retreat from the stage like my feet were on fire.

The goat was chill for about two songs, until our DJ pumped the beats about 20 bpms faster. At that point he became possessed and started spinning around and dancing like he didn't give a fuck about anything. I didn't mind that part, except for the fact that he left a trail. He basically ran across the front of the stage at full speed, shitting himself the whole fucking way. Dude pulled so hard on his chain and collar that it slipped out of my hand, and he ran right into one of my boys, bucking him straight in the ass.

There we were, the Fugees, the next big thing, with a stage full of goat shit and a room full of disgusted girls waiting for Jodeci. We had two more songs to do, too. They would remember us, alright. The promoter and Jodeci's manager nearly broke the door to our dressing room afterward.

"What the fuck is wrong with you people?" their manager said. "That was some disrespectful shit!"

"We didn't mean that to happen . . ."

"Is that how you do it in Jersey?"

When you're the leader of a group, everyone is quick to tell you their opinion of your ideas after it's passed. When you fail miserably, they tell you sooner.

"I told you that goat was a bad idea, man," Pras said. "I told you this shit wasn't going to work, but you don't listen to people. You just do what you want to do." Pras sold me out, which wasn't like him. We were always very all-for-one. He was really trying to get through to me and teach me a lesson.

"Ayo," another of our friends said. "You just cost your group their career."

None of our crew would even sit next to me in the car. I'd failed everyone.

And all I could think about was getting rid of the stinking goat so I could forget about this mess. I'm not proud to say that in that moment I wanted to shoot that thing on the spot. I didn't own a gun, so I asked Chop Chop to pull over so I could leave that stinking Mexican bastard at the side of the road.

"No, man. That goat's your problem. You've got to take care of this yourself. Don't bring me into this shit."

When we got back to the Booga I went to see a guy in the 'hood who was a hard gangster, and I asked him if he'd take the goat and kill this thing for me.

"You out of your mind? I can't kill no animals," he said.

"Why not, homie?"

"What if we come back to this world as animals?" he said. "I ain't going to risk that shit by killing some goat for you. You want it done; do it yourself."

This dude was like the Tony Montana of our neighborhood, and I'd seen him do some cold shit. But killing that goat was too much for him. He was right, though. Don't ever do what doesn't feel right.

I ended up tying the goat to the fence in the backyard. I don't remember what I told my aunt, but I made up some story about watching this pet goat for a friend for a little while. There was a crack house on one side, a gang hangout on another, and our block was full of kids two steps from jail. With so many criminals and troublemakers all around, you'd think that something would have happened to the goat after just one night. I thought I was going to wake up to a chain and an empty collar. I wasn't that lucky. Nobody wanted that goat for themselves.

I did wake up to about a hundred kids from around the way, all hanging out, petting that thing like it was Bambi. The Booga now had a one-goat petting zoo. And the goat loved it. He was still ugly but he looked happy now.

"Ayo, what the fuck you all doin' in my backyard?"

"We here to see him," one kid said, pointing at the goat. "We heard you had an exotic dog!"

"Aw, man, that's no dog."

"This ain't no dog?"

"No."

"What is it, then?"

"It's a goat. It's a Mexican goat."

"Can we give him dog food anyway?"

"No, you can't do that. But you can give him grass. That's what he needs. Goats eat grass."

"Okay!"

Our goat might have crapped all over the stage and scared all the girls clear to the exits but he did get us noticed. That afternoon the DJ on Hot 97 mentioned the Jodeci show and he had this to say, too: "Jodeci was hot, but before they came out, there was this group from New Jersey called the Fugees. They came out with a goat wearing a t-shirt and some glasses and this thing crapped all over the stage. I don't know what the hell they were thinking. Here is their single, 'Boof Baf.'" That's all I wanted—and I made sure Pras and Lauryn understood that the goat was a success. The DJ even got our name right on the radio.

I took care of the goat and through him I learned to respect animals. He and I got into a rhythm with each other and I started to enjoy hanging out with the goat in the yard when I took a break from working on music. I even got him a Spuds MacKenzie Bud Light doghouse to hang out in, because in spite of the stink, that goat was a cool dude.

The one thing I didn't take into account as far as the goat was concerned was winter. All of this went down in early fall when the weather was still nice enough for the goat to enjoy the backyard. Sometime around early December the weather turned cold, and I realized I had to find a real house for this guy. Spuds's plastic hut wasn't cutting it. And there wasn't enough room in the Basement for both of us. He really didn't like it inside anyway; he probably had flashbacks to the club.

Before I could figure out a solution we got a blizzard in the middle of the night while the goat was still outside. An old Jamaican man lived next door and he always yelled at us about the goat and how we didn't take care of it the way we should. So when the snow started he called the cops who called the ASPCA who came and took the rare Mexican goat away. I was in bed down in the Basement when these guys broke in like a SWAT team, all of them dressed in black.

"Who is the owner of this house?" they yelled.

"He's not here," I said.

"Who is responsible for that goat outside?"

From a very young age I had learned not to trust any kind of organized army, especially those dressed in black.

"What goat?" I asked. "Nobody here has a goat."

"We are taking the animal," they said.

They covered the goat in blankets and off he went in an Animal Rescue Unit vehicle. Our eyes locked as they were loading him in and I swear to you his expression said it all: "If only I could talk, I'd tell these motherfuckers what you did to me, taking me to a club, putting me in a goddamned shirt. Fuck you."

Whatever, goat, you'd have been stew if it weren't for me.

. . . .

THIS IS HOW HUNGRY we were as a support group. We once opened up for KRS-ONE and after our last song we dropped the instrumental of "The Bridge Is Over" and freestyled over it. KRS's DJ, Kenny Parker, ran out from backstage, snatched our DJ by the shirt, threw him away from the decks, took the record off, and walked offstage with it. We deserved that because it was a ballsy thing to do, freestyling over one of his biggest hits, basically his theme song, just to prove to him personally that we could rhyme over his beat. We wanted to show him we were coming in, and that we'd thought we had arrived. That was cocky and tasteless.

We opened up for Biggie and Puffy, too, just after they'd come out with "Warning" and were really starting to get on. We were all at some college show. At that time record labels made all of the acts they were breaking do college tours, because back then the colleges had money to bring in concerts. In the nineties everyone had more money.

"Hey yo, here's how it's gonna work tonight," Biggie said. "We're going on before you."

I wasn't expecting that one.

"But we're opening for you," I said. "They all came to see you."

Biggie was walking around our dressing room, picking up a few percussion instruments we had.

"What you think is gonna happen after you come out with all these cheap tricks and cymbals and shit and get the people excited running around making noise like you do? I'm gonna just stand there and do my songs? You'll be banging on all that shit and take the crowd with you. I'm going first."

We were flattered because Biggie was such a huge talent, man. We knew it, even then, just like anybody who ever saw him or has heard his records can say. This was too much for us to hear him say that we were too good to go on first.

"No, man, we can't do that," I said. "We don't have hits like you do. We love you, man. We want to open up for you. You're the star, man. You've got to let us play first."

"Not tonight, homie," Bigs said. "I'm up. You're next. That's how it's going to happen." And that's how it went down. You've got to hand it to him; he saw how it was and did right by himself. I guess that reputation of us being the killer Fugees had gotten through to him.

We opened for just about everyone that meant anything in nineties hip-hop: Nas, Wu-Tang, Onyx, Naughty by Nature, you name it. But once we became known as the opening act that stole the show, everybody was less friendly to us when we showed up that night.

We were just happy to be out playing and touring Europe and America, no matter how small the shows were or how chilly the reception from the headlining act. We discovered who the Fugees really were on the road—in every way—because we loved to perform. With some studio experience under our belt, I started to put together a sound in my head for our next album. I was going to capture our energy the right way and translate that live feeling directly to our new music. I hadn't developed the skills yet to create it all myself, but I was on my way.

It wasn't easy for me to explain it. Besides, we were working with Khalis Bayyan, who had sold 100 million records with Kool and the Gang, so I kept saying to myself, *What the hell do you know?* For me to have gone to Khalis and tell him I thought the tracks should sound different would have been like a nobody telling Dr. Dre he could teach him a few things. I'm not saying I hate *Blunted*. I'm just pointing out that of all the songs only three of them—"Vocab," "Some Seek Stardom," and "Giggles"—reflect the true sound of the Fugees because those were the only ones envisioned entirely by us as producers.

We had something going on that record to be sure, but it didn't showcase everything we had to give. It wasn't who we really were and how we had come together as performers. We were learning, still new to the recording process, and we weren't experienced enough to drive that train ourselves. We needed to make some changes, to get our onstage sound onto a record and to keep playing bigger markets. We had a reputation for being the opening band nobody wanted to book, and we weren't going to get large-scale gigs on our own unless we had a radio hit. We were never going to rise higher in terms of our profile as a live act no matter how great we were, and if we did nothing about our recorded sound we'd just fade away. The one person who understood this was our product manager at Columbia, Jeff Burles. I recognized the problem, yet I had no solution for it. But our man Jeff did: he hooked us up right away with a producer named Salaam Remi to do a remix of a song on *Blunted*. We meshed so well with Salaam that—out of no disrespect at all—we left Le Jam and Khalis and signed a production deal with Salaam. We loved Khalis and how far he'd taken us as our mentor, but the truth was Salaam Remi understood exactly who we were and how we wanted to sound. We didn't have to explain ourselves and we didn't have to argue or try to convince anyone in the studio that what we were hearing was something they should consider. With Salaam, we were all on the same page before we even opened the book.

Working with someone like-minded behind the mixing board was a breath of fresh air to us. Salaam was more current and closer to our age, and at the time he had produced a few songs we connected with. He did Super Cat's "Ghetto Red Hot," some stuff with Shabba Ranks, and other artists like them that bridged the gap between rap, dance hall, and early reggaeton. We felt cool with him, just comfortable off the bat, so we were able to stretch out and create musically. The first day we hung out with him was incredible; it was like that scene in the Ray Charles movie, *Ray*, when they recorded "What'd I Say." He just put on a beat and said, "Clef, go in there. I want to see what you can do. I want to hear what your voice is." He let it roll and we explored every idea we had musically.

I freestyled for about twenty-five minutes, and Salaam still has that track today. It's a priceless piece of off-the-cuff, free-associa-tion rhyming—and those are his words. Within that twenty-five minutes, at one point I said, "Yo, Mona Lisa, can I get a date on Friday and if you're busy I wouldn't mind taking Saturday-ay-ay." And that one minute is what became our first big hit. Salaam heard it all. He was the guy who plucked that diamond from the mine. I sure as hell didn't know that was a dope hook. I was too busy going off on my own trip. I don't even remember why I was even think-ing about the girl I called Mona Lisa. I hadn't thought about her in years, and that day, there was no reason at all why she should come to mind. But that's the way creation is, and you can't question it when it comes.

After I was done going crazy, Salaam put Lauryn in the booth, then Pras, and he took notes about what we did the whole time. Only after he'd heard all of us, and everything we spat out that day, did he come back to that Mona Lisa line. Honestly, all of us had forgotten about it; it had gone by that quick.

"That line is gonna be the hook to this song."

"Who did that again?" Pras asked. I felt the same way—and I had sung that shit.

"Listen," Salaam said, "your group is so talented that we basically gotta dumb y'all down. We gotta bring it for the knuckleheads first. And then, after you win the knuckleheads over, everybody else will come. We gotta keep it knucklehead right now. Save that other shit for later. This hook is perfect, it's got melody, it sticks in your mind, and nobody gonna forget it." He was so right about that.

Before we set that loose on the world, Salaam started doing his thing by remixing "Nappy Heads" off of *Blunted*. We listened to him and focused on our flow and kept our rhymes basic and simple but never stupid, like A Tribe Called Quest always did. They are the best example of a group that always took you on a journey with-out confusion. They said what they had to and did it with wit and intelligence without flaunting their wordplay. They didn't shy away from vocabulary either. Tribe was always a group that hit the balance right. We went for that same ideal on this remix and I think "Nappy Heads" captured the essence of who we were. It started making a whole lot of noise at college and major market radio and because of that, we immediately went back to Europe and then kept touring small markets around the United States.

Here is a deep Fugees story to inspire all the kids who want to be entertainers of any kind. After we recorded "Nappy Heads," the number-one station in New York City was Hot 97, and the number one DJ at that time was Funkmaster Flex. Salaam was a friend of his, so he brought the record to Flex personally. He gave him the original remix with our voices on it and an instrumental version with no vocals. Flex told Salaam he'd play it. So for the next two weeks, we listened to his show every night, waiting to hear it. A couple of days passed and he hadn't played it, but we kept listening anyway. Every night we were like "Flex is about to play our shit."

Finally, he put the instrumental on, as he talked over it. We were freaking out. "Aw man, he's never going to play this thing; he's playing the instrumental!" We called our friends, but we weren't sure if we should be excited or not because our song was being used as background music with no rapping. Is that something to be proud of?

And then out of nowhere, after ten minutes of Flex gassing us, he dropped the verse, and we went wild.

"Oh, Mona Lisa, can I get a date on Friday?"

Our song was being played on the number one station in New York. My life was complete as far as I was concerned. That was in 1995. I had no idea what was coming next.

ANYTHING WAS POSSIBLE AFTER that, and we all felt it. We'd delivered our song to the knuckleheads and they liked it. That moment was when things got real for the Fugees. We went back out on the road, continuing our grind 24/7 from that moment until we broke up. It was as if getting our song on Hot 97, in our home market, was the pistol at the beginning of the horse race. It didn't matter what we'd done before that. Afterward, everything was different: everything was faster and more intense than we could ever have imagined. It was a roller coaster with loops and corkscrews that never let us off. I'm not lying when I say this: the Fugees never took a break. The Fugees kept going. Then they just broke up.

5

THE SCORE

I feel like an old man every time I tell a young gun what the music business was like in my day, when my group's biggest record came out. I'm not even talking about how it was back in the days of Grandmaster Flash or even Public Enemy and A Tribe Called Quest. I'm talking about *my day*, which was only fifteen years ago—but that's how much the world of music has changed. That's a blink of an eye in the history of the business, but back then the things considered impossible today were still possible. Back then, in the nineties, a record could come out and sell 15 million copies if it struck a chord with the world at the time. Back then, radio could still make a somebody out of a nobody, and you couldn't get recorded music for free unless you taped it live off the radio. People would line up to buy an artist's new CD the day it came out, because to hear it, you had to own a piece of plastic with that song recorded on it.

A record that talked about what was going on at the time was something that everyone had to have back then because it was more than a record: it was a moment. Dr. Dre's *The Chronic* was one of those records. Biggie Smalls's *Ready to Die* was one of those records. Tupac's *Me Against the World* was one of those records.

Jay-Z's *Reasonable Doubt* was one of those records. And the Fugees' *The Score* was one of those records. Everybody who loves hip-hop has a memory from the summer of '96 involving one of the singles off *The Score*. Don't even try to tell me y'all don't. And unlike a lot of those other records, songs like "Ready or Not," and "Killing Me Softly," crossed over to pop fans, too. Our second album was one of those records responsible for bringing hip-hop into the mainstream, and making it the driving force in music for the second half of the nineties into today.

In 1996, there was so much great music out that for us to sell 15 million records worldwide really meant something. Hip-hop and R&B were at their best that year: Biggie and Tupac had just released their masterpieces, Jay-Z was heating up, TLC was at the top of the charts with *CrazySexyCool*, and Wu-Tang had us all in check. D'Angelo's *Brown Sugar* was out, and Michael and Janet Jackson had just dropped "Scream." We had to have skills to take those charts by storm the way we did.

The Fugees were raw talent and passion, and it shone through. The musicality was there because we had lived side by side with each other since we started rehearsing in front of that mirror back in Jersey so many years before. There was love in that music, too, the love between Lauryn and me. We had become a real couple, even though I was with someone else at the time. It didn't matter; she and I had our own musical and romantic language, and you can hear that in the music we made together. That's why it touched people; that's why it's so real. You can hear the tension in the music, all of that impossible love. It was like we knew it wasn't going to work from the start, but we couldn't shy away. It's not that it was wrong; it's just that it was too good to be true. The way we related we couldn't sustain because it was this whirlwind of creativity, this success, this performance. It was a fantasy that we engaged in because it was almost as if the music and the group and what we were doing drew us in. It was like all of that depended on this love we shared. But it wasn't real-life love. And we found that out—boy, did we.

The Score is raw storytelling: it's a candid picture of who we were and the times we were living in. We didn't make it in a slick upscale studio; we made it in a basement in the 'hood in New Jersey. Our recordings were pure—no tricks in sight—and it connected with music fans around the world. We had built our fan base one country and one city at a time, so when we came at everyone with The Score, they were ready.

I remember after we did the remix for "Nappy Heads" with Salaam Remi, we went out on the road to Germany to do a gig with Das EFX. It was weird. They were some big hip-hop group in a very traditional style, and we were opening up doing our thing, with all our instruments and all that. We were always about having a band and a DJ because we were so much more than just rappers: we were a group. The live instrumentation sparked our performance, because we were musicians in every way. Our drummer at the time was a cool cat named Johnny Wise, who is known for how well he plays break beats. That was his main thing; overall his drum skills were pretty unique and not exactly technically perfect. But that was all good to me, because having a nontraditional drummer was important to me. It didn't matter if he couldn't play rock or jazz as well as what he did with us: the point was, no one played the breaks in our songs better. When Johnny got on the set and started laying it out, L, Pras, and I lit up and we did our thing. I had to feel that shuffle beat he laid down, because I was the Cab Calloway of the Fugees, leading everyone, showing them which way we were going to move.

Those German shows were unusual because no one was expecting us. We'd smash them usually, but there was one night that we were in some area overrun by skinheads. I don't know who booked a hip-hop group in that bar, but we walked in and the word "nigger" was spray painted real big on the wall. That was an interesting welcome. Honestly, I had no idea why or how that shit got there. Coming from the States, it made no sense to me. I didn't think racism like that existed outside of the United States, because why would it? Racism here, and that word specifically, is a product of slavery and American history. What did Germans know about "nigger"? But fuck, there it was, on that wall for all to see, in the depths of this country. We were far from home but that same hate was all around us.

We opened up and the show went alright, and then these German hip-hop groups played, who were dope and cool, but nothing could really offset that racism vibe that we felt the minute we walked in and saw that word on the wall. So it was a weird night. I didn't feel like I was in danger, but I didn't feel welcome or comfortable either, and there were all these German groups performing music that was invented by black people from the Bronx and the Caribbean. Still, I've got to hand it to those German rappers. I remember thinking how no one at home was going to believe me when I told them that I saw German hip-hop acts who knew what they were doing. I could hardly believe it myself.

Our European travels took us to France, Iceland, England—just about every festival going on at the time—and that is how we built our name from the ground up. The funny thing was that when we landed back in New York with Das EFX, who we'd been supporting, all of us heard our song on the radio in the car on the ride home.

"Yo, yo, this is the Fugees with 'Nappy Heads,' on Hot 97, where hip-hop lives!"

We had been opening up for these guys and there was our song coming out of the radio. Apparently it had become one of the most played tracks in the few weeks we were gone and nobody had told us. Our stock had gone up from being in tenth place, playing support slots on European tours, to being the headliner right there in our hometown.

That summer we played Jones Beach and I was about ready to lose my mind. It felt like we'd spent years rehearsing for that very moment, and this was something I couldn't deny. No one could take that moment from us, standing there on that stage with the ocean behind us, playing our hearts out to a hometown crowd. All that rejection, all of that choreography learned in front of that mirror, all of it to go from a room in Germany with racist remarks on the wall to a sold-out crowd at Jones Beach. The minute I opened my mouth and sang, "Mona Lisa . . ." the entire audience sang the rest with me. They knew every single word. Our success didn't come overnight, but when it came, it came faster than the blink of an eye and it was overwhelming, like the top of a roller coaster.

The whole time, Lauryn and I were falling into a daring kind of love, while I was already in love with my future wife, Claudinette, across town. I need to rewind the tape a bit to explain all this.

I met Claudinette when I was about nineteen, and she is a few years older than me. She was fly, she was established, she was modeling in New York, and just so she wouldn't pass me by, I tricked her and lied about my age. I said I was twenty-two or something, so she'd go out with me. Her family is very religious and traditional, so I brought her to my dad's church and courted her the proper way and we started dating. This was about the time when I started rehearsing with the Fugees and moved into the Booga and started spending time with Lauryn. I spent all my time with either one or the other of them, you know what I mean? Lauryn and I were pursuing a dream together, and that goal, as well as our mutual love of music, was the language that brought us together. And there was an attraction there; I'm not going to lie and act as if it was just because we spent time together that we ended up together. Lauryn's beautiful, and because of her looks and her talent and everything we shared with each other—from songs to books to lyrics—love was bound to grow. I was with both of these incredible women at the same time, which isn't something to be proud of but it was definitely unavoidable. I couldn't say no to either of them. I mean it when I say I loved them both, because I did. I knew this situation couldn't last, but I didn't care; I was going to try to work it for as long as I could. And I think most men in my position would have done the same. I now know it ended up causing more trouble than anything—for all of us—but at the time that was the last thing on my mind.

By that time Lauryn was driving and she had a Jeep, and after we worked in the studio creating, we'd take her Jeep up to Eagle Rock Mountain, which is a state park that borders Montclair and West Orange and has a view of Manhattan in certain parts. It was like Lover's Lane where I grew up: you'd drive up there and make out and look at the stars. If you had a Jeep you could take it off the beaten path and feel like you were in nature, so we'd do that, just look at the stars and talk about our hopes and dreams. It was romantic, but my main attraction to Lauryn wasn't just her beauty: it was her mind. Her age and what was in her head did not match up, and that's what people always said about me. I've always been called an old soul, because the way I think and talk about life is the way an eighty-year-old who has seen everything would. Lauryn is like that, too, so we connected in every way all those nights under the stars. It was inevitable that we'd fall in love.

Claudinette to me was like Wonder Woman: she was modeling and making money and I didn't have a penny. When I lied to her and told her I was nineteen, she didn't believe me. Not for a second. She knew I was a kid but she didn't care. She was smart and going to school and I had barely graduated high school. And she believed in me; that made me feel like a million bucks. Actually I used to borrow money from her to go to the clubs because she wanted me to hear what was going on so that I could be better at what I wanted to do. She was mature and supportive—beautiful, driven, and independent. She came from a good family and she loved me as much as I loved her. She fell in love with the real me: the comedian, the character, the silly, witty kid.

Before I moved into the Booga full-time, when I was still trying to live in my dad's house, Claudinette's family would take me in when my dad and I fought and he kicked me out. She'd hook me up with some blankets and I could sleep in their basement as many nights as I needed to. In return I got her hooked up in my dad's church, where she began to sing and became an important member of the congregation. Our relationship was natural and it was comfortable. But on the other side of town, something else was going on. With Lauryn, just being in the studio so much together, working on our music as a team gave us an attraction toward each other. Being part of something bigger than you can do that, and sometimes there's nothing more to the relationship. It's like a romance on a film set that ends at the wrap party. But that wasn't what we had. It was more than that. Spending all our time together brought us together. It started in the studio, working on those routines and our rhymes. I mean there was one time when I was around Lauryn twenty out of the twenty-four hours in a day. The thing I have to say about my wife, Claudinette, is that she supported all that hard work I was putting in. She trusted me and loved that I had a purpose, a goal, and a team to pursue that with.

During that time, Lauryn and I ate, slept, woke up, ate, slept, and did music; that was our world. And when we began to tour together, every night was like a fairytale world and we were living in our dream. We'd each have our rooms but we'd always end up in the same one. It felt like that relationship was real, and it was. It was love; it was lust. It was more intense than some teenage romance, because we knew ourselves. It was the type of pure love that burns bright but burns out fast.

Our friendship began as a mentorship where I taught her to rhyme and brought her into rap culture. And like I said, she ate it up. She was a natural. Pretty soon she was better than me at memorizing my own rap sheet. And her delivery wasn't something I could teach. She became my muse; she became this creative chariot that pulled me along and inspired me to be the best artist I could be. We lusted for each other. We were making the best songs we ever had—lyrics flowing out of us—and our love was all tied up in the music.

I was a big-brother figure to Lauryn until it turned romantic, and the soundtrack of our relationship is *The Score*. That album came out the way it did because of our passion. You take us both and intertwine us and put it on a piece of vinyl and that's what you get. The emotion is real, and I believe that is what connected with so many people. We made fans out of people who had never listened to hip-hop. None of them knew what was going on behind the scenes, but they felt that passion in the music. The music came with a kiss. Our physical relationship was an important part of what inspired the music. I'm not saying that we couldn't have made an album like *The Score* without being together physically, but I think the tension and passion and emotion that you hear in the singing was there because it's the sound of people experiencing something. If someone is in love or sad or angry—just experiencing something intense—you hear it in the intonation of their voice. You can't fake that. If you're really feeling it, the vocals will sound different. Listen to Billie Holiday: even if you know nothing about her life, you can tell without a doubt that her blues are real. She is singing from a broken heart. Lauryn has that quality to her voice naturally. Think of a song like "Me and Mrs. Jones," by Billy Paul. That track takes you there. Lauryn does the same thing, every time.

Lauryn and I had a *True Romance* kind of thing: it was like we were two outlaws in love. There was a daring kind of vibe to our relationship and we always felt like it was us two against the world, each and every day. There was no going back and no surrender; we were going to defeat the odds against us. It was all tied up with the group, because at the time, she, Pras, and I lived every victory and every defeat as a unit. When people said we were whack and we needed to get back on the banana boat, it affected all of us.

The three of us had made a pledge not to quit years before and we weren't going anywhere. When the critics wrote that the girl should go solo, Lauryn's reaction was that they could go to hell because Pras and I were her brothers.

"I ain't going nowhere," she'd say. "We make it together or we don't make it at all."

That kind of commitment breeds natural attraction, as does natural talent. The more Lauryn evolved as a musician, the more I fell for her. I loved her voice and always thought she was beautiful, but as she became a great rhymer and performer, I couldn't help myself: I fell in love with her again for her skills. It felt like we shared a mind, because we'd have long conversations, all day every day, and we got to know each other deeply. Lauryn is very intelligent and she taught me a lot about things I wasn't familiar with creatively. We were two artists speaking the same language, which is a romantic and intimate thing to share.

I remember the day things changed, and it was my fault. I slipped up. We were talking about some music stuff and I couldn't hold back any longer.

"You know, you kinda attractive," I said. "You know, you a pretty smart girl."

"Stop it, my brother," she said.

"Nah, nah, I'm serious. You a hottie."

That was the moment. It sparked a different tone in the way we spoke to each other. From there we started getting closer and flirting with each other for the first time. Little by little, that innocent flirtation became obvious attraction, and the little gestures between "brother" and "sister" became flirtation between lovers. It all changed step-by-step, the tension between us growing, until one day, it just happened. I'm the guilty party. I'm the one to blame. I definitely went for it first; I ain't going to lie. Lauryn tried her best to keep me in that brother place. Maybe she'd thought about what would happen, too. I don't know. All I know is that I was the one who made the move to the other mode. I knew it was wrong, too, because I was with Claudinette. And I loved Claudinette. There was just no way I could avoid falling in love with the little world of music that Lauryn and I shared.

Physically falling for her was easy: she is beautiful, but there was a lot more to it. Artistically, Lauryn gave me soul music, which is where her true gift lies. She shared that knowledge with me: the Jackson 5—the deepest part of Michael Jackson's career—Marvin Gaye, the Delfonics, Barry White, all of the soul music I had missed growing up was our thing. That music was too explicit to be played in my father's house, because it certainly wasn't Christian. She opened my eyes—and that was some romantic shit to be bonding over.

I remember telling her, "Every time I sing, I sound too world-music. Teach me how to sing your kind of stuff."

She'd give me lessons: R&B singing lessons from Lauryn Hill, imagine that; I don't care who you are.

She taught me circle runs, which is when a singer delivers a line in a melodic circle rather than a straight line. Instead of holding a note, you bend it, the way an R&B singer does. That's how they get to the pain in their soul, and that's what Lauryn taught me to do. We fell in love with each other's minds, and it was a no-holds-barred conversation between us always. We were always together and we talked about everything. Pras still blames me for wrecking the group by getting into a relationship with Lauryn, but the truth is if he had the option to, he would have done the same thing. Believe me, any man would. Our group chemistry was like this: Pras was the little brother, I was the big brother, and Lauryn was my girl. And it was all good—on the road at least.

The Score is a tragic Shakespearean romance because it was destructive and all consuming at the same time. As it was coming to life, I decided to marry Claudinette. I loved her, I knew it was right, but the timing was a reaction. It was the effect of a cause that caused further effects. And further drama came with that, do you dig?

It's hard to explain, but I was in love with both of them. I was torn between the impossible love affair, the whirlwind artist romance, and the solid, good woman who demanded respect. The solid woman had her passion, too. So my life became crazy, because I was in the middle and each of them was passionate about me in different ways. One side was all bound up with music and discovery and my own self-expression. The other side was all about intellect and wisdom and helping me to mature. I did not know what to do; I just knew I had to do something. It was one of the hardest decisions I've ever made in my life. It wasn't clean and simple.

It's going to be easy for people to read this and say, "Why did he do that to Lauryn? How could he not go with her? He broke up the Fugees!" I wish it were that easy to explain away, but it's not. Claudinette was with me when I had nothing, and she stood by me and helped me to be the man that I have become—the man I wouldn't have been without her. That man is the one who created *The Score* and *The Carnival*, and I don't think he would have been here if he had gone with Lauryn. We wouldn't have been the same; we wouldn't have evolved apart if we didn't explode together. It's easy to listen to the music and hear the romance and love in there and think of what could have been. But the music is the best expression of my relationship with Lauryn. The rest of it wasn't smooth at all. We were either deeply in love or fighting; there was no middle ground. It was a passionate roller coaster ride, every single day. We had fights on planes. We had the police called to a hotel where we were staying in Germany because our arguing was keeping the neighbors awake. I know fans like to believe in things like that, but they have to remember that they're basing what they think we could have been on the Lauryn and Clef they saw in the limelight and heard on the record. The real Lauryn is much more complicated than what comes through in her art. Same goes for me.

In the face of that, I went with the woman who was down-to-earth, who had always and still tells me to believe in myself, and who believes in me and what I want to achieve—even after all I've done and all I've put her through to this day. She knows all the wrong I've done and she's forgiven me and we are still together, because nothing can come between the love we have for each other. Claudinette is the woman who listens to the music I make and who tells me what she thinks of it, honestly. She's the woman who gave me money to go out to the clubs when I was still a kid so that I could learn what the music industry was about. She's the one I'd ride my sister's BMX bicycle across town to see before I could afford a car. There was something enchanting about Claudinette, too, because she was what I consider my first experience with a woman. She was older, she was together, and she had it all figured out. She was untouchable, but I found a way to get to her, and when I did we fell in love.

My father married Claudinette and me in his church and Lauryn was there at the ceremony, the reception, all of it—and that was definitely heavy. Lauryn respected the day so there was no confrontation because I'd told her that I'd made up my mind and that was it. Of course later, when we were on the road again, I fell back into indulging myself with her.

My wedding was traditionally Haitian, which is to say that it was as big a party as the Greeks have, just with a whole different flavor. Entire families come. They eat, they talk, they laugh, they tell stories, and it goes on all day and night. My dad didn't want any dancing in his church, though, so we all had to wait for him to leave to start partying. We even went so far as to have another secret reception in another room where there was a band and everyone was dancing. My dad, of course, heard about it and showed up there, too, and he suspended the musicians in the band, and all the women he caught celebrating, from coming to church for a month. As I've said before, the church band was a big deal in our neighborhood, and by then those musicians were getting paid to play, so getting banned for a month was real punishment. He was a serious dude, my dad.

If Lauryn and I had a rocky relationship full of breakups and make-ups before, my getting married turned up the heat 100 percent. Like I said, when we got back on the road, she and I took up with each other again, and it was crazier than ever, fueled by the fact that I was married. I tried to keep from going there, but I've got to be honest: I didn't want to end my romance with Lauryn. It didn't feel natural to stop it. It was at the heart of our music; that love between us was the soul of what we were doing. It didn't seem right to us to be on the road creating and living our musical life without that bond between us. It was impossible for us not to be drawn back into it; we were like pieces of metal, and that thing we had as two artists on a journey together was a magnet that pulled us together beyond our control. But one day it was love, and then the next day she would be chasing me down the street somewhere like Australia, beating me to the ground out of jealousy.

Lauryn would keep it all inside and act like she was cool and we would be together the way we used to be and then, *bam*, she'd explode without warning. It was a constant cycle. I tried my best to keep my home life out of her face and separate, because that was sure to start a fight, but even if I had done that perfectly, those blowups would have happened. That's just who she is: she's a deep, soulful artist and she feels everything intensely. So she might have acted like it was cool, but she was thinking about it, and when she felt that jealousy or had enough with being cool, she'd let me know about it. Didn't matter where we were or what we were doing; if she felt something strongly, I was going to know. I had a wife at home and a girlfriend on the road. That is not a new story in the music business, but this is one more case that proves that it will never be easy.

We were touring: back to living together, eating together, performing together, sleeping together. Our relationship, our intimacy hadn't changed within that bubble, but everything outside of it had. It was hard. Every time we were together, Lauryn would ask me, "How come you're not with me?" I never knew what to say, because part of me was with her, and but more of me was with my wife. There was the part of me that understood her the way she understood me. But it didn't change the fact that I'd made up my mind to go with the rock, not the feather.

Lauryn and I always seemed to get into the most heated conversations about our relationship while we were traveling, usually on airplanes, and it never ended well. We had huge fights, and a few times when it went down she started swinging at me right there in the seats. People would scatter. We never got arrested, but we came close a few times in Europe. It's a good thing this all happened before the iPhone. Airport security came on the plane in Germany once to make sure we were okay and weren't going to hurt each other. That is the way it always was; we were emotion turned up to ten. Lauryn would go from extreme passion to extreme anger with little warning. The two of us were just crazy; that's all. She is a Gemini, and anyone who has known one intimately can tell you that they can flip like a switch.

She and I started out in a friendship that was beautiful, and over time it developed into a deep romance. And since it didn't work out—and it tore her up emotionally—a lot of people have blamed me for Lauryn's emotional instability and artistic inconsistency afterward. It's sad but true that she's not been herself as an artist in the years since *The Miseducation of Lauryn Hill*. No one is more upset about that than I am. I mean it; I am her biggest fan and I always will be.

I've been told by many angry people who are also her fans that if I hadn't messed with her she would not have gone so insane. My response to that is: you can talk as much as you want to talk, because talking is easy, because you're not the one who was in my shoes.

You're not the one who had to be around that beautiful woman 24/7 sharing genius space with her. We shared a creation, one made of our passion, molded into music that went out into the world and became an album that seized the times. It's the yin and the yang; there is a give and a take. We gave of ourselves, we put ourselves together to make something, and what happened was the price we had to pay. I wouldn't take that back if it meant taking back what we did with the Fugees. I can't speak for her, but I hope she feels the same.

THE SCORE WAS THE soundtrack I'd had in my head for a long time, and the album that Lauryn, Pras, and I were destined to make. It was driven by my relationship with Lauryn, but let me say right now that we couldn't have done it without Pras. Out of the three of us, he was the hustler, he was the business mind, and he was the most like a record-label visionary. He was like our L. A. Reid or Clive Davis: he had the vision to bring us together because he felt that magic would happen. It was his idea to get my voice on that first record, because he knew that if he got me into the studio with Lauryn and Marcy and him, something really good would come out of it. Along the way he contributed all kinds of pieces to the puzzle that needed to be there. He brought that rock element to the group and always had great production ideas in the studio because he loved rock music, from Metallica to Guns N' Roses. The sounds of those records and the way they were produced was something that affected his idea of recording and it kept our music fresh. Pras was always an equal partner, and he was always the glue that kept the three of us together. Pras suffered a lot because of that, too. He had to deal with all of the emotional ups and downs going on between Lauryn and me. He had to play the middle, sometimes on my side, sometimes on hers, depending on what was going on. He had to see both points of view and then do what it took to keep the train moving. I know his attitude as things got more intense with Lauryn and me was always, "Damn, I didn't create this shit to have to deal with this shit." He got the short end of the stick. He put all that frustration he was feeling aside while we were together doing our thing, but after we dismantled the group, all of it came out. And he had every reason to be angry, because an incredible group that he put together got taken down by a romance.

No matter what was going on, though, the Fugees never, ever fought about music. We had complete synergy and complete respect on that level because our attitude was that a song wasn't right until all three of us felt comfortable with it. If somebody was uncomfortable, it was wrong and we had to keep working. There was a lot of trust between us at the time on a musical level, so even when Lauryn wanted to kill me, she'd respect me if I said she needed to do another vocal take and know I wasn't just saying it because we were fighting. It was the same way I respected her when she told me I needed to change a line in my verse or adjust the musical arrangement. I never for a minute thought that her motives for saying that or not agreeing with me were anything but pure. I knew that just like me, Lauryn's first love is music, and that she'd never let her other feelings get in the way of the art. I was the composer, Lauryn brought the soul, and Pras brought the over-the-top rock element. And we knew that about each other and we knew that formula worked because it allowed our individual talents to shine within our group dynamic. We were all for one and one for all where it counted.

We brought all of our talent—and all of our drama—to *The Score*. There is no better snapshot of who we were as a group than that album. By the time I sat down to get the music for the album together, I had learned my way around a mixing board from Salaam Remi and Khalis Bayyan and, courtesy of Renel Duplessis, I had all the vintage gear I needed to get the sounds I heard in my head onto tape. We were of one mind about that, because we'd spent so much time together. This next album was going to be us on the road, right in the studio, telling the story of who we were and the world we lived in. We weren't going to let a producer shape us into anything other than ourselves, because no one was better fit for the job. I was the composer, so I led the charge.

I started collecting samples from old records and made beats on my MPC. I was always really into jazz, ever since my days in the high school jazz band, so Miles Davis and John Coltrane had a lot to do with how I set about composing the music. Just listen to *Blue Train*, *Giant Steps*, and *On the Corner* and you'll know everything there is to know about me as a composer and producer from that point until today. Those cats knew musical space inside and out, and I hope I've taken even a little piece of that wisdom and put it into what I do.

I wanted the depth of jazz, but I wanted a pop sensibility, too, so my reference there when I started writing the music for *The Score* was "Nights in White Satin" by the Moody Blues. I listened to that song over and over and it was a hugely inspirational theme to me. It had the mood and vibe that I wanted for the album—something beautiful and grand. I wanted that orchestral sound and those sad melodies behind Lauryn's vocals. I wanted to capture how important a song like that sounds. The only problem was that I didn't have a philharmonic orchestra in the Booga Basement and I sure as hell couldn't afford to hire one. I didn't even know enough string players to fake a quartet. But that didn't bother me because I had always gotten by on what I had. I took a few weeks to go through records I had to create samples that captured the grandeur of an orchestra, and I married them to beats that reflected the gritty attitude of the streets.

The place where *The Score* was made is the backdrop to the album; it defines it more than fans can probably understand. The Booga Basement was a unique space, and the 'hood was a character all its own. The people that came in and out of that place every day all those years—the thugs, the dealers, the gangsters, the murderers, the innocents, the hustlers, the lost souls, the good, the bad, and the ugly—they are all a piece of that record. Their energy was in that room because the door to the Booga was always open. I'd learned that from my grandmother back in Haiti: leave your door open to everyone in the neighborhood so that no one will steal from you. If you make your home their home, all will respect it. Some days I woke up to rats running all over the basement and the room where I slept; some days I woke up to someone from the neighborhood crashed out on the floor. It was never boring.

The everyday sounds of our neighborhood were part of the music as if they were nothing special, but in that context they became epic. When I listen to those songs today, now that so much time has passed, I appreciate it all the more. In the skits on the album you hear Chinese voices, which were very much a part of our world. We hung out at the Chinese man's grocery store and we had watched kung fu movies from the time we were kids. I'm a huge fan of the marital arts, and Asian stars from Bruce Lee to Jackie Chan. In my mind, I've considered myself a ninja forever, and if you're laughing as you read this, go ask anyone who grew up with me. I'm agile and I always have been—I'm telling you. On *The Score*, when you hear the voice of Shannon Briggs on a skit it's no joke. That's him. He is a boxer we knew from around the way who came in and ad-libbed for us. He said, "Yo, my name is Shannon Briggs. I get paid to knock people out." It was the truth.

The album was all that we were; it was where we were from, all the sights and sounds, and all the drama between us. I heard love songs, I heard true stories, I heard a score. I heard an extension of the Shakespearean play that Lauryn and I had been in together, set to our personal story. We had become an opera unto ourselves and now we had the ability to sing it out in our own way.

When we got off the road and back to the Booga and started in on working, it became serious real quick. It was like the intensity of touring—of proving ourselves night after night—had nowhere to go, so we focused it on the songs. You'd think we'd want to chill for a while and relax, but we didn't. Grinding was instinct at that point. I think after, like, one day of sleep I was restless and ready to work, and so were Pras and Lauryn. We got right to it, locking ourselves down in that basement for hours. The studio was our canvas and the album came together naturally. All that we'd worked out subconsciously on the road flowed through us once we were there in our own backyard.

I sampled almost everything you hear on that album using an Akai S900, which is the cornerstone of all hip-hop created from the late eighties through to today. For those of you who don't know what that machine is, it's the first sampler that was introduced to the mass market. It was affordable, it was basic, it was the Sony Walkman of making beats. I'd say it was like the first iPod, except that the S900 didn't change much from the time it first came out in 1986 until it was updated in 1996. It allowed you to record thirty pieces of music no longer than ten seconds each onto its memory chip, and if you have enjoyed any hip-hop record released between 1987 and 1999, I'm telling you, most of what you are hearing is the Akai S900 at work, from De La Soul to A Tribe Called Quest to Outkast to Dr. Dre. It should be in the hip-hop hall of fame.

My other go-to machine was a Linn 9000, which is one of the oldest and still one of the best-sounding drum machines money can buy. Roger Linn was a sound engineer and instrument designer who created the first real drum machine, the LM-1 in 1979. He recorded a session drummer playing a real drum kit and converted it into digital samples, so the machine sounded like a human being. All of his machines, including the Linn 9000, can be heard on every great early-eighties synthesizer-oriented album, from Michael Jackson to Prince to all the New Wave English bands. In the late eighties, Linn's company went out of business, but Roger was recruited by Akai where he invented the MPC 60, which combines sequencing and sampling with performance pads—basically making it the perfect drum machine. It is now called the MPC 3000 and it's still used onstage and in the studio by hip-hop artists everywhere.

When it came out, the Linn 9000 was expensive—it was about five thousand dollars—but by the time I was putting the Booga studio together in the early nineties, it was old. Everyone was using MPC 3000s and a lot of cats didn't know how to use a Linn. I had learned that thing backward and forward from Khalis, so I was all about it. I could get drum sounds from the same era that Lauryn was channeling. It was perfect.

The way the Fugees worked never changed: our producer would give us a beat and when we all felt it, we'd take turns freestyling until the song presented itself to us. Lauryn always found the melody, and a lot of the time she'd come with the lyrical hook, too. Then we'd all find our way around the song and the subject matter. We were used to having someone guide us in the past, and we'd needed it before, but times had changed. We had evolved out there on the road playing shows all over Europe, at college campuses all over America, and we knew who we were now. We knew what we wanted to say and how we wanted it to sound. We still needed a producer to feed us a beat, but this time that producer was me.

One of our greatest moments of creation was unexpected, and like the greatest surprises, it yielded one of the greatest songs we ever wrote. The way it went down is a real inside look into who we were, and it's a moment I will never forget. The song I'm talking about is "Ready or Not." The main studio at the Booga was downstairs in the garage. That is where we did vocals, and that is where the mixing board, keyboards, and microphones were. Up on the first landing, still in the garage, before you got into the house, there was a small storage room and that's where I slept most nights. That little closet became my home away from home. It was almost like a monk's room in a monastery, with nothing in it that would take away from my pursuit of the music. I had a bed, my sampler, my Linn, a TV, and nothing else. The room had no insulation, so it was cold, but I didn't care: it was my crib. And I was in there one rainy day, watching *Sleepwalkers*, one of my favorite movies, which is based on the Stephen King book, while I worked on a track. One of my brothers had put me on to Enya, whose music I still love to this day. When I first heard her I became obsessed, so I was in there messing around with some samples of her songs because I loved the moodiness of them. I had a simple hip-hop break beat going on my Linn 9000 and was looping an Enya sample over it on my MPC.

Just then my door burst open, and Lauryn Hill was standing there.

"Hey," she said.

"Hey."

She scanned the room, and then looked me in the eye. "What's that?"

"I don't know yet. I've got a beat and a loop. I'm just messin' with this."

We both sat in the semidark just listening. The sample came back around, and then the beat kicked in—*doom-cha, doom-cha*. And then Lauryn started singing.

"Ready or not, here I come, you can't hide . . . I'm gonna find you, and make you love me."

I got shivers all up my spine. It was magic. We both knew it.

"Keep goin'," is all I could manage to say.

That song was born in that small room, just the two of us alone in the dark. She closed the door, she kept singing, and as the beat rolled on the words flowed out of her. It was natural, it was beautiful, and I fell more in love with her on the spot. That moment in that closet I called a bedroom was one of the most meaningful times we ever shared. When we finished the final recording a few weeks later, Lauryn cried during one vocal take, after she'd run through the song a few times. The version you hear on the record is the one where she cried, because there was none more honest. She and I were going through our shit, and that song and her performance says more than I could ever put down here on this page.

The way I justified being with Lauryn in the studio and doing music the way we were and being with my wife at the same time was that I loved what Lauryn and I had while we were creating. She was my muse and we did beautiful things together, but I loved being at home with someone who had nothing to do with the music industry or the art of music at all. Claudinette loves music, but she and I barely talked about it at home. She was the woman who made me believe, like she did from the beginning, that I was going to get wherever I wanted to go in the crazy industry she let me run wild in. She wasn't with me because of what I did; she was with me because she loved me for the funny, witty character I am.

"READY OR NOT" BECAME the Fugees' anthem, the first song music fans around the world remembered us for. Though, in my opinion it's not the essence of *The Score*. To me, "Zealots" is the most important track on that album. It's not the most pop friendly, but it lays out our philosophy. I took a sample of "I Only Have Eyes for You," by the Flamingos, which is a classic, beautiful, orchestral love song. The lyrics to "Zealots" are deep because I worked on my verses with my brother Sam, who was in law school at the time. Sam was always a scholar, whereas I never was, but we understand each other when it comes to the meaning of life and human knowledge. I wanted to write a verse that referenced all of the great thinkers that mankind has known, but I'd not read the books enough to know the great from the fake. Sam did, and he gave me an academic's take on a battle rap.

> *I haunt MCs like Mephistopheles*
> *Bringin' swords of Damocles*
> *Secret Service keep a close watch as if my name was Kennedy*

Abstract raps simple with a street format
Gaze into the sky and measure planets by parallax
Check out the retrograde motion, kill the notion
Of biting and recycling and calling it your own creation
I feel like Rockwell, "somebody's watching me."

That was what Sam inspired. He kicked that knowledge my way. He gave me the word "parallax," which is the difference in the apparent position of an object viewed along two different lines of sight. I love that whole concept: it means what you see may be something else if you change your perspective.

The Score is full of consciousness on that level but the three of us didn't set out to make a record like that. We wanted to speak to our lives and the times more than we had on *Blunted*, but we didn't try to project any message directly. We wanted to make music that moved the population, and we wanted it to move us, and be fly. We always knew that we would never talk garbage; we wanted to speak the truth without being preachy. All we ever talked about was how to just be ourselves, and how to let our own beliefs, such as they were, come through us by focusing our minds on the music. We were and we are three different people, so we knew that the messages would be in the same spirit, but definitely different. So we never set out with a goal for a particular song; we just trusted in each other to be what we were, and trusted our collective mind to make something real. The messages in the music came through straight from our souls, from our subconscious, not guided by any conscious decisions.

The Score is a yearbook; it's the growth of three individual talents. At the time, Pras was in Five Towns College and Lauryn was attending Columbia University, so they were reading and learning, becoming educated and enlightened. They grew beyond the street-corner rhyming we did on *Blunted*. I had to keep up so I relied on my brother Sam, like I said. *The Score* was very philosophized, and I think that's why there has not been another Fugees album. After all this time, and even though we don't speak about it, I believe that we all know what it means to make a Fugees album. The synergy of the three is the Fugees. We know how it is supposed to sound and we know how deep it needs to be, and that's not there between us now. Doing anything but our best would be an insult to what we've done.

Our synergy was unique, and you can hear it all over our music. It was born from all that time we spent together, and we don't do that at all anymore. Back then we knew each other's every thought and I don't care who you are; you can't just walk back into a studio after being apart for so long—after not even talking for years—and expect that magic to be there. We're all three different people, and different in different ways. On the cover of *Blunted* was a three-headed baby and a hand holding it down: that was the Fugees. We were tied at the hip 24/7, until that knot came loose.

LOOKING BACK AT WHAT inspired me musically and lyrically during the creation of *The Score*, I have to say that one of the biggest influences on me personally was the church. I had left my father's house, but he still had hopes of bringing me back into Christian music, so he sent me Jimmy Swaggart books and all kinds of things to read, acting like he didn't know where I was or what I was doing. The truth is, as much as we disagreed, I missed my dad and I missed the church, but I wasn't going to stop making hip-hop. So Christianity was on my mind when I was writing lyrics. I had read the Bible cover to cover several times by then and all of those stories were a part of what I was writing. Listen to my rhymes, on songs like "Manifest":

> *I woke up this morning*
> *I was feeling kinda high*

It was me, Jesus Christ and Haile Selassie
Selassie said greetings in the name of the most high
Jah Rastafari
Christ took a sip of the Amaretto
Passed it down the table, said today I'll be betrayed by one of
  you 12 disciples
Give me a clue who could do this to you?
The kid on the block who makes less money than you.

That was my version of the story of Judas betraying Christ for the gold.

I'll never stop being impressed by how much Lauryn came into her own on *The Score*. She was the caterpillar that became a butterfly. On *Blunted* she was still learning how to rhyme, so lyrically she had the training wheels on. Pras and I held her back because she wasn't ready to be unleashed. In the years between, she wrote, she practiced, and she became a true artist. She is one hell of a rapper, and that came shining through on *The Score*. Just like I'd been waiting to shine as a producer, she'd been waiting to do it as a rapper, so once we both got our chance, we ran with it. We did it our way.

ONE OF THE THINGS that helped Lauryn to rap better was something that helped all three of us become better rappers. It is what I call our training, and it involved a group from New Jersey called the Outsidaz. We used to hang with them a lot, just passing the microphone, ciphering, doing what people call battle rapping. They were fixtures at the Booga and in our lives back then and we all took pieces of what they did, because they were the best.

The Outsidaz are legends in nineties hip-hop: everyone from Eminem to Big L references them in their songs if you go deep enough into their catalogs. Those guys were like the Shaolin monks of freestyling at the time as far as I was concerned. They were the Wu-Tang of New Jersey, but they never got the recognition, because it takes more than talent to be successful. RZA is one hell of a business man, and unfortunately the RZA of the Outsidaz, Slang Ton, ended up getting shot before he could really get things going for them. All I can say is that if you've heard the earliest, nastiest, most out-there rhymes that Eminem threw down back in the day, these guys were leagues beyond that. They were just ill and completely insane. Eminem name-checks them on his first album, because he had to; he is a continuation of what they started.

The only way I can describe them is to say that the Outsidaz were 'hood thug nerds, if you can imagine that. They were street, and they were tough, but somehow they had spent years in the library and had greater book-smarts than all the kids who stayed in school. They were the kids who dropped out of school because they were bored but who learned about the world by reading every single book they could find on the subjects that interested them.

When we were making *The Score*, Young Zee and Pacewon and Slang Ton, rest in peace, came to the Booga all the time. Their swagger was nothing you could even describe. Slang read a lot of science all the time, so he based his rhyme structure on a metaphoric logical style like Killah Priest from Wu-Tang Clan. When Slang Ton rapped, you would understand two out of every five sentences in the precalculated equations he spit. But that's exactly what he wanted: he intended to grab your attention and make you think, but he didn't want you to know for sure what he was talking about. He wasn't keeping secrets, because if you asked him what it all meant, he'd break it down for you like a professor to a student. But he was all about avoiding the obvious when it came to lyrics.

Slang Ton was also very high all the time. As someone who gets high, listen to me when I tell you that he was real high. The guy was so high that he once spit on my dog. I had a German Shepherd mix named Black that I got for protection when I started living in the

Booga full-time. The dog kept watch and let me know when someone was coming in, but overall he was pretty relaxed. Except when
Slang Ton came around: that dog would sit in front of that dude
and growl the whole time until he got up and left. Black just hated
this guy. Slang Ton tried to ignore it, until the one day when he'd
had enough and just spat full in my dog's face. The dog snapped his
jaws at him, as I would have if I were a dog.

"Man, what did you do that for?" I asked him.

"Fuckin' dog was looking at me funny." And he said no more.

WHEN THE OUTSIDAZ CAME around, it was a chance for the
Fugees to learn a few things, because, like I said, they were free-
style gods. They were like Mr. Miyagi from *The Karate Kid* for us:
we couldn't understand how they were so good, but we sure as hell
knew they were good. So we knew to pay close attention to everything they did. They loved to battle rap, and they'd do it everywhere they went, whether or not they had opponents. When they
didn't, they'd just battle among themselves, and those moments
were when the learning happened for observers like us.

We went head-to-head with them whenever they were around,
and as much as the Fugees lost, which we usually did, we learned
a lot. Those ciphers were like being on a team with the world's
toughest coach, or learning how to play a sport from a professional
athlete when you're still a kid. In those cases you'll never be better
than your teacher or your opponent, but that doesn't matter. The
act of battling them and losing teaches you more than the average
coach would. The Fugees were never going to be better than the
Outsidaz, but their skills pushed the limits of our rhyme abilities
into new territory. Believe me, we tried, but there was no beating
those dudes. They had already thought about what they were going
to say to you three or four sentences down the road while they delivered their first line. And the more they got to know us, the more

they knew how to take us out, because they learned our moves. It got to the point where they were in our heads, responding to what they knew we were going to say about them before we even tried to spit it.

There is only one thing you can do when you come up against talent like that: if you can't beat them, you join them. And so we asked the Outsidaz to do a track called "Cowboys" with us on *The Score*, and then we made them a part of our crew, the Refugee Camp, and got them an album deal. I came up with the concept for the song "Cowboys," because that's what I do. I told everyone to come in and build a verse off that theme and came up with the beat and music. Young Zee, he just talked right out of his brain on that track, man. His verse was amazing. There's no mystery there: when the Outs hooked up with the Fugees, all kinds of weed was smoked. I'd fill this huge tobacco pipe, and those guys always came through with a few types of shit. We'd put all that weed and all creativity in one room and we always walked away with something special.

OUR FORMULA WAS PERFECTED on *The Score*, and that's why it crossed over into more markets around the world than most rap albums at the time. People responded to Lauryn's voice, which is beautiful, like an angel. What she did was calm the group and the music down. Pras and I had so much energy and so much to say that we were lyrical chaos: we made sense but we ran around yelling everything to make our point, because that's how much passion we had. When Lauryn dropped into a song, everything relaxed. She was the element that kept Pras and me in check. She held it all together and made everything we did lyrically make sense.

I know why Pras and I were so noisy: we listened to a lot of Metallica at the time. Don't laugh; it's true. We liked their intensity and their phrasing. Metallica knows how to get their point across.

So if you look at our group as two MCs with too much energy and a lot to say, and one gifted rapper and soul singer who kept it all in balance, the Fugees will make sense to you. Our music was both types: conscious hip-hop and love songs, all in one.

You can hear it all on "Killing Me Softly," which was sampled and reinterpreted from Roberta Flack. You can also hear it on the song "The Score,"; that one was my concept, too. It is a sample of every other song on the album, as if the album is a movie and the song "The Score" is the soundtrack.

The song "Family Business" came from Salaam Remi and it's a basic Fugees track, while "The Mask" came out of me telling everyone to come into the studio with a lyrical mask for themselves to wear in the song.

When we made *The Score*, I was in what I've come to call my scientist mode: I was in the lab, and on an adventure. I was experimenting, mixing things up, trying all the combinations I could think of until the music was right. It was a collaborative atmosphere, so there are certain things that I feel people took credit for in the making of that record that really came from me. At the time I was so concerned with getting it all together and driving us forward without losing all that momentum from touring that I didn't take credit for a lot of things that were all my idea. Now that I know more about publishing and songwriting, a lot of the credits on those songs would have been listed differently. I'm not saying I didn't get my credits. I am just saying that the collaborative environment among the people within the group and the people hanging around our studio during the creation of the record, that got more of them listed with specific credits than should have been.

This doesn't apply only to me, by the way. My cousin Jerry "Wonder" Duplessis, who I gave that nickname, was a big part of those sessions. He earned that title during the recording of *The*

Score because he brought wonder to the tracks. He did so much more than he's credited with, too. He was the spirit of the project and he was the backbone of that record, but since he wasn't some huge producer yet, his contributions were downplayed. Jerry's skills tripled through the making of that record and he came into his own afterward, but I was still fifty yards ahead of him.

I had new ideas about everything we did. On my cover of "No Woman, No Cry," I decided to detune my electric guitar completely so that it sounded like an acoustic. I didn't have an acoustic at the time, but if you listen to that song you'd never know it because I was able to make my guitar sound like the original. The song "Manifest," which is the outro of the record, I wrote from the perspective of a composer or a screenwriter-director starring in his own picture. I had the whole record in my mind, and at times I was like a dictator, telling Lauryn and Pras, "This is the story we're telling; this is how our movie is going to be." If you think about *The Score* as a film, I am the one who wrote the plot and assigned everyone their roles. I gave them their motivation when they didn't know what it was in a particular scene. I was always the one driving things, but everyone else's role was equally important; that's for sure.

One song that brings that whole period of time back to me is "Mista Mista." It's a simple tune, just me and my guitar, but I'll never forget the night I wrote it. It wasn't something I pored over; I just came home to the studio drunk out of my mind after a long night out at a club, so what you're hearing on that track is the sound of Wyclef recording intoxicated.

I don't remember where I was, but I stumbled home that night, passing a homeless guy that was one of the local crackheads we all knew. He asked me for a dollar, because he always asked me for a dollar.

"Mista, can I get a dollar so I can get the hell off this street?"

"No, man."

"Can I get a dollar so I can go get me something to eat?"

"No, man. You know damn well if I give you a dollar you gonna go smoke crack."

"No, no, Mista, I don't do that no more. I'm drug-free! I'm drug-free!"

His words and his face kept going around in my mind all the way to my door. When I got to the studio, I picked up the guitar, pressed Record and what you hear is what came out. Sometimes it's just right the first time.

That wasn't the case with Lauryn's masterpiece on *The Score*, "Killing Me Softly." Getting that song done was an album unto itself. If you want to know the meaning of perfectionist, go into the studio with Lauryn Hill when she has her mind set on something. That woman is a visionary and recording that song, to her, was paying respect to the history of soul. She spent a year on that song, because she'd been talking about it on the road at least that long, deciding if she wanted to do it—and if she could do it right, but make it her own.

Taking on a classic like that was stepping out for sure, and it didn't matter how much Pras and I encouraged her, she had to make that decision for herself. We knew she could do it, but only her vote counted, you understand?

I think the turning point was our relationship. As things got more complicated between us, that song came alive to her because she felt it in a very real way. It became a symbol of what was wrong and what was right between her and me, and because of that she wanted her version to be completely perfect. The thing was, we didn't have session musicians on hand to recreate that song properly for her, so we worked and worked on it to get the backing track to sound as close to the original as we could. It took weeks, all while she and I went through our ups and downs, so that process alone became a love affair of the deepest kind, in both heart and soul. We both had to get this track right; it meant everything. We didn't let ourselves say why, but we didn't have to. We both knew.

I enlisted what I call the Defender Rhodes to make that song swing the way it does. That's a series of pads on the S900 that when you sync them to your keyboard, it sounds just like a vintage seventies Fender Rhodes organ. I played it until I got the part right, and I messed with the drum tracks until it all came together.

Pras was the one who understood that the beauty of this cover was going to be its simplicity. I kept trying to add more sounds, more instrumentation, trying to capture the grandeur of the original. I wanted it to keep up with the depth of Lauryn's soul on those vocals. Pras was the one who turned my head around.

"No, man, we don't need any more music. You got to scale that back," he said. "Fuck the music. All we need is the break beat and the bass."

"You crazy, man," I said, shaking my head at him. "Do you hear what she's laying down? We can't just leave that out there without nothing else."

"You got to trust me, man. Just try it."

He was right. The break and the bass carried that whole record. Lauryn needed nothing else. On top of that simple arrangement made on my Defender Rhodes, Lauryn's voice is a dream, and I don't care what anyone says, I think she sounds better than Roberta on the original version. Maybe that's just because I feel the yearning in her voice, because I know where her pain is coming from. I'm sorry for causing it, but at the same time, I'm proud that we made something so beautiful out of a confusion we just couldn't help.

Let me give you an example of how intense this situation was. I knew that Lauryn and I were like fire and gasoline. I'm being real: when I decided to marry Claudinette, I made a life choice because she was the right woman for the life I wanted: a safe one. But at the same time I knew that our getting married wouldn't mean the end of Lauryn and me. That would be like asking the sun to shine only between the hours of noon and 5:00 PM, you understand what I'm saying to you? What I thought would happen was that Lauryn and I would continue to be together on the road, as a part of what we did together musically, until she fell in love with someone else and got married. That would be the only out: once we were both married, this affair would come to a natural end and we'd just be friends. Her marriage and pregnancy is what put an end to what we had, so I suppose I was right. Unfortunately the friendship part didn't come along the way I'd pictured it would. But long before that, everything came to the surface—which I didn't count on at all.

Claudinette knew that there was something going on aside from our musical relationship, and she called me out on that. She told me she wanted to talk to Lauryn face-to-face, not just one-on-one: she wanted me right there beside her, because, according to her, that was the only way she'd be able to understand what was really going on between us. So one night, when Claud and I were at home and this topic came up, she made me call Lauryn and ask her to drive over to our house. It was more like Claud had hijacked me: the whole time I was on the phone with Lauryn, Claud was hitting me over the head with the phone, nonstop. She needed this to happen before any more time went by. She was over this shit and she was going to figure out what the hell was going on.

Lauryn drove over in her car, and Claudinette and I came downstairs. Claudinette jumped in shotgun, right next to Lauryn, and I got in the backseat, thinking I'd never get out of there alive. The gig was up, man. I started sweating. I don't think it was summer—I have no idea—I don't even think Lauryn's car was heated, but I was sweating like I had malaria. I could not deal with this situation on any level. I had a death fever leaking out of me from head to toe.

"All I want to know is one thing," Claudinette said. "What is going on between the two of you?"

"We're making music together." Lauryn said. "That's what we do, it's intimate."

"It is," I said. "We have our own language." I could feel the sweat spilling over my brow and down my arm pits.

"I want to know what's going on besides the music," Claud said. "Is there something else going on between the both of you?"

The silence probably didn't last long, but in my mind it took ages and ages. No one was saying anything. I couldn't take it.

"I am in love with Lauryn, Claudinette," I said. "I'm *in love* with her."

Claudinette got out of the car and slammed the door as hard as she could. Lauryn turned the engine over and pulled away, driving down the street. I was still in the backseat losing my God-damned mind. I had spoken from the heart but I didn't know what I was saying. I was feeling; I loved them both and I had no idea beyond that.

A block later Lauryn pulled to a stop.

"Get out," she said.

"What?"

"Go home," she said. "Now. Get out of the car and go home, Clef."

I don't know if that's what I wanted to do but that's what I did.

Lauryn sped off, and I didn't look back as she did. I had one thing in mind: I ran back to Claudinette, back to our house. I got upstairs, but she was not willing to have anything to do with me. I didn't care; I started talking *at* her, just like a babbling idiot, but all that I said in that moment came from the heart. I meant all of it; I didn't want to lose her—no way. I knew that. Yet I also loved Lauryn; I knew that too. But I knew I'd be nothing without Claudinette. It was as if Claudinette was my foundation, my rock, and Lauryn was my dream. At the end of the day, only the foundation exists, only the rock can hold your weight.

I loved them both in such different ways, but how could I hope to say that? And I'd already looked Claudinette in the eye and told her that I was in love with Lauryn. Here she was sitting before me.

"Claud, let me explain," I said, "I know what I said, but I don't mean it. I'm in love with Lauryn. I am in love with her because we made music together. I know that doesn't make sense to you and I hope all you can do is let it go, but we made something together musically that is bigger that both of us. It's important and it's beautiful, and I love her for that, but I don't want to spend the rest of my life with her. We don't have that kind of love, like you and me. It's something different. I know I said I love her, but it's something different."

Claud was not having this. She just kept shaking her head slowly, looking like she wanted to kill me.

"This piece of music we are working on, Claud," I said, "it's incredible, you'll see. Lauryn and I made it together and that is why I love her. That is how I love her. It is really about the music."

There was no getting away from Claudinette's tractor beam.

"Get the fuck out of the car," Lauryn had said.

That moment, with both of the women I loved in one car, calling me out, defined my character. It put me to the test that I've done my best to pass ever since. I've been blessed with the kind of life where temptation is always in the wings, and I've done my best to avoid what brought King David down. Luckily when I've strayed, my life, Claudinette, has been my rock. We are together and we will never be rocked.

6

FUGEES ON FIRE

The Fugees were a family coming apart just as everything we'd worked for creatively was coming together. The drama between Lauryn and me threatened to tear us apart before the record even came out, so the success that followed was often hard to enjoy. All of the pressure that came with it was like dynamite tossed on a bonfire.

The Score got rave reviews everywhere, from *The Source*, where we got the coveted five mics, to *Vibe*, to *XXL*, to *Rolling Stone*, to the *New York Times*. The Fugees were called the second coming of conscious rap; a next generation's A Tribe Called Quest. We were different from Bigs and 'Pac and everything else. We were musicians, we were referencing soul music, we were talking about our times, and we had a female rapper as strong as the males.

The other side of having someone like Lauryn in the band, with a voice as beautiful as hers, is that critics immediately said that she should go solo and leave Pras and me behind. Her voice is something special, they said, while we were just a couple of average rappers from Haiti. The biggest haters said we should get back on the banana boat we rode over here and let the girl have a real career. That always bothered me, because in terms of composition and production, that album was mostly my doing. I've made a lot of music and I've won a lot of awards, and I've thought about all of this before now. But looking back on *The Score* today makes me call into question *The Source* magazine's rating system. Back in the day *The Source* was the bible of hip-hop, and we lived and died by those ratings. Four or five mics in *The Source* meant everything back in the nineties. We got five mics for *The Score*, but what I'm saying is, considering that I came up with the ideas for most of the music and a lot of the hooks, shouldn't I get five mics just for myself?

All that noise didn't matter; that shit didn't touch us at all, not even Lauryn. Because even though we were in the middle of our issues, she was loyal, and there was no way she was going to abandon her brothers after all we had done and been through together to make it.

The Score was the result of so many people's contributions, musically and in terms of the vibe that surrounded the Booga. But the truth is that album is nothing but the three core elements: Wyclef Jean, Lauryn Hill, and Pras Michel. Anyone can say what they like about which of us was more important and who has more talent, but if you took any of us out of that formula, that record would not be what it is. We were a team and if you take one out of the equation, you lose the magic.

That's not to say you'd never have heard of us otherwise. If it weren't for the Fugees, would Lauryn Hill have become famous? *Yes, she would have.* Would Wyclef Jean have become famous? *Yes, I would have.* I don't know what anyone else involved in the record would have done, from the musicians who played in the studio to the guest rappers to Jerry Wonder, even. They all might have gone on to do great things on their own. I do know that because they were involved with us, they went places faster, and got places they might have never been. *The Score* changed the game by taking intelligent hip-hop to the top of the pop charts. And it changed the lives of everyone associated with it.

If the Fugees had never come to be, Lauryn Hill would still have become a star, but I'm not sure if I would have become a professional musician. I think I would have ended up in the ministry in some way. I know I would have been a leader, because just like the men I'm named after, it's in my blood. If I devoted myself to the church, I would have risen high in those ranks because that is who I am. I've always been the son of a preacher man.

We came out strong on *The Score* and we made it big. To this day people still say that Lauryn was the real star and that Pras and I rode her coattails. If they want to believe that, I'm not going to waste time stopping them. If they look deeper at all of us as talents, they'll find the truth. We might have been one thing as a group, but if you look at us individually, you see where the talent is by what we did after the Fugees. If a group has hit songs together, you have to look at who has hit songs afterward. Who has the most? If you look at what I've released myself and what I've written for other artists like Shakira, I do. Lauryn and Pras had their moments, too, but I have the most hits to my name as a writer and producer. I'm not saying I'm any better; I'm just saying those are the facts.

When I think back on the Fugees, I realize that our album covers say it all. *Blunted* depicted a three-headed baby tied together, being held down by the hand of The Man. On *The Score*, that three-headed baby had cast itself in its version of *The Godfather*. We were out to settle the score—with all the critics and haters who'd heard our first album and thought we were shit and had nothing to say. Our album hit number 1, we had multiple hit singles, and less than a year after it came out, we'd sold over 6 million albums in America alone. We won a Grammy for "Killing Me Softly," and we stayed on the charts for the rest of that year and most of the next. All of the hip-hop critics who hated on *Blunted* became our biggest fans.

That album is fifteen years old and it still sounds fresh. When I hear it, I'm taken back to those times and to that little room where we did it all. The Booga Basement isn't there anymore, but the building still is. It's a house, but it's not the same house because a fire took the original down to the foundation. It doesn't matter; the soul of the Booga lives on. And all of that equipment we used is with me in my new Booga Basement, which is in a very humble room in Bloomfield, New Jersey. I do my mastering and proper recording in my studio in Manhattan, but I like to create and vibe out in a space closer to my roots, in the basement of a building that you would walk right by and not think twice. I feel anonymous there, and I like coming and going as I please. At Platinum Sounds there is a legacy of hits and plaques on the wall to prove it, but I don't want to see that when I'm creating. I write from my heart and I don't look to the past, only to what's inside and what is ahead of me that I have yet to achieve.

It didn't take us more than a few months to record *The Score*. *Blunted on Reality* took much longer, which seems crazy. The Score is who we really were, and putting yourself out there honestly is easy if you know yourself. The only pressure we felt making that record came from ourselves.

We hit the road to promote as soon as *The Score* came out, because we expected it to be another uphill battle over the course of a few years getting the word out there. But then our single charted, and then it hit number 1. Then our next single hit the top 10. Soon that tour schedule had no end in sight and we were playing huge venues in countries we'd never been to before. "Killing Me Softly" hit number 1 in the States while we were on tour in France, playing Paris. The French had loved the Fugees from the first, so it was nice to celebrate that milestone there.

"Hey Paris," I said, before we started the song. "Y'all always embraced us, so I'm happy to let you know something before anybody else in the world. This next song we gonna play for you just hit number 1 in America. I think you know the words, so let's do this one together."

The entire audience stood on their chairs and danced. They were jumping up and down, breaking those seats in two. They sang every word with us, and I'll never forget that moment.

As the tour offers kept coming, our label began to love us like they never had before. The minute "Killing Me Softly" hit the top of the charts, they packaged and released "Ready or Not," which was fine with me, because that was the only thing that could follow up Lauryn's performance on our first big hit. We had to come with something original, too, because we had made that first single our own, even though it was already Roberta Flack's hit.

The Fugees' train was rolling, and because we were making money for Columbia, I finally got my wish: a meeting with Tommy Mottola, who was the head of Columbia at the time and a legend in the business in his own right. I had asked for a meeting with him when we first got signed, but he had no interest in sitting down with some Haitian kid from the little Ruffhouse imprint. It took a number-1 single to get that meeting, and that's cool. I always told Lauryn and Pras we'd have a number 1, but the truth is, as great as I knew *The Score* was, I expected to sell something like five hundred thousand copies. I had no idea we'd do 20 million.

Meeting Tommy Mottola was more than just a symbolic thing for me, because I had been after a meeting with a guy with his kind of power ever since I interned at RCA Records back when I was fifteen. Working for Jan Berger, walking through those offices, all I kept wondering was, *Who is the guy at the top of all this? What's his office like? What is he like? What does it take to be the man on top like that?* I've always wanted to be a leader and I wanted to know what a guy who ran a huge international record label looked like. When I finally got my chance I discovered that Tommy was a real gentleman. He had us up to his office and I think he fed us some spaghetti. It was straight out of *Goodfellas*, and it was over before I knew it.

We kept going around the world, because our next single, "Fu-gee-La," hit the charts hard, too. The video for that song honors one of my favorite films, *The Harder They Come*, starring Jimmy Cliff. It's about a reggae star coming from nothing and making it out of the ghetto in Kingston, and becoming one of the top music stars of his time.

We were touring so much that being tired became my everyday state of mind. We were on planes, on buses, never stopping, always doing press or performing, making appearances, and being photo-graphed. It got to the point that a few times I even asked the road manager how many minutes we had to play to fulfill our contract, and I'd make sure we did not thirty seconds more even if we had time for another encore. It got to the point where one night, somewhere in America, I faked passing out at the side of the stage, just to cut the show short so I could get some sleep. I was put on oxygen and taken away in an ambulance. I got a little nap in there, then when I got to the hospital, I told them I was alright and asked to be taken back to my hotel. Pretending to pass out was the only way to not get sued by the promoter that night.

During that tour, in Amsterdam, I experienced my first coffee shop and being able to smoke as much weed as you want in there. There was liquid weed, cookies, and all of that, but that didn't in-terest me. I went for some variety called El Niño, around noon. Next thing I knew it was midnight and I'd not even left the place. I spent twelve hours there, until someone from the crew came and got me. From there we walked through the Red Light District, just looking at all the beautiful women on display. It felt like Sodom and Gomorrah or something.

When we played Shepherd's Bush Empire in London, I could not believe just how huge we had become. I looked over and I saw Mick Jagger in the balcony watching us. So I did the only thing that made sense to me: I climbed up the rigging to say hello to him. Mick fucking Jagger! I got right into his booth because I'm a maniac when

I perform and said, "Yo! Mick Jagger in the house!" And then our DJ dropped the beat to "Satisfaction." Moments like that change your idea of who you are and what your music means to the world.

As the energy of the Fugees spread further, our shows became events. We had always thrown ourselves into the performance, but now that our songs were connecting with people on a larger scale, the energy that came back at us every night was more intense than anything we had ever given out. All of this fueled the drama, too. The band and our tour was a pressure cooker waiting to explode. This strange kind of energy took us over, and it made the shows more intense, because we were performing songs that told the story of our relationship, all while it was still getting played out. Things between us went in cycles, so as we toured the world, certain countries ended up seeing us at our most raw, just because that's how the stars aligned. Our Japan dates stand out in my mind because they were really crazy. Japanese fans are intense to begin with, so the second we stepped off the plane we were like Michael Jackson or the Beatles to them. People swarmed us wherever we went and at every show the crowd knew every word to every song. Having those songs about Lauryn and me sung back to us like that was too much sometimes, and she and I got into it offstage like we never had before.

We discovered sake on that tour, too. We didn't know what it was; we were just kids from New Jersey. We were told it was made of rice, but we had no idea it was stronger than wine. It tasted refreshing and it looked like water, and we drank it like there was no tomorrow. Pras really got into it, and one night, we found out how much onstage.

It didn't seem like anything was really wrong until we got to Pras's first part in the first song. Lauryn and I finished our parts, then all of a sudden there was silence. I looked over to see that Pras had fallen off the front of the stage. He liked to party but he didn't have a drinking problem, so this kind of behavior was new to us.

But there he was, trying to go on with the show, lying there on his back, on the floor in front of the stage. It was a mess. He got out some of the words, and I filled in the rest of his verse. We made it through the rest of the set, because hitting that concrete definitely sobered him up. It was gonna take more than sake to take us out.

Back in the States we did photo shoot after photo shoot and in every interview, Lauryn and I kept our business out of the press. We never even had to talk about it: we knew what was best for the group, because that was bigger than both of us. Our little problems had no business being involved in our business, and we honored that. When we did interviews, we said that "Killing Me Softly" was so soulful because all of us were going through some issues at the time. Both Lauryn and I even talked about the fact that she is crying on the lead vocal take; we just didn't say why.

For me at least, it felt like if we stopped at all we'd lose momentum and everything would end. Opportunities kept coming at us, and I saw no reason not to take them. We lived every moment to the fullest, hopping planes for gigs overseas, award shows, magazine cover shoots, tours of our own—just about everything. I was aware that this moment was special and that it was a peak that might not last, so I decided that we should do something that would mean everything to me and Pras while that window was open. I realized that we had to give back to the culture that had shaped who we were and we had to use our influence while we had it.

"We got to go to Haiti."

I know that a lot of what I say sounds like I'm bragging, but without my ambitions I would have died quietly a long time ago. I always held Bob Marley in my mind as a role model who represented his culture, and now that we had achieved some success and I had the attention and influence to do so, I organized a concert down in Haiti. This was the beginning of my efforts to bring the world's focus to my native land, which is something I intend to do for the rest of my life.

Bob Marley, like Jesus Christ, led a life that has inspired just about everyone his music has touched. He united the poor in Jamaica and devoted his life to informing the rest of the world about the plight and culture of his people. As a man who began his life in a hut with a dirt floor and now lives in a mansion in New Jersey with Grammys on the mantle, I feel that it is my responsibility to do all I can. I'm not a legend like Bob Marley, but I am going to try my best to do for Haiti what he did for Jamaica. If I can do a fraction of that I'll be satisfied.

We had the attention of MTV by that point, so I approached them and asked them to fund and to broadcast our concert. They agreed, and before I knew it, we were at the mayor's office in Port-au-Prince. Then we did a show for something like half a million fans. You can see it on the telecast: there were people as far as the eye could see. Everything we had done to get there was worth it and of all the shows we ever played, that one meant the most to me.

It was the most appreciative crowd we saw in our entire career. These were people who looked to music as a language that they shared, who struggled every day just to survive, so this was a tremendous event for them. That day I felt the energy of the people because I was home. That spirit of togetherness is what will carry Haiti into the future because it has always been in our character. That moment planted the seed and drove me to start my charity, Yéle, and years later, get involved in Haitian politics. Yéle is a term that I coined that means, "Cry freedom," and that is what I hope all of my work and influence will help the people of my homeland to do.

We sold tickets for that concert but the money we were hoping to raise didn't reach the people the way we intended it to, which is the most important lesson I took away from the experience. After our Haitian relief show, we went off to Europe to accept at an awards show and to start another leg of our tour, so we weren't on top of the situation. When we got back to America a few weeks later, I learned that somehow no funds were donated. We had organized everything through the government in power at the time, and trusted them to collect money for tickets. When we came to them asking how no money had been made on the show, they claimed that somehow every single one of the half a million who came to see us had slipped through the gates. When a system is imbalanced, no matter what your intention, it is always those who need the least that receive the most.

I never forgot the lesson I learned: if I were going to help my native land, I couldn't trust the system, even the members of it who embraced me with smiles and open arms. The only ones I could trust to take care of business were those I'd entrust with my life. If I were ever to build a bridge from America to Haiti, I needed to start from scratch and lead by example. It wasn't an easy solution, but it didn't scare me. I understood that it would take years to get it right, but I didn't mind because I was ready to give all the time I had.

AS A MAN I have a purpose, and that focus came to me back then, because I realized who I really am. I am a Haitian first and an American second, and that feeling for my homeland has centered me ever since. I have always been concerned with my trajectory as an artist, but from that point, at the height of the Fugees' career, I began to take into account my responsibility to the culture that shaped me. I also began to see that I could use the influence of my success to focus the attention where it was needed. That desire within me felt natural and at the time, it was one of the only things that I knew without a doubt to be stable and unchanging.

It wasn't easy to see something that had begun so beautifully become so destructive, but that was the truth and there was no running from it. My relationship with Lauryn had become too intense for either of us to continue, and it was putting stress on both my marriage and the group. The tension was there when I was home and the drama was there when I was on the road. I was a part of it all and all of it was nonstop—this never-ending roller coaster—because I loved two women but I could only have one. I loved them both for who they are, and I loved them so differently because they are so different—and both so beautiful. I'd made a choice and I was sticking to it, but my decision didn't put an end to the story because you can't just stop loving. It has to fade away or die because something happens to kill it. You can't cut love off overnight because the heart wants what it wants, and it sure as hell don't heed the mind. Lauryn and I weren't going to leave each other alone, plain and simple.

After *The Score* and the Fugees had taken over the world, after the awards were won and the touring was over, we all took a break, because we needed that more than you know. We had won a huge victory but we had fallen to pieces in the process. Lauryn and I could hardly be in a room together when we weren't performing, because we had no more words to say; if we started, it was anyone's guess where we'd end up. She wanted to be with me and I still loved her, so we were together sometimes, even though I was married and she hated that. It wasn't fair to her, but we didn't stop it—because we couldn't stop it. To make matters worse, even though I was married, and I knew once she was married all of this between us would stop, I still got jealous when I knew she was interested in other dudes. It's not rational thought, and I don't expect you to understand it, but the kind of passion that defies logic is the type of love she and I had together. Something dramatic had to happen to our relationship because we both knew that I wasn't going to leave her alone and she wasn't going to leave me alone.

Let me rewind here for a moment, because I need to tell you that our concert for Haiti was a pivotal moment for the Fugees internally, too. Afterward, nothing was the same, because it captured the pivotal event that changed everything between Lauryn and me. Anyone who has seen the footage might notice that Lauryn Hill was pregnant at that time. While we played those songs I believed that her child was mine, and I'd believed that for the eight months leading up to that moment. That baby wasn't mine, and thank God it wasn't, because I didn't know what I was going to do if it were.

Only after her son Zion was born did I learn the truth, but now when I look back at things, I know what went down. Of course I'm only guessing, but I remember when we had a quick break between shows, months before the Haitian concert, Lauryn went to Jamaica while Pras and I went home, and then the three of us all met up again in England to continue our tour. Lauryn spent that time with Rohan Marley, who she remained with for years, but after that trip she told me that she'd been with him romantically. I would have known it even if she'd lied because she showed up with an acoustic guitar that wasn't hers. It was sitting there deliberately on display in her dressing room.

"What's that?" I asked her, when I walked in.

"It's a guitar," she said, leveling her eyes at me.

I went over and picked it up. It was well worn and broken in. "You don't play guitar, and this one isn't new. So it belongs to someone who played it a lot."

"Maybe I'm going to learn."

I felt my blood boiling. "Who got you that fucking guitar?"

I was mad as hell because I knew she'd been with that dude, and I knew it wasn't fair, but I was jealous and mad at her for it. We got into it, and eventually she told me the truth. When I heard it, I got so upset that I smashed the wineglass in my hand on the table, and the entire stem of it went into my palm. I started bleeding everywhere, and though I was in pain, I kept yelling at her. I couldn't control myself even though I knew I had no right. In the end, we talked it out, and she made me feel comfortable with whatever had happened by telling me the least that she had to. When you love someone you are willing to believe things that make no sense, or that you might not otherwise believe if you are thinking clearly. I came into the conversation feeling the truth, which was that they had been together, but I left her room believing that nothing serious had happened between them. That's what I wanted to hear, even though I knew it wasn't true. I let my heart trick my mind, which is a dangerous thing to do.

For the next nine months, I assumed her child was mine. It was easy to do as we rode the wave of success. In my mind, it was complicated and dangerous, but it was beautiful, too: if Lauryn and I had a child together, it was, to me, a product of our music and everything we'd worked to achieve. It made sense to my heart, as much as I knew it was wrong in my mind. If that's what it came down to, I knew I would be honest with Claudinette and hope I didn't lose her, just the way I knew I would do right by our child and so would Lauryn. I was proud of it when we performed in Haiti, because Lauryn was visibly pregnant. So to me, we were playing a concert for my people with our child growing inside her.

When Lauryn gave birth, I learned the truth: the child wasn't mine, it was Rohan Marley's. And in that moment something died between us. I was married and Lauryn and I were having an affair, but she had led me to believe that the baby was mine, and I couldn't forgive that. This killed our trust in my mind, and it caused us to start drifting apart. But the reason the Fugees broke up—or faded away—wasn't just that. Things changed when Lauryn had her child; that event broke the spell between us. After that we both saw that she and I were going separate ways. I saw it when she deceived me, but when she had her son she saw clearly that she was going to do her thing and I was going to do mine. She could no longer be my muse. Our love spell was broken through her creation.

As all of this came to a head within the band, my marriage was hitting the rocks as well. Claudinette could tell that I was distraught over Lauryn's child with Rohan and she confronted me about my feelings for her and whether we had been together in the recent past. I didn't lie to her about anything, so she did what she should have done: she told me to move out and figure out what the hell it was I wanted. I already knew—I wanted her—but I moved out like she asked me to, into an apartment on Sixty-Sixth Street on the West Side of Manhattan.

I remember sitting there in my new living room, looking around, peeping out the window at the view. I could see Central Park, all of that, and to the naked eye, I should have felt accomplished. I had come from living in a closet off of a basement that I called a studio to traveling the world, playing for millions of people, and enjoying an expensive view of Manhattan. I had more friends and contacts than I could count and my new home had everything I'd never had in terms of comforts, but I had never felt so lonely in my entire life.

That is where I started writing the music for *The Carnival*. I didn't know what my life was going to become, and I thought I'd lost both of the women I loved. I was alone for the first time since I was a kid, and I wondered to myself what was going to happen to me. I still had feelings for Lauryn but I knew I didn't even want her, and I was pretty sure she didn't want me either. Claudinette and I didn't have any children, so we could part without hurting anyone else. I was thankful for that but I didn't want to get my head around the idea of losing her at all. I had moved into a beautiful home, but I felt like a man with no home at all for the first time since that winter night my dad kicked me out. I had nowhere to turn, so I did the only thing I could do: I turned to music and I turned to writing lyrics and I started pouring my heart out in song.

Lauryn was doing the same thing. She wrote *The Miseducation of Lauryn Hill* during this time and if you look at both records, each is like a mirror of the other. She might not agree, but that's my opinion. Those two records are the end of us. They are what was left from that beautiful star going supernova.

I locked myself in my new apartment with all of the records that had ever meant anything to me. I had all of my mom's country records, all the soul music Lauryn had given me, and all the reggae that Renel and his family had exposed me to. It literally was everything that had influenced who I had become as an artist, and I sat there going through it all, trying to forget the Fugees. I tried to forget my success because I wanted to start fresh. As far as I was concerned, all that I knew before was gone. I had nothing, not even an idea of what kind of music I wanted to make as a solo artist. It's hard for me to even remember which song I wrote on *The Carnival* first, because all of it was a big blur. I was there alone: wife gone, *The Score* was over. Too much drama had delivered me to this place. It was me and a room full of records, doing music to help my mind escape, which was my cure in the end.

The Carnival sold over 5 million copies and had a bunch of hit singles, including, "Gone Till November," "Guantanamera," and "To All the Girls." That last one really spelled out where I was at the time.

> *To all the girls I loved before*
> *To all the girls I cheated on before*
> *It's a new year*
> *I got a change of gear, I swear*
> *I can see clearly now, the clouds disappeared.*

Meanwhile Lauryn was writing *The Miseducation of Lauryn Hill*, which she recorded for the most part in Jamaica, at Tuff Gong Studios, where the Wailers did most of their work. She was there with Rohan, with whom she went on to have four more kids, even though he was still married to someone else. I can't speak for her, but I don't think Lauryn knew about this until she was already pregnant. Rohan had gotten married years before, had two children with that girl, and when things didn't work out, never divorced. He and Lauryn kept having children and just continued on unmarried because he couldn't legally marry her. The perception in the media, though, is that the two of them were a married couple, because over the years Lauryn openly referred to Rohan as her husband in the press. These days I don't think they're together anymore, but what do I know.

She might have been with him in Jamaica at the time, but musically and lyrically she was still with me. Her whole album was about her trying to make sense of our relationship, and when I listen to *Miseducation*, it's like reading a diary of our personal history. There are lyrics and references that only two people in the world could know and understand, and you're here reading one of them. Her album went on to sell 7 million copies. She also won five Grammys and hit number 1 on the album charts her first week out. After that album, which was a major work for that year, Lauryn disappeared from the public eye and has remained pretty private as an artist ever since. Every single fan and friend of hers has their theory about why she's done this or how this happened, and I'm sure all of you reading this have yours, too.

A lot of people blame me for what has become of Lauryn since then, and the fact that she's not out and about in the music industry. If you've read this far, you have to understand that she and I had a very complicated relationship, and I'll take the blame for my side of the pain and confusion. No doubt, my marriage to Claudinette hurt her, but the fact that she more or less left music behind can't be explained away that simply. Her relationship with Rohan Marley changed her life, as did becoming a mother five times over. I think she's had a hard time in her relationship with Rohan and faced her challenges raising all of those children. It just makes me sad that Lauryn hasn't been out there making music, because she's got a real gift and I wish she would share it with the world.

Pras is someone who definitely blames me for the Fugees breaking up. We never really broke up, by the way, we just stopped talking about getting together to record again. In any case, Pras has made it clear to me that he thinks I'm responsible, and I understand why he feels this. It's because he had to manage Lauryn and me when we became a couple on the road. Every time we fought, he was in the middle, keeping us focused, telling jokes, doing whatever he could to stop things from getting too crazy. Pras was the glue that kept the Fugees together. He did everything he could, but there was no helping it from self-destructing, and he's bitter about that. I understand, but I don't think he's asked himself the most important question: if he were the one in my shoes, would he have thought twice about doing as I did? Would he have resisted being with her? He's never answered that question, but I don't care what he says. He'd do the same thing I did, and I wouldn't blame him for it if he did. But that's just my opinion of course.

Everyone always wonders about a Fugees reunion, probably as much as I do. I wouldn't put it past us, but I wouldn't put my money on us either. We have many rivers to cross if we're going to find our way home. First of all, the thing keeping it from happening is bigger than Lauryn and me. It's all of us.

Pras has to realize how important he always was to the musical chemistry of the Fugees. I don't think fans even understand how important he was to the artistic connections within the band. Pras loves music, and he always heard things in the studio and added to what we were doing in ways that are not obvious to the people listening to the result. I think Pras feels that he was like the Tito Jackson of the Fugees—included in everything but forgotten by all. That wasn't what it was like. Whenever Pras came in and did his 8 bars of rapping on our tracks, it added something we needed. I always tried to make his additions strategic because for me, whenever Pras was going to lay it down, things might get weird in the sense that the entire tone of the track might change. It would usually be a good thing that opened up your eyes and ears, but if it arrived in the wrong place, it might take the song to pieces.

That is why I let Pras do his thing when we did try to get back together, following our reunion for the film Dave Chappelle's *Block Party* in 2006. We hadn't played together in over seven years and all three of us loved doing our songs for a hungry crowd in Brooklyn. It had been long enough that it seemed like we could start again, so we went into the studio and tried to record some music. We did one track, "Take It Easy," and I let Pras go. My intention was to do a mix tape together, and let Pras do a few tracks even on his own if he wanted to. If we were going to come back, I felt like we had to drop some shit for the streets since we'd been away for so long.

None of that came to pass, even though we did a bunch of music together before we hit a wall. Each of us had reasons why we couldn't go on, but looking back, I think there's only one: the chemistry wasn't there. And now that I've had time to think about it, I know why.

Lauryn is an amazing talent, but she needs to be directed. She needs a strong influence that she trusts to steer her creatively. Back in the day, she trusted me in the studio, but that trust is gone. After all we'd been through, it didn't matter how much time had passed, she wasn't going to let me fill that role again. She wasn't going to turn herself over to me as her producer. It's sad that we can't get back to a place where she can just think of me as her big brother. I know that is asking the impossible, but the Fugees are used to accomplishing the impossible. I really thought we could get there after that much time apart, but I was wrong.

I didn't expect things to be just like they were fifteen years ago when we got in the studio together again, but I didn't expect her to be as opinionated about the direction she wanted everything to go. She wasn't ready to bend from that, not even on one detail, so the sessions couldn't progress at all. She and I knew what was fresh and what wasn't, just like we always did. But when I talk about direction, what I mean is that she didn't want to take any direction from me—like nothing, not even a suggestion.

It's too bad, because in every country I go to, I'm always asked when the next Fugees album will come out. In some places we are like the Beatles. That is why Bono once called us the hip-hop Beatles, and I've never forgotten it.

That was an impressive thing for him to say, because I never saw us that way. I just saw three kids talking about their generation. We wanted to show people our age and everyone else that kids from the suburbs and kids from the 'hood could get together, and that we had more in common than we had differences. We showed them that kids from the 'hood weren't savages and that the stereotype of what was being promoted wasn't always true. We showed the world that kids like us could sing passionate songs. We could smile, make love, and be happy. Life could still be fun for us and we could all have the same dream and pursue the same life, all of us together. We took that message across the water and around the world. Hip-hop didn't have to be about thug life; it could be just about life. And we should celebrate that, because life is a precious gift, and everyone's life is different.

I never say never, but I don't think we'll be able to get the Fugees back together. I'd like to, but I think the magic is gone once and for all. It comes down to trust, and that is what we lost when we followed our hearts where our minds told us not to go.

7

WHEN THE
CIRCLE BROKE

There was just one thing more bittersweet about my success than my drama with Lauryn: my father and I were not able to celebrate all that I achieved as it happened. I had gone against his wishes, and made a career in hip-hop, which he considered bum music, so he did not really want to hear about what I was doing. He understood that I had a group and that I was touring and that my music was supporting me as my occupation, but he did not ask questions about it, and he had no idea of the magnitude of the impact my music was having.

As for it being bum music, all I can say to that is that anyone who has listened to a Fugees song understands that our group was the furthest thing from bum music, by which my father meant gangsta rap or anything that glamorized the drug trade and violence. Bum music was what the hustlers and dealers in the 'hood listened to, so he associated anything that had the same beat and the same swagger with the culture that was destroying the community. The Fugees spoke the same language, but we weren't saying the same things.

We were conscious and we had a message; we told our own stories and those stories represented what much of our generation was going through beyond the street tales that we heard on the radio all the time. Critics called us the most cohesive unit since Tribe Called Quest, and said that our eclecticism set us apart from every other group of the day. Even if he had read those reviews, it wouldn't have made a difference to my father, because that boom-bap hip-hop break beat meant nothing but bum music to him.

When I was home from tours, visiting my parents, he and I spoke about the church, about our relatives, about the family, about everything but what I was doing on the road. It was like I was still in school and living at home: I was expected to come to services, and I did, and that was that. My mom understood things a little bit more, maybe because my brothers and sisters explained it all to her. She was proud of me and I think she understood how popular the group was, but still she didn't really translate that to my dad. Or maybe she did; I don't know. All I do know is that my father acted like it wasn't any big deal, almost like it wasn't making me a living. It didn't matter that we were playing sold-out shows and making money; he saw it as a waste of time or some little diversion like Exact Change.

I wanted him to understand the magnitude, not only because I was proud of what my group was doing, but also because I wanted him to know that I had made something of myself. I wanted him to be proud that how he'd raised me worked; he may not have raised a church man like John Wycliffe, but he'd raised a leader like Toussaint Jean. I was a visionary in that sense, like he was. And like my father in his own way.

I wanted to find some way for my father and me to get on the same side of the invisible fence that stood between us. I wanted him to realize, as I had begun to, that he and I were more alike than different. It should be clear by now that my father was a proud man, so proud that he never believed in taking money from his own church for his salary. Until the day he died, he always worked at least one day job. When we were kids, he worked a few. He did janitor shifts at a few local hotels, cleaning bathrooms in the bars and lounges on weekends. I used to go with him, and I remember hearing cover bands doing songs by Bruce Springsteen. I learned to love songs like "Born in the U.S.A.," which had a whole other layer of meaning to an immigrant like me.

During the years that the Fugees were at the top, my father worked for Donald Warnock, who owned a car dealership. My dad drove cars from one location to another, he worked in the garage doing oil changes, he washed cars, or he took care of anything else that needed to be done in the service and delivery departments. One day he was working with this Mexican brother, both of them under the hood.

"Hey Jean," the guy said, because all of the Mexicans called him Jean. "You know something? You look like this guy who is a singer. He is in a group called the Fugees."

"I don't know what you are talking about," my father said.

"Jean, you look like this guy. His forehead, it's just like you. His nose, it's the same as you. And his last name is the same as you, too."

"What is his first name?"

"Wyclef."

"His name is Wyclef?" my father said. "That is my son."

"Wyclef Jean is your son? Then what the hell are you doing here, man? He is a big superstar! You're funny, Jean. That's not your son, man."

"I am telling the truth. Wyclef Jean is my son."

"Okay Jean! Sure he is. If Wyclef Jean was your son, you wouldn't be working at Don Warnock. You would be owning Don Warnock!"

My father called me that night, out of the blue, which was unusual. If it weren't an occasion of some sort, that usually meant something was wrong.

"Everything alright, Dad?"

"Yes, everything is fine. Everyone is fine. I have a question for you."

"Alright."

"What is it that you do?"

I wasn't expecting that, and I wasn't sure how I wanted to answer it either. We'd had this kind of unspoken agreement to not talk about the bum music I'd made it my life's business to make. I hadn't prepared for this day at all because I never expected him to ever ask me about it.

"Dad, you remember when I was younger and I told you I was into rap and that I'd joined this group called the Fugees, which was short for refugees?"

"You were making the bum music, the rap music, yes? Is that what you mean?"

"I know you think all rap is hoodlums and thugs and street music and gangs and drug addicts, but it's not, Dad. It's just a style of music and a way of telling stories. I write lyrics about my life, but all of my inspiration is from the Bible."

"I only hear bum music. Those kinds of people are the only ones I see listening to this kind of music."

"I understand that, but it is not all the same. My group does something different and I think you'd really like it. We don't talk about any of that. I turn to everything I learned from you in the church when I write lyrics."

"That is good."

"I think if you let me play some of it for you, you would understand."

He was silent for a long moment. "Okay," he said. "Come to church this Sunday. After the service we will sit and talk about what it is you do."

When my dad opened the door that day, I was ready to walk through it. Our differences weren't that much different than what had kept him and his father from seeing eye to eye. And though my father never told me directly how that affected him in his life, I know that it weighed on his mind. He never had the chance to build that bridge before his father passed.

"Dad, hip-hop doesn't have to be all about drugs and violence," I said. "It's a way to tell a story. It's just the backdrop, like a Bible song that retells something from scripture in a different way."

"And do you need to use profanity to tell these stories?"

"Sometimes I do. Sometimes it's necessary to make a point."

"What is the story that you are trying to tell people?"

"We talk about our lives and who we are and where we come from. We talk about the world around us. It's just life, and out in the world, people do use profanity once in a while, Dad."

"Try not to do that, son."

"Okay, Dad, I will. What most of my songs are about are Bible stories. I look at people I know or situations I come across in my life, and the first thing I do when I go to put them into a song is to think of which Bible story relates to my story the most. Then I use the knowledge in the Bible as my guide and my metaphor when I write my lyrics. It's just like what you do in your sermons."

He scratched his beard and looked at me a long time. "I think I understand this. You keep putting the Good Book in your words and you will spread knowledge."

"That is what I'm trying to do, Dad. I also tell everyone that will listen about Haiti and where we come from. It's a very big part of what we do."

"And the people like your music? They come to see you play?"

"They do, Dad. A lot of them. All over the world."

He nodded at me. "Then this is okay with me, son," he said. "But one thing."

"What, Dad?"

"Try not to use profanity."

Something passed between my father and me that day, and from that point forward we had a man-to-man relationship. He and I were so alike that we had to oppose each other while I was growing up, but in our hearts we were the same. We might have chosen different churches to worship in to spread our gospel, but as different as they were, our goals as leaders were the same.

Now that my father is gone, I am grateful that he and I found a way to see eye to eye, because if we hadn't, he would never have seen me play Carnegie Hall. It was a concert I called the All Star Jam that I organized to raise money for underprivileged inner-city youth through the Wyclef Jean Foundation in 2001. My debut double album, *The Carnival* had been such a success that I leveraged that attention to get this event together, and managed to get some big names as well, from Stevie Wonder to Eric Clapton to Marc Anthony to Mary J. Blige to Macy Gray. And it all went down on one of the most historic stages in the world. Carnegie Hall has a long history of classical music and jazz performances, but in terms of rock and roll and pop music, only the very best like the Beatles, Ike and Tina Turner, and Pink Floyd have played there. There is nothing like that building and that room; the acoustics are perfect and every seat in the house is, too. I couldn't believe it when my manager at the time said that the Hall had agreed to host the show there.

It was going to be a night to remember for me, but still I was nervous that my dad might not come. I called him right away and begged him to come to see it. This was a big thing, because in all these years, he'd never come to see me perform my own music anywhere. I hoped that since he'd heard of Stevie Wonder and Eric Clapton he'd realize that this wasn't some ordinary concert for me. The best thing I had going for me was that it was Carnegie Hall—he would definitely respect that—but I still had only a fifty-fifty chance.

Let me explain something: my father didn't care about how important some event was to anyone else in the world; he only did what he wanted to do. I'm talking about a man who turned down an opportunity to come to the White House with me to meet Bill Clinton. It's true. I was invited to an event there and was allowed to bring my parents. My father's response? "I do not want to meet Bill Clinton. My question to you is this: why do *you* want to meet Bill Clinton? He will not do anything for you! He is going to use you for his own image. I do not go. And you—you should not go!"

My father was so stubborn that he refused to go to the hospital or the doctors' office regularly even when he felt sick. "Why would I go to get checked up?" he would ask. "I already know I am sick, just as I know I will get well. If I go to the hospital now they will take my blood, and I will see that blood no more. They will have that piece of me and they will put that blood in a blood bank. Then they will sell it for money. I do not go!"

What I'm trying to explain to you is that I had to come up with some kind of a pitch to get this guy to Carnegie Hall. Anybody else's parent would have gone even if they didn't like their child's music. They would have gone just to see their kid lead an all-star cast for charity. That wasn't going to be enough to get my father there. So I told him that I was performing jazz and world music with the Philharmonic Orchestra, and that it wasn't rap at all. This wasn't true, but it worked.

He was silent for a long time, the way he was when he was considering something. You never knew which way he was going to go. "Are you doing church music, too?"

"Yes, Dad, we are doing church music. I've got Whitney Houston coming out to do—"

"I do not know that person."

"She's a singer, Dad. . . ."

"What kind of music does she sing?"

It went on like this for days and weeks, until finally he agreed to come. I felt like I had climbed Mount Everest single-handedly.

My dad and mom sat in the balcony with the rest of my family in a box overlooking the stage, which I couldn't see at all when all of the bright lights hit my face. I wasn't positive that he was even there when the show started; with my dad you never knew if he might change his mind at the last minute. But he didn't. At that point in his life, my father had a long white beard and that night he wore all of his ministerial robes and looked like a regal Haitian diplomat. My siblings said he sat there very stately, taking all of it in, not really reacting to anything all night. That wasn't unusual; he was a serious and stern man, who always looked unimpressed and unmoved by anything that didn't involve his faith.

In the middle of the performance, when the show was really cooking, I stopped everything.

"Hold up, hold up. This is the best night of my life," I said to the audience. "Want to know why? My dad is in the balcony, y'all!"

Everybody started cheering.

"He's right up there. Can we get a spotlight on him? Everybody, say 'what's up' to my dad."

The audience went crazy, shouting and hollering at him, and in that spotlight I saw something that made all the hard times between us worth it: I saw my dad break into the biggest smile I had ever seen on his face in my entire life. He was beaming from ear to ear, belly laughing, taking it all in. He put his seriousness aside for just that moment, and he relished all of the love coming his way. Seeing him with his guard down, enjoying this time with me, still means the world to me. For that moment, he allowed himself to stop being Gesner Jean, the minister who must demonstrate piety and devotion by example. For that moment, he was Gesner Jean, the proud father of the young man onstage. I feel so lucky that I was able to see him in that light. He and I were on the same page for once. It felt like he understood and it felt like he respected and accepted me.

After the concert my dad came backstage and, God bless him, he was still smiling.

"Now let me tell you something, son," he said, his smile fading into his usual serious stare.

Oh no, I thought. He hated it.

"Do you know what it means to finally make it?"

"I do not know, Dad. . . . Success?"

"No, there is something greater than success, because success is only what others give you. Success comes from what they think of you, not from what you think of yourself. Only you can define your success. There is something more. If you have every race in one place: if you have black, white, and Asian, if you have dignitaries, if you have presidents of corporations all in one place to see you, and none of them sees your color, they only see the man, then you have finally made it. That should be your success. Only then when your color is invisible are you the man. And that, my son, is what I saw here tonight."

I thank God every day for that moment.

ON SEPTEMBER 7, 2001, I was in the studio working on my album *Masquerade* when I got the call. I was in the middle of figuring out a part, playing something and seeing where the music took me, so I ignored the flashing light, which meant an outside call was coming in from the switchboard.

My engineer answered it and from the look on his face I knew it was serious. It was my mother.

"Your father is in an ambulance and his pulse is very weak," she said. "They aren't sure he's going to make it to the hospital. There has been an accident."

I doubled over, because my stomach had fallen through my feet. Tears poured from my eyes before I could even get a word out.

"What . . . happened to him?"

"He was pinned under the Bentley."

The rest of the day was a daze. Jerry Wonder got me into a car and we drove to the hospital.

As I've told you, my father had always worked on cars. He loved them, and he understood the mechanics, the engineering, and everything about the history of the automobile. Long after he needed to, he kept his job at Don Warnock's dealership and never even accepted promotions because he liked to get his hands greasy in engines. He was the kind of guy who could tell you what year a Cadillac or Chevy from the forties or fifties was from half a block away, so as soon as I was able to, I gave my father a gift that I knew he would appreciate and would never have gotten for himself, even if he were able to: I got him a 1991 Bentley.

That gift killed him, a tragic accident that still haunts me to this day. The morning was cold, so he turned the engine over to let it heat up while the car was still in the garage. He was going to take a drive with my mother. He didn't get all the way into the car to start it, instead he opened the driver's door, turned the ignition, and then reached one foot in to push down on the gas pedal to rev the engine. In the process of doing this, he slipped the car into reverse, so when he pushed down on the gas, the car was launched backward. Since he was half in and half out of the car, the front wheel rolled over one of his legs, pulling him out of the car and onto the ground. The Bentley kept going until it hit the garage door, rolling right over my father's chest.

As Jerry sped us to the hospital, I felt in my heart that he was already gone. I just knew it. It was like a black cloud in my heart and there was no lifting it. The doctor at the hospital didn't even have to open his mouth. His face said it all when he came out of the operating room.

"We lost him."

I fell to my knees, inconsolable, crying. Then I rose to my feet and demanded to see his body. They brought me to the room where he had passed. His body had been severely injured and I understood that, but to me he still looked so strange: the strongest man I'd ever known with the life crushed out of him. This couldn't be happening. His face, though, was at peace. That gave me some sense that things were okay. I took him in for the last time. I went up and kissed his forehead.

"Good-bye Dad. All is good now. I love you."

I MOURNED MY FATHER every day after he passed, because he was always close to my heart and in my mind, even during those years when we couldn't find a common language to speak to each other. We finally understood each other, and in the year before he died I believed that we respected each other in a way we never had before. It made his passing weigh even more heavily on me in every way. The days after he died were surreal, because four days later was September 11, 2001, a day no American, New Yorker, or citizen of the world will ever forget. While mourning my father, I mourned the terrorist attacks on the Twin Towers. It just felt like a bad dream I couldn't wake up from. Not even Psalm 23 could save me.

I'm not a man who cries often, but at my father's funeral I broke down and couldn't stop. I felt like the foundation I had built my character on was taken away from me and I lost all sense of focus in that moment. It was a very trying time for the world in general. I responded to all of that loss by forgetting who I was for a time, and making a series of mistakes for the next few years. I betrayed my marriage and I went astray. It's taken me even longer to make those errors right, but I learned something valuable every step of the way.

My wife, Claudinette, always believed in me, back when I had no money, when I was just a teenager and she already knew what she wanted out of life. Both she and her family supported me financially and emotionally since the day they took me in. That kind of compassion and loyalty are why she and I are still married today. She always gave me shelter, she always nurtured me, and she made me believe I could do what I wanted to do every time I doubted myself.

In 2005, Claudinette and I adopted our daughter, Angelina, and she brought us even closer together. If you look into the lives of many of our world leaders, you will find that the woman that stays with them for life is a woman that they met when they were young, who knew them better than anyone else. No matter what happens during their career, no matter what skeletons come out or what trash is thrown around in the media, the most dedicated women stay with their men. Those couples have an understanding that runs deeper than the average boundaries of a marriage.

I have not been faithful, several times over, but my wife and I have always found a way to work it out. In the eyes of the world, and on the blogs and Internet message boards, people are always asking, "Why the hell does she stay with him?" People even write to Claudinette directly, saying, "You should have left his ass a long time ago." There are women out there everywhere who flap their gums around Claudinette telling her that they'll fix me. They'll get Vodou too, saying things like "I'll get two chicken legs and pepper and your man will be running down Main Street butt-naked once I'm done with him. I've got something for that bitch he done you dirty with, too! Call me, girl." Claudinette doesn't need any of that, because she knows she's got me, and I love her, and I'm not going anywhere. That doesn't mean what I did was right, but it doesn't mean that I don't value my family. It doesn't mean I can't change. I already have.

In those years after my father died, like I said, I made many mistakes. The worst of them was to get into a relationship with the woman who was my manager at the time. That affair damaged everything: my career, my family, my creativity, and my professional reputation. I had been unfaithful before—and I'm not just talking about being with Lauryn—but this relationship was a tremendous blow to my wife because it was so publicly in her face. It almost cost me my marriage and it should have; it wasn't right. There were items written about it in the New York newspapers and my former manager denied the allegations—and because of that I can't say too much more about this—but we all know the truth. It was all in the papers: there was the issue of a naked picture she sent to me that Claudinette intercepted. My wife found it on my BlackBerry and then asked me if I had been involved with this woman sexually at all. She asked if we ever got into orgies or anything like that and when I said no, she confronted me with the picture. My wife was a woman scorned, so she then sent that picture out to a few of her friends and one of them must have put it up on the Internet.

My former manager claimed that the picture was a nude shot taken by a photographer for a book of artistic portraits. I'm pretty sure that book never came out, but I wasn't going to throw her under the bus publicly, so I didn't say anything more about it. I didn't even make a public statement on the matter at all. I don't know if that was the best thing to do, because all the headlines in the gossip columns made it worse. After I fired my manager, some of the media even claimed that my wife had forced me to fire my manager because of the affair, which made Claudinette furious. That wasn't true at all. I did so because of a few bad business decisions on her part, and I also didn't agree with her management style. Even if those two issues hadn't been there, my mixing business with pleasure was miserable. Firing her as my manager was the only thing I could do after crossing those lines, because business could not go on as usual between us any longer.

This event was a crossroad for Claudinette and me, and after we got through it, everything in our relationship changed. People can say what they want, but what they will never understand is the mystery of how deep the love between Claudinette and me runs. As much as I've ever wilded out, whenever she has said she's going to leave me, I've done whatever it takes to keep that from happening. If she left me, I would lose my best friend in the whole world and the only person who has been with me since the beginning. I would lose that girl who made me want to ride my sister's pink bicycle across town to see her, not caring about how much shit I'd catch from the thugs on the street. When I'm old and gray I'll still have that excitement within me. I still feel that thrill when I see her now, every single day. My wife knows my heart. She knows that I'm the kind of person who would take out my heart and give it to you if I could, and that is why she's with me. I will give my last dollar to someone else and I'll sacrifice myself for mankind as if my life doesn't matter—as if I don't even exist. She knows that is my soul, and I know hers is beautiful and compassionate and understanding. We can do this until the end of our days. I know this.

My wife comes from a very magical place in Haiti called Jéré- mie, which is the city of poets, far on the western part of the island. She has an intuition like no one else I know: she has talked about things that ended up happening ever since we were kids, in the way that a medium or a fortune-teller does.

What that has meant in our relationship is that whenever I've lied to her, it's only been a matter of time until she's found out the truth, because she already knows it, sometimes before it happens. We have been in bed together and she has woken up in the morning and said to me, "I've had a dream," and whatever she has told me pretty much became reality.

My wife foresaw her mother's passing long before it happened and she's seen everything that ever went on between us—both the good and the bad. She prays a lot and she has a lot of faith, and there isn't anyone else in the world like my Claudinette. And as much as she's truthful with me, so much of her nature is still a beautiful mystery to me. She makes things manifest, so she only says some of what she sees in her mind.

When I look back at our relationship and everything I have done wrong, and every time Claudinette has known the truth before I even told her, I see that she was teaching me a lesson. I had to learn this lesson over and over until it finally manifested itself within me. I have finally grown up, and I have finally realized all of the blessings I've been granted because of her. I understand her wisdom and why she stands by me, because the two of us cannot be divided, no matter what our trial. We are meant to be together because we are one. In her wisdom, she knew this truth before I did, but now I understand.

I have a wife, I have a daughter, and my little girl really looks up to me. I began to realize that it wouldn't be too long before my daughter would be able to read all about her daddy on the Internet, and if I didn't change my ways, what she'd find out wouldn't be good. She'd know that I'd messed up and I'd hurt her mom. That's why I'm laying it all out there now. I want the world to know the truth about everything I've done wrong so that no one can say I didn't own up to my mistakes.

Sometimes only the possibility of losing everything can make you learn a lesson. That is what needed to happen to me, more than once, but now that lesson has been learned. In the same way, tragedy wakes us up and demands that we value our lives and loved ones. And the earthquake in Haiti did that to me as well. Those twenty-four hours changed everything in my life. It was like I woke up to who I really was all along, for the first time.

It is easy to be a careless young man in show business. That kind of behavior is encouraged! But being treated like a star doesn't teach anyone to learn what's important in real life; it only feeds the ego, which keeps you in the mind-set of a teenager. Lifting bodies into trucks in my homeland, with the woman beside me who had stood beside me from the start, made it clear to me what life is all about. I realized that it was time for me to forget Wyclef and become Jeannel, a family man who my father would be proud of, and a Haitian who did everything he could for his homeland.

Working together on the relief effort, side by side, on the ground, brought Claudinette and me together in a whole new way.

When we returned from that first trip, I changed everything: I fired the manager I'd had an affair with and I made a new start. For a long while I had no manager, no representation, and I just focused on raising money for Haiti and nurturing my family and my relationship with my wife back to health. Past mistakes became corrected and past problems found solution. I will no longer do what I did because I don't want to lose my family and I don't want to lose my country.

I had been working on a record that was a return to the rap game and I put that to bed. There was nothing else I could do. I had left that Wyclef down in the rubble and returned with a new purpose. I wanted my music to reflect the culture that defined me, because that is who I am. I wanted everything I did to give back to my homeland. And it did. Everything became clear to me and I haven't let it go. I admitted my mistakes and I have confessed to my lies. Believe me, if you have the strength for that, your life will be the better. If we can all do that, this world stands a chance.

8

WYCLEF FOR
PRESIDENT

In the aftershocks of the earthquake, my charity raised millions
of dollars in just a few weeks. It is the most important thing I've
ever done. I had been building Yéle in Haiti since 2005, and we had
been making moves toward becoming an NGO, a nongovernmental organization like Unicef, but we hadn't achieved that goal quite
yet when tragedy struck. NGOs were established by the United
Nations in the late 1940s to define groups that work outside of the
government but often do benefit from government subsidies. It is
the best way to operate: you have the blessing of the government
but you are somewhat free to follow your own agenda. When I
first started flying first class with the Fugees, I remember the host-
ess passing the orange box down the aisle asking for donations for
Unicef, and that image stayed with me. I wanted Yéle to be just
as established, accepted, and understood. When I began to look
into it, I realized that Haiti didn't have one NGO operating in the
country. There was no global organization devoted to Haiti, no organization with millions of dollars in the bank to draw from when
an unforeseen event struck. Haiti had no sponsors looking to build

and improve its infrastructure—no group to rescue the people in times of need. I saw this void before the earthquake, so I had been doing all that I could to build up a support system, while spreading awareness of the country's need internationally. When the quake hit, we weren't even close to our goal, but in terms of aid groups on the ground, we were the most organized and most visible one there, and I am proud of that.

After spending the first forty-eight hours after the earthquake on the ground in Port-au-Prince, I returned to America to rally more support. And when I got off the plane I was met with accusations from a few media outlets that all of the money Yéle had raised via text messages, online donations, and corporate sponsors was a fraud. I was accused of running a company that stole from the rich and kept the money for itself while the poor starved. Single-handedly we had raised 1 million dollars in twenty-four hours just by asking people to text YELE 510 510, all of which, my accusers in the press claimed, was going to me and to my staff. According to their allegations, those funds weren't going to provide shelter or clean water to Haiti. This wasn't true.

I thought of what my father had always said when he talked about Martin Luther King Jr. and the civil rights movement in America. He wasn't directly a part of it, but my father felt that struggle personally, and he always told me how Reverend King was accused of using NAACP funds to support himself and his family. My father said that this kind of malice went back to the time of Jesus, and it was what the weak men in power resorted to when they felt threatened. Jesus was the man. He was a true leader of the people, which was fine with those who governed until he brought his message to Jerusalem, the seat of power. Once he took his beliefs to the top and rode into the capital on a donkey, he was accused of everything and murdered because his teachings were too dangerous. My father always said that no matter what the situation, I should always think long and hard before riding my donkey into Jerusalem. He said to be sure the cause was worth wearing a crown of thorns, because if it were, even if they killed you and nailed your beliefs to a cross, your words and your example would go on. He was trying to tell me that no cause can be defeated if it speaks to the people and if you give yourself over to it completely.

I thought of my father's words when I returned home from Haiti after the earthquake. But even those moments of reflection couldn't have prepared me for the crucifixion that awaited me. From the plane I went directly into a press conference, and aside from my father's funeral, in that room, I've never broken down into tears so honestly in front of other people. I had been so caught up in all I had experienced over the previous two days, and so overwhelmed that for the first time I let the emotion go. If they had seen what I'd seen, if they'd been where I'd been, if they'd held their country-men's bodies like I had, they would have wept beside me.

I had not expected to answer accusations, which is what I learned I would be doing in the press conference. As I walked through the airport, a kid, college age, yelled out to me.

"Clef, I donated to YELE 510 510. I know you doing right, but they trying to throw dirt on you!"

"How?"

I was serious, I had no idea what he was talking about. In the days since I had left America, the media had investigated Yéle for sup-posed nonpayment of taxes. They had seen how much power we had with the people, so of course they had to find some way to bring us down. The same people that were there to listen to what I had to say about the conditions on the ground were also there to accuse me of collecting the money for profit, not for aid.

The focus was Haiti, but I had to take time away from that to clear my own name and the name of Yéle. Then after that, the affair with my manager came to light publicly. My image could not have

been worse right at a time when I was poised to really make a difference in my homeland.

That first day back was complete darkness for me. In that press
conference I cried for myself, I cried for my people, and I cried because of the misrepresentation. I poured out my emotions honestly,
and whatever the reporters had thought of me when they came in,
they asked no further questions after I was done speaking. All I
could do was tell them about the horror I had just seen. I walked out
of there to dead silence.

In the end, the media didn't find anything wrong with our tax
situation because there was nothing wrong with it. We were behind
on our payments for a few years before the earthquake. We were a
small charity and that's how things go in the beginning stages, but
suddenly, once we had managed to raise so much money so quickly,
we drew their attention. We were expected to run our organization like we'd been together for years and had always run the show
in Haiti—in the midst of the biggest national natural disaster the
country had ever seen. It is true; we had a few outstanding financial
issues to deal with, but our accountants took care of them right
away. We laid our books open to every news source that wanted
to see them. CNN investigated us thoroughly a month later and
admitted that they found nothing wrong.

The way media works today, however, is that the first story is
the one people remember most, and a lot of the time, when it's
all cleared up, they've moved on to another topic. Our news jour-
nalists deliver bits of sensation but never stay with a story long
enough to follow it through to the end. And that's what happened
to Yéle's mission. Less than a month later, there was an earthquake
in Papua, New Guinea, and the focus of the news and the world
shifted there before they got the chance to hear the whole truth of
our story. Much of America will only remember that Yéle stole the
money it raised, and that Wyclef doesn't pay his taxes. My father

always told me to face things honestly and that is what I do. Honesty always prevails, he said, because honesty is what separates men from giants.

From the start, I came clean about the mistakes we had made. I was accused of accepting a $100,000 payday for a benefit concert, funneling $250,000 to a media company of mine, and paying $31,000 in rent to my studio, Platinum Sounds. Why would I do any of this? I have a watch collection worth $500,000. I would never need to take the money from my own charity to cover operating costs like that. The truth is that Yéle has real influence: we raised 1 million dollars in twenty-four hours and I think the show of unity we inspired made powerful people uncomfortable, which led to unfair scrutiny. There was only one thing to do, which was to keep going hard, to disprove these shady allegations over time.

The truth will prevail, and even those who still doubt us will see that Yéle is Haiti's greatest ally and asset. We serve to rebuild, to empower, and to educate. Since our start we have been doing work that will continue beyond the earthquake relief. We've been putting kids through school, starting with the 3,600 scholarships we provided to children in Gonaïves following the devastation of Hurricane Jeanne in 2005, our first year in operation. In our second year of operation we doubled our number of scholarships and spread the wealth throughout Haiti and we've been growing ever since. Yéle is in Haiti to stay, just as my heart and all of my efforts as a man and artist will be focused there for the rest of my days.

Haiti was the first black republic in the world and having that heritage in my blood has allowed me to become a successful artist and entrepreneur in the United States and in the rest of the world. How could I not do everything in my power to repay my roots?

. . . .

I RETURNED FROM HAITI after several visits in the wake of the earthquake as an entirely different Clef. It was as if every trip there confirmed something that had always been in me, but that I had not recognized until then. Down there amid the suffering I became part of the effort from the ground up, and realized that my family came first and my home country came next. People think I decided to become a statesman overnight, but the decision wasn't spontaneous. It was the end of a journey, as it was also the beginning of one—one that started the day my father passed away. That moment was my first awakening. I realized that I should be doing more with my life than music. My father gave all of himself to others, and I realized that I should do what I can to be as useful as he had been.

And so I began to think of the coming election in Haiti. There was much that I could do through Yéle, but there would be even more I could do in office. I could turn the types of institutional programs that bring education, food, and water to the country's neediest regions into national institutions. Yéle had a successful infrastructure and I wanted to re-create it within the government to whatever extent possible.

I had some more work to do on my public image first, because damage had been done. The main allegation that came up during the tax issue centered on Telemax, a television production company in Haiti that I own with Jerry Duplessis. Yéle paid Telemax to create television ads for the organization in order to spread awareness of our programs. Some saw this as my foundation paying me directly via a company in which I own a majority share. Technically this is what happened, but to think that Telemax profited from the ads is ridiculous. Yéle money was used, but it was the bare minimum of what was needed to cover the operating costs of creating and running the ads. Let me put it this way: a company may decide to give a vendor a deal on its rates, but that doesn't mean that the company's employees agree to a wage cut for that week. These mathematics were not accounted for in the media reports. The discount Telemax gave Yéle covered the operating costs, but there was no profit whatsoever. Some people saw this as a conflict of interest, and while that may make sense in the first world, that doesn't apply in someplace like Haiti. It comes down to this: Telemax is the best, most organized television production company in the country, so there was nothing wrong with employing them to make the best advertisements possible. It was a guarantee that Yéle would get the best work for its money. I'm an entrepreneur, so if I own a television production company, and the best ads will be made there for the cheapest budget possible, that's what I'm going to do.

After all of the negative attention from the national press, accusing me of living high off of Yéle money and using the charity of others to funnel profits into my other companies, I decided that the only way to keep this from ever happening again was to go above and beyond what other charities, nonprofit organizations, and nongovernmental organizations do to allow donors to follow the trail of their contributions. We undertook a full restructuring of Yéle Haiti and made our work entirely transparent. It's right there on our website, so that anyone who is interested can see how we are set up to provide aid from start to finish. I invite the world's curiosity.

We now have a bigger board of executives and we employ one of the most respected accounting firms in the world to oversee our books and control the money. All of the funds we raise—from individuals, governments, or private companies—are held by that accounting firm until the proposals for the various Yéle projects are approved by the board of directors. Once a project is approved and the budget is put into place, the money goes from the accounting firm to the committee in charge of the program. Yéle may have grown too fast and made some mistakes, but we have made changes to improve our operating procedures and they are there for all to see.

I own eight businesses in Haiti, because I'm trying to lead by example in the eyes of the international business community. I want global investors to see that profitable, stable businesses can exist in my homeland. The only way for Haiti to enter the modern age is for foreign capital to become a permanent part of our business infrastructure. Many celebrities have charities, but not every celebrity charity is a nongovernmental organization. Declaring yourself an NGO means you are stating that you want to handle the types of internal responsibilities to the people that the government usually takes care of. That is my goal with Yéle: to provide what the government cannot, until the government can. And as a celebrity, I intend to lobby on behalf of Haiti everywhere I go.

My vision with Yéle was simple when I started it, and even now with so many challenges ahead of us it remains the same: to bring civilization to Haiti's most rural areas by providing education, creating jobs, and convincing kids to trade their guns for work that will provide a future for their nation. The foundation came from my brain and contains my soul. I spent the years before the earthquake making influential people like Brad Pitt and Angelina Jolie and Matt Damon aware of Yéle, and I got them all to come down and see our scholarships in action. We were providing close to seven thousand scholarships to send kids to schools and universities. It was basic education, that cost us about a hundred US dollars per kid, and we funded much of it through Voilà and our partner company, Comcel (both cellular phone corporations that have since merged). My belief was always that teaching kids to read and write wasn't enough. To have a self-sufficient nation, they needed higher education, too, and those who were too old to start classroom learning needed vocational training. Think about it: if a kid is nineteen, he doesn't want to head back into a classroom, but he may respond to learning a trade, something practical that can provide him a living and a new life. These are not bad things in any country at any time.

We put all of these things into effect on our own, but unfortunately we were still virtually an underground movement until the
earthquake, and the fallout from the tax misunderstanding put us
on the map, in the wrong way, in the eyes of America. I regret that
when we hit the big screen and got our mainstream exposure it
was for that reason, but you know what they say: bad news travels
quicker than good news. I'd raised money for Haiti before, after the
floods in Gonaïves, and I'd been providing education to Haitian
children for almost ten years, but that didn't matter to the public,
at least at first. I stayed strong during that time, and I remembered
what my father once told me: "When you are being tried, and the
eyes of the world are upon you, never use your color, you blackness
as an excuse." I stayed strong because I knew in my heart something else he told me: "If your hand is clean you have absolutely
nothing to worry about."

IN THE FIRST FEW weeks after I returned from the devastation,
I went to a few meetings at the White House to speak to one of
Obama's political strategists about how to most effectively get aid
into the country and save lives. I also spoke to members of the
Black Caucus, because I was a firsthand witness at that point, and
they wanted to know the real deal of what it was like on the ground.
I told them all of Yéle's plans to rebuild and what kind of resources
we had—and what we needed. I told them about my larger plans to
get the country up and running again and how I wanted to devote
myself to educating the international community about the culture
and the needs of Haiti.

I got a call from George Clooney around this time, which was
really cool. He had an idea for a show to raise money and he said he
couldn't do it without me. So we started to put together the concert for Haitian relief. Every good thing you've ever heard about
George Clooney is true: he is a man of his word and a man with a

real strong character. He wasn't an actor producing a self-named telethon; he was someone who wanted to come out and do his part. He was a part of every e-mail and phone call that I got from that point. He was such a good manager and event producer that I kept asking him if he had a day job we could replace.

Around that same time I got a call from Oprah, whom I'd always wanted to talk to. I mean she's Oprah Winfrey. That woman has achieved so much in her life, she should be an inspiration to everyone, no matter who they are. She and I stayed on the phone for an hour or more, talking about the conditions in Haiti and the best way for her to help out. I'd wanted to be on the *Oprah* show my entire life. Oprah is special; even speaking to her on the phone you can feel her warmth. She is one of those people who is truly tuned in to the world and she has a light about her, this natural light that people gravitate toward. She didn't want to go to Haiti for the photo op; put it that way. She wanted to do real work.

"Clef. Call me whenever. I mean it." She don't say that to just anybody, right?

Oprah pours herself into what she does, and that's how I'd approached Yéle. I remember meeting Harry Belafonte in 2004, the year before I founded Yéle. He told me to read an amazing book called *Pillar of Fire* by Judith Tarr, which is a historical novel based in Egypt that explores the idea that Moses and the pharaoh Akhenaten were the same man. He said it would teach me about what it means to be a leader. Harry is a wise, serious man, so when he looked me in the eye I listened to everything he had to say.

"How deep are you willing to go in? That's the only question you need to ask yourself," he said.

"I want to go in. All the way."

"Do you? Be sure that you do. Because once you take that step, you must not turn back."

"I will not turn back."

I went in deep from the start. Within the first two years of running Yéle, I found myself in situations that other men might not have walked out of alive. When I think about them, I'm still not sure how I did it. My only explanation is that the spirits who watched over my father all those times he walked through the 'hood in Coney Island untouched were now there watching over me.

The most dangerous position in which I found myself was acting as mediator between two gangs in Cité Soleil—one of the worst, most violent slums in all of Haiti—in 2005. I was on tour in Paris at the time when someone in my circle handed me a phone.

"Clef, somebody named 2Pac wants to talk to you," he said.

"What the hell you talkin' about? 2Pac is dead!"

"I know, I know. This guy says he knows you. He says he's the Haitian 2Pac and that it's important. He says he's got to talk to you."

I had no idea what this was going to be about, but like I told Harry Belafonte, I was ready to go in.

"This is Clef," I said into the phone.

"This is Clef?" he said. I could tell he was a just a teenager.

"Yeah it's me. What's going on, young brother?"

"Clef, we're in Cité Soleil, we have over five thousand guns, and we have a standoff. We want to put down our guns, but we need someone to come talk to us and the only person who can do that is you. We listen to your music, and remember you said in your song, 'The guys from Cité Soleil are not scared of anything.' That's truth. We're really not."

"I believe you."

"We need you to come talk to us, Clef, because we don't want to fight, but we feel like if we don't, the other gang's gonna kill us. I know they'd kill us. We want peace; we got people starving in here because we're all fighting every day."

"Be strong, young brother. When I get off the road I'll come down and talk to you."

It was an urgent situation: the gangs were controlling the food and water supply, and their fighting was keeping innocent citizens from receiving any aid being bussed in by organizations like Yéle and the Red Cross. This was right after President Jean-Bertrand Aristide lost power, so the infrastructure had fallen apart, and in regions like Cité Soleil, chaos ruled the day. It's too bad his regime fell apart. I felt like his rule was a moment of hope for Haiti, because his plans for the future were progressive.

People were starving and I was the one to put an end to it, so I went to Cité Soleil with just two friends and a backpack. There was constant gunfire every day, tires and garbage burning in the streets, and fear in the air. You can see it all in the documentary *The Ghosts of Cité Soleil*. It was a human hell on earth.

I walked into Cité Soleil with my father's spirit inside me and so I was unafraid. I went in and slowly people started to follow us; the further I went, the more people joined the crowd like I was some kind of Pied Piper. By the time I thought to turn around, it looked like a crowd of ten thousand were behind me. They were chanting and singing my songs and moving as a huge mob. The leader of the gang, a guy higher up in rank than Haitian 2Pac, came to me then. His name was Labayne. We left the crowd behind us and went inside a building to talk.

Lebayne was a hard gangster with a nasal voice who talked with a distinctive twang. "Do you know my favorite song?" he asked me. And then he started to sing a few lines from "Sang Fézi" off my album *The Carnival*.

> *Ki ayisien kap di'm map mache New-York san fezi*
> *Mwen di ou messie nou menti*
> *L bum yo ginbe ou yo devore ou se l ou mouri police vini.*

In English that means: "Which Haitian is going to tell me to walk to New York City with no gun? / You're lying because the police show up after the thugs are done robbing me." He said he listened to it every night before he went to sleep.

"I wrote that song about people stealing my sneakers back when I was a teenager. I'm sure it means something different to you."

It's hard for me to think of something everyone has seen that compares to what Cité Soleil was like. What comes to mind are pictures of Somalia, Baghdad, and maybe North Korea; in all those places, the news outlets printed pictures where every kid fifteen or older had a gun, and they were all out in force. That's what this place was like, at least until we got there.

"You're not scared?" Lebayne said. "Because millionaires don't come down here to talk."

"Well it's a good thing I'm not a millionaire," I said. "I'm a revolutionary, and that's why I'm here."

He gave me a good long stare and then he burst out laughing, and as he continued to laugh I heard rounds of ammunition going off, over and over, outside.

"My friend," I said, "I am here to talk to you because we need to bring peace to this place. People are starving and only you can stop this. At the end of the day the future of the country depends on what happens here."

At that moment Haitian 2Pac came up to me. I gave him a hug.

"Clef, thank you," he said. "Only you could do this. After we're done here, we've got some music for you to listen to." He was just like kids in the States; he saw a chance and he was right there with his demo tape. He wanted to put his guns down and try to keep the peace with us rappers over here; we're people who have the privilege of not facing life-or-death moments every minute of every day.

I had made my way in, but I had to get this side talking to the other side, because making friends with one wasn't going to solve a thing if the others didn't come to the table—and I had to make that happen by charm and force of will. Just like gangs in the States and around the world, all of those kids threw signs with their hands. They were different from East Coast–West Coast shit, but it was all the same language.

"If I create a sign for peace, will you respect it?" I asked.

"Yeah, Clef, we will."

I made a sign that was like a peace sign but all my own. I threw my hands up in the air. "Stop the violence. Peace. Don't put up a gun."

The word spread throughout Cité Soleil and the other gang leaders; they came to us, and I was the middleman and I brought them together. Within a few days all parties agreed to let Yéle truck in some rice and water. I am happy to say that lives were saved.

I flew American Airlines back to the States at the end of that trip, and a man I'd never met before came up to me on the plane.

"You don't know me, but I want to tell you how lucky you are."

"What do you mean, brother?" I said.

"I know where you just were and I know what you did. There were three assassination attempts on your life, but they were all stopped. You are lucky to be alive."

I thought he was making it up—until he gave me names and days. He knew exactly when I was with Labayne and Haitian 2Pac and he knew exactly where we held the meeting. He mentioned a guy who had come in waving a gun, acting crazy.

"He was supposed to kill you," this man said. "One of the smaller gangs wanted you dead. You said something to him that made him change his mind, though. What did you say to him?"

"I just told him to come and sit with us at the table and help us figure out how we could get the people fed."

I've walked into rooms that charged since then, and I've done what I did that day and so many days like it when fear has threatened to stop me from my intended mission. At those times I do what my father taught me to do when I felt spirits present: I recite Psalm 23 (maybe not out loud, but always in my mind). I keep saying "The

Lord is my Shepherd, I shall not want." And the Lord has seen me through.

THE DAY I DECIDED to run for the office of the president of Haiti I thought of a moment my dad and I had shared many years before, when I was still a boy. It's a hazy memory, but I was chasing him and he fell down and I asked him, "Dad, are you okay?"

"Yes. Listen to me," he said. "I'm fine. Thank you for helping me up. But don't do this for everyone you consider to be your family."

"Why not, Dad?"

"You must do whatever you can for your fellow Haitians, son, but don't ever make the critical mistake of trusting them."

"Okay, Dad."

I didn't understand exactly what he meant then, but I sure as hell know now. He was trying to tell me to keep my countrymen in my heart, and to aid them as much as I could, but to do so from a distance, no matter how much I might want to go in. I'd need three eyes to work inside Haiti and not be taken advantage of. I've never forgotten those words, because I've had to learn that lesson a few times over. I regret none of it, because my mistakes have made me a better man.

In my family we always said that we'd never let politics divide us, and that is how I approached things when I decided to run for president, particularly because my uncle Raymond Joseph was running for the same office. He had been the ambassador to the UN for Haiti for a few years, and through him I learned so much about the government and what the country really needed. Uncle Raymond was my entry point into aiding Haiti, and how I got my feet wet with Yéle. He was always supportive of me; in fact he was the one who told my mother—his sister—that she should let me move out into my other uncle's house to pursue my music. He understood me from the start, even though we didn't spend a lot of time together during my youth.

After the earthquake, when Yéle became a tangible force in Haiti, I met my uncle and told him all about the youth movement we were organizing down there and how all of the kids we were reaching were crying out for change. We had a program called Fas-A-Fas, which means "face-to-face" and was meant to motivate the youth to become politically aware and vote in the next election. They wanted education and jobs and a future—and my movement was at the center of it. At the time, my uncle knew he was going to run for president and told me all about his campaign. That thought hadn't crossed my mind; all I cared about was motivating the youth to become part of the political process and rebuilding the nation. I wanted them to take charge of their world, because it is theirs to inherit.

The first thing I did was step down from the board of Yéle so that there would be no conflict of interest. I also gave up my title as ambassador-at-large, which the former administration had given me in recognition of my fund-raising on the country's behalf internationally. I hadn't told my uncle about this when I entered my name in the race. I also neglected to tell Michel Martelly, the man who eventually won. He has been my friend for twenty years; he is the one I wrote about in the song "Sweet Mickey" on *The Carnival*. I should have told both of them. I don't know why I was secretive; I just decided to fly down and enter my name in the ballot. I was inspired, thinking about my brother and I growing up in our village and how much I'd achieved and how I'd like nothing more than to give back by serving. I felt like I was running for the office of president of the world, it meant so much to me. I knew my uncle and Michel would find out anyway, and I didn't want them or anyone else trying to convince me not to run.

I was foolish to think that this wouldn't be a problem. Both of them got pissed off, so the media blitz that came turned into a face-off between me, my uncle, and my friend of twenty years. The slogan of my Fas-A-Fas movement, "face-to-face," came true alright. It became very strange between my uncle and me. I would get e-mails from him saying things like, "We're on the same team, so I'm going to do this interview and make sure that people understand that politics will not divide our family. You must make sure you do the same." Meanwhile, he didn't realize how tuned in I was. I'd listen to his interviews and hear him take little stabs at me when they'd ask about running against his nephew. Mostly he didn't seem to be taking my campaign seriously and talked about it as if it were just some crazy thing Wyclef the rapper was doing.

The truth was that I came into the race so strong that every other candidate was scared. I had tremendous support from the youth, and everybody knew that there was a good chance that I would win. So I'm not surprised that they found a way to get me out of the race. I got taken out on a technicality having to do with my residency, since I hadn't lived in the country for five consecutive years. If we had decided to fight it, we could have won, because I have maintained a residence there. The law states that you don't have to live there so long as you maintain a residence and consistently come back to Haiti. If I had been in the country and had my presence known more than I had over the past few years, I probably would have been allowed to run for president.

I was driving back from Port-au-Prince to the village where I grew up when I heard the sad news on the radio. They were announcing the final slate of candidates and those who had been rejected. My name came up last.

"Jean, Wyclef: rejected."

I felt like my whole world came down.

I had to adapt and decide what was best for the country. I had a populist movement behind me, a majority that would follow me if I said, "We're going to fight this." That wasn't going to help anything. Haiti has been divided for so long that I didn't want to see whatever unity I had brought become a force for more division. That's not what I started Yéle to do.

The next morning I made my announcement.

"There are laws in this country and that is what we all must respect," I said. "So I ask that everyone who supports me to be nonviolent over this decision and vote for the remaining candidate you think will be best."

In the end they removed my uncle from the race as well. I suppose they figured anyone from our family would be trouble. They probably figured that if the uncle won, the nephew wouldn't be far behind and soon there would be one family ruling the nation again.

Michel was harmless—just a popular singer—so he stayed in. I'm sure the powers that be never thought he'd win. And Jude Célestin was another candidate who wouldn't disturb the status quo if elected. I didn't support any candidate in the first round of elections, and Michel won by 51 percent. The natural thing for me would have been to support Michel, my friend and fellow musician, and just go rock out with him, but I didn't want to do that. It was not because I don't support him as a man or as a politician, but because I've realized that politics is not music. I needed to sit back and watch my friend and truly believe in what he stood for philosophically before I threw in my support. We're cool as friends, but politically I was still waiting to see what happened.

He won the first round but when it came to the second round of elections I went to see him. I have known Michel since I was twenty-one; I first met him at the Cameo Nightclub in Miami when the Fugees were on one of their nonstop tours, but still pretty much nobodies. He pulled up in a white Mercedes with a big smile on his face in his bald head and apparently he went up to the bouncer and said, "I hear that there is a group here tonight called the Fugees and they're Haitian. Where are they?" They let him into our dressing room, because Michel is charming like that and he just walked up to me and asked me my name. We got to talking outside the club and when he saw me staring at his car he tossed me the keys.

"Take it for a ride, Wyclef."

"For real?"

I had never even been in a car that nice before.

I don't think he regrets it, but he still talks about how long I went cruising around South Beach in his ride. Man, I was having the time of my life! I never forgot that: he wanted fellow Haitian musicians like me to know that I could have those things, too, if I put in the work. He had never heard our music before; he came down strictly because he heard we were Haitian. He was inspirational to me, and in all the years I've known him since, he's always been about the Haitian people. So in the end I threw him my support and asked all of my followers to do the same. If he could inspire the country the way he inspired me that night, he would be a great leader and bring about positive change.

Michel walked into a real nightmare for any leader. Being the president of Haiti is not a glamorous job. It's probably the worst job you could have in modern politics. It's more of a sacrifice than an occupation. The country is in pieces in every way and all eyes are on him to rebuild and inspire. His first one hundred days were devoted entirely to education, which I think was a wise move. Michel has reinstated my ambassadorship so I've been doing all I can to help out, working on programs that are sustainable, that will hopefully become permanent, centering on vocational training. Haiti needs to train the youth to rebuild, giving them the tools to support their families and move the nation forward. It must start with moving rubble and building houses before we tackle the larger infrastructure. I'm also focused on tourism, and helping to create a market for the world to come and enjoy all of the natural beauty in Haiti. I have my work cut out for me there. It's going to take years for people to feel safe coming down again.

CONCLUSION

Looking back at your life is an odd thing to do, and I wasn't sure I was ready to do it at just forty-two years of age. But when I look at where I'm from and where I am, at how far I've traveled and at what I've achieved with no head start whatsoever, I realize that my story is something special after all. It's something I hope will inspire others like me to make the most of themselves, because anything is possible if you have faith in yourself and a higher power. I want Haitian kids to see me living in my mansion, knowing I was born in a hut just like theirs.

When I look back at my life I ask myself what I would have changed, and the answer is that I wouldn't have changed a thing. There are millions of kids who begin their life the way I did, but I am the one who made it, so it is my duty to be their leader. But what kind of role model am I? What kind of role model could I ever be? I am human and I am a man like any other. I am not perfect, but I try to be the best that I can. I have made many mistakes and I have learned my lessons. I am lucky to have my wife and my family and I will honor them as I will my homeland of Haiti for the rest of my days.

I hope that my stories have done what I intended them to do; I hope they have inspired others like me to dream greater and to try harder, and that they have enabled everyone who has read them to connect with themselves in a deeper way. Reflection has helped me to understand my life, my journey, and what it is to be me. Now you've met the kid who became the man. Now you understand that I've always done my best to live my life the way I saw fit: as if every day were the last, as if every move I made meant everything. Now you know that I've lived my life as I have since my first breath and as I will to my last—with purpose.

ACKNOWLEDGMENTS

Thank you to my brothers, sisters, and cousins, and the one brother, my guardian angel, who took me in after the earthquake in Haiti destroyed us all. You helped me find my musical side once more. He may be an angel, he may be a man. Either way, you blessed me. You brought me back into the science of music, my brother, my blood—Sedek!

To all of my managers past and present, thank you for working for me. Thank you to all of the agents that made my career and this book possible. We wouldn't be here without you. To my true friends, who I can count on one hand, I thank you: Seth Kanegis, Jerry Wonda, Brad Horowitz, and those who know they are true friends—you know who you are. Also Melky Jean, Rose Jean, Samuel Jean, the Yéle Haiti team, the Thebaud family, the Martelly family, the Mignon family, the Pierre family, Harry Belafonte for his wisdom, Quincy Jones for inspiring me to be a better musician, Bill Roedy and his family, Cara Lewis, and Clive Davis, who was a tremendous inspiration to me. I'll never forget that he took the time to come to my dad's funeral. Thank you to Chris Swartz and Ruffhouse Records for signing the Fugees and to David Sonnenberg for sticking with me from the beginning. Thank you also to

Jimmy Iovine for believing in my skills as a producer and giving me a shot.

To the people in my homeland of Haiti: I live and breathe and sleep for you. All of you—every single one—are my inspiration. I will never stop working on your behalf.

To all the Fugees fans around the world, and of course to the three of us, Lauryn, Pras, and me—the mighty Fugees; I wish everyone One Love. We did it. They can never take that away from us.

To all the Wyclef fans, One Love. To everyone around the world, One Love. To everyone reading these words, One Love. One Love. One Love.

Wyclef Jean
May 2012